THE DOCKERS

Class and Tradition in London

THE DOCKERS

Class and Tradition in London

STEPHEN HILL

Lecturer in Sociology,
London School of Economics

HEINEMANN

LONDON

Heinemann Educational Books Ltd
LONDON EDINBURGH MELBOURNE AUCKLAND TORONTO
HONG KONG SINGAPORE KUALA LUMPUR
IBADAN NAIROBI JOHANNESBURG
LUSAKA NEW DELHI KINGSTON

ISBN 0 435 82416 3

Published by
Heinemann Educational Books Ltd
48 Charles Street, London W1X 8AH
Printed and bound in Great Britain by
Morrison and Gibb Ltd, London and Edinburgh

To Jane

Preface

Several people have helped me at different stages of my investigation into the London docks. Henry Bradford, a shop steward at Tilbury when I first tried to gain access to the industry for the purposes of sociological research, was largely responsible for persuading other stewards and managers to co-operate and allow me to undertake this study, and ever since has greatly contributed to my understanding of the docks. Peter Powrie, then of the National Ports Council, and Jack Harper of Scruttons Maltby Ltd. also helped to smooth the way, at a time when the industry was particularly concerned with its internal affairs and the people in it were unreceptive to outside observers, especially academic research workers. Professor David Glass was co-supervisor of the London University doctoral thesis on which this book is based and taught me to respect rigorous empirical research. Ron Pluck persevered in teaching me the rudiments of data analysis and showed me some appropriate techniques for handling the material presented here. Professors David Lockwood and Donald MacRae both read earlier versions of the book and made valuable suggestions which I have tried to take into account in writing the final manuscript. Keith Thurley has seen the book through from start to finish, first as co-supervisor of my doctoral thesis and latterly as a colleague and friend, and has always proved a constructive critic.

London School of Economics and Political Science, September 1975

Stephen Hill

Contents

CHAPTER 1

Introduction

The first aim of this book is descriptive: to give an account of the social and industrial behaviour and attitudes of London dock workers, a group of men who have often been maligned by the press and misunderstood by sociology. The second aim is more theoretical: to define and explain the position of dock workers in the British class structure. Anyone who undertakes the first task is necessarily led from an examination of docking as an occupation to a description of the industrial and social settings in which attitudes and behaviour occur, so this book is also about the Port of London and the communities in which dock workers live. The second aim, to understand the place of dock workers in the class structure, is carried through by comparing the sociological model of the 'traditional worker' with the reality of docking, and by further comparison within the occupation between the men and their foremen. The importance of the social division of labour for the analysis of class is emphasized.

The Docks' Background

Two major changes have influenced the development of the port industry over the last fifteen years. The more widely known and discussed change has been the long-term decline in employment opportunities for all grades of employee. The decline began in the early nineteen-sixties, as the result of changing patterns of trade in British ports and improvements in handling techniques which reduced labour requirements, but it only became a subject of public concern towards the end of that decade. The other change was the restructuring of the basic institutional fabric of the industry at the end of the nineteen-sixties, which resulted from the recommendations of the Devlin Committee of Inquiry into the port industry.[1] Following these recommendations, the labour force was decasualized and the number of employers reduced during Phase 1 which started in 1967. Phase 2, introduced in London in 1970, was a pay and productivity deal similar to many others in different industries, which provided a high guaranteed wage in return for more productive working methods.

[1] *Final Report of the Committee of Inquiry under the Rt. Hon. Lord Devlin into certain matters concerning the Port Transport Industry* (London, 1965), Cmnd. 2734. This will henceforth be referred to as the *Devlin Report*.

1

The declining market for dock labour in the industry as a whole and in the London docks specifically can be seen in table 1.1. This records the number of workers on the register each year and, in London, the distribution of workers between the various dock sectors which make up the port. This table in fact overstates the number of men who are fully employed, because the size of the labour force has been run down by means of natural wastage and voluntary severance, neither of which has proceeded as quickly as the decline in work. The sharp rise in the numbers quitting the industry during and after 1972 was the result of increasing the financial compensations of voluntary severance. Within the London docks, there has in addition been an extensive redistribution of labour downriver, mainly to Tilbury but partly also to the Royal Group. Various upriver enclosed docks have closed since 1967, namely the London and St. Katherine docks between 1967 and 1968, the Surrey Commercials in 1971 and some parts of the West India/Millwall system in 1972. Nearly all the riverside wharves have also closed in the last seven years. The men displaced by these closures have been employed elsewhere in the remaining sections of the port. Meaningful figures concerning the exact nature of the shift downstream are not available, however, because men are still frequently recorded according to their original sector even when they work elsewhere: the Surrey Commercials closed down several years ago, but several hundred men are still registered there who work in the downstream docks or across the river at the West India/Millwall.

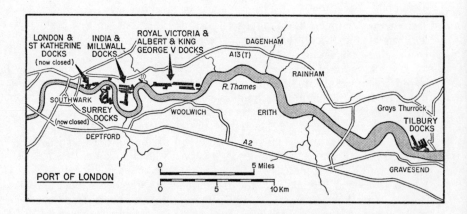

The causes of the overall decline in job opportunities in London and the shifting distribution of the work which remains are changing transit practices, changing cargo-handling techniques and changing patterns of trade between the various ports. The three are frequently related. For example, the decline of the riverside wharves and the London and St. Katherine docks, which together used to handle the short sea traffic to Europe, has mainly been caused by the growth of modern road networks in Britain and Europe, the growth of roll-on/roll-off lorry ferries and the expansion of the small southern and eastern ports. The use of lorry ferries means that cargo is handled only at its points of origin and destination, while the ports now used are those closer to the Continent and involving shorter sea voyages. As trade with the six original Common Market countries is the most rapidly growing section of all U.K. trade, its loss has deprived London of a significant amount of work.[2] A second example can be found in the decline of the Surrey Commercials, which was partly the result of new techniques of packaging timber into unit loads rather than transporting and handling the timber as individual pieces. These packaged units are designed to be moved by modern mechanical handling devices, which required more space and more modern facilities than were available in the Surreys, while the new ships which carried the loads were too large to enter the dock. Thus Tilbury has developed as a large handler of 'packaged' timber. At the same time, much of the timber which formerly entered the London dock system now goes to other British ports which are nearer the final destinations.

Technical developments within the industry have played a large part in the changes which have occurred. There have been several innovations over the last fifteen years which have progressively simplified docking operations, speeded work flow and raised labour productivity. Quay cranes which lift heavier cargoes and run at greater speeds, wider ships' hatches which reduce manhandling in the hold space, the introduction of fork-lift trucks on the quay and in the sheds, the palletization of many commodities, and new berths which reduce congestion have all combined to increase the amount of cargo one man can handle on conventional operations. Increased technical efficiency partly accounted for the declining job opportunities, because fewer men were required even when trade patterns remained constant and the same amount of business continued to enter the same docks.

Towards the end of the sixties, there were further innovations in London which dramatically altered labour requirements over the course of about four years. They broke the established pattern of a fairly long-drawn-out process of change which made men surplus to requirements rather slowly. The consolidation of cargo into unit loads

[2] The *total* U.K. non-fuel trade, imports plus exports, grew at an annual rate of 2·2 per cent between 1962 and 1971. It has been predicted that this rate will be 3·6 per cent annually between 1971 and 1980 (National Ports Council estimates). The growth rate with the E.E.C. (6) was 4·9 per cent annually in 1962–71 and is estimated at 6·4 per cent in 1971–80. The E.E.C. (6) share of the total U.K. non-fuel trade was 12 per cent in 1962, 15 per cent in 1971 and is estimated to reach 20 per cent in 1980.

(containers, pallets, lorry loads, and 'packaged' timber and paper pulp) means that the manhandling involved in consolidating goods for shipment, which used to be done in the docks, now takes place outside. The new methods greatly reduce the demand for labour by removing the labour-intensive part of dock work outside the industry altogether. This leaves only the residual tasks of transferring unit loads between ship and shore. One rule-of-thumb guide to the possible savings suggests that a man becomes ten times more productive on containers than on modern conventional work. Unitization obviously causes a direct drop in the labour requirements of the industry.

The indirect impact of advanced cargo-handling techniques has been to facilitate the diversion of trade to other ports. Unitization simplifies dock work and reduces the importance of traditional expertise. The London labour force was always the most efficient and productive in Europe, when the port was working and not stopped for some reason, but such efficiency is less important in a unitized system when machine-driving is the only skill required. Thus shipowners and shippers can now choose between ports on criteria other than labour efficiency.

London has managed to sustain a fairly constant total tonnage of cargo over the last decade,[3] but rival ports have made inroads in certain of London's traditional trades since 1968, in addition to the short sea and timber trades already mentioned. Containerization on the North Atlantic route allowed Felixstowe to take part of this trade from London, and the same was true of the movement of much of the Far Eastern business to Southampton. Within London, the containerization of refrigerated meat led to the expansion of Tilbury at the cost of the Royal Group, which had long been the centre of the meat importing business. Such changing patterns of trade have had an uneven impact on London, leading to the decline of some parts of the system but leaving the rest untouched. This can be seen most clearly in the West India/Millwall, where many quays were shut down at a time when others were being expanded to cope with increased business in their particular trades.

Unit load cargo transit had existed on a small scale in different parts of the world for several years prior to the recent boom, notably on the coasts of America where it was particularly widespread and successful. By the mid-sixties, British shipowners had become convinced of the savings they could make from unitization. The proportion of a ship's life spent in port would decrease, thus increasing the amount of sea-time when the vessel was earning money, reducing the proportion of total costs due to labour, and reducing the number of ships needed on

---

[3] The stability of London tonnage figures has to be seen against the background of annually *increasing* trade for British ports as a whole. The figures also exclude the fuel trade, which has declined in London but which has had virtually no impact on the enclosed docks.

any route.[4] Unit loading of trade with Europe grew throughout the sixties as the result of new roll-on/roll-off ferries, so that 59 per cent of all trade to the six original members of the E.E.C. was unitized by 1969. But the unitization of the deep-sea trades could only get under way if port authorities agreed to spend large sums on the alteration of existing facilities, because unit loads could not easily be handled by existing equipment nor were existing berths large enough to store the units. The Port of London Authority foresaw the potential demand and spent approximately £30 million on an extra dock and a new lock, new berths and cranes at Tilbury. Tilbury was the only place in the London system with sufficient depth of water for the new container vessels and sufficient land behind the operating areas to store and handle containers (which require a lot of space).

Once the initial break-through was made in terms of capital investment in new port facilities, unitization grew rapidly as shipowners built new vessels or converted old ones. By 1970, overtonnaging had already occurred as new vessels and port facilities expanded more quickly than the available trade. This kept shipping rates artificially low on the relevant lines and encouraged shipowners and port authorities to put pressure on their customers to unitize their wares. Rather than an orderly progression along the road to unitization, there was a sudden rush which caught many unawares. Table 1.2 gives the National Ports Council's estimates of market penetration on selected routes for certain years. Between the end of 1969 and 1971, unit loads increased their share of the U.K.-E.E.C. trade by 12 per cent and took a further 17 per cent of the North American trade. By the end of 1971, 37 per cent of what was estimated as the potential market for unitization on the Australasian run had been containerized. This was less than two years after the inauguration of the service from Tilbury (though much of this growth was trade diverted from Holland which had been containerized for some time). Total share of the estimated potential market rose from 17 per cent in 1969 to 27 per cent in 1971 and an approximate figure of 44 per cent in 1973. World-wide, the number of deep-sea container ships (roughly defined as those carrying more than 200 20-foot containers) increased from 81 in 1968 to 339 in 1973.[5] None of these figures relates specifically to London, nor are data available, but they give an indication of how unitization has spread since the middle of the nineteen-sixties. However, London can show how rapidly shore facilities for the unitized trade have grown. For example, Tilbury

[4] Experience on the Australasian trade route shows that 75 per cent of a new container ship's life is spent at sea, against 60 per cent of the conventional ship's life on the same route.

[5] The annual figures (National Ports Council) are as follows: 1968=81; 1969=136; 1970=175; 1971=220; 1972=310; 1973=339. All figures refer to the year's end. Throughout this period, there have been more than 5,000 conventional cargo ships on the seas.

provided three berths for 'packaged' timber and paper pulp, four container berths and two roll-on/roll-off berths between 1968 and the end of 1973.

Statistics such as these often create a false impression of the speed at which the work performed by dock workers has changed. It is still the case that most men do *not* work on advanced, capital-intensive methods but perform fairly traditional tasks on conventional operations. For example, out of a total of more than three thousand men working in Tilbury in 1973, a maximum of four to five hundred worked on the new berths. It is also very clear now that the future penetration of unit loads on deep-sea trades will advance more slowly, for a variety of reasons. Labour costs form a smaller proportion of total costs on the deep-sea trades than they do on the short sea ones. The loss of stowage space which results from containerization can be serious on the large ships now used for intercontinental trade. Many less developed nations prefer to employ labour in their docks rather than spend large sums of money in order to reduce labour needs, while facilities for inland distribution are often less effective in economically less developed nations. At the same time, the building of modern, conventional 'break-bulk' cargo liners continues to flourish. The introduction of standardized designs which are relatively cheap to purchase and which incorporate up-to-date cargo-handling techniques makes conventional operation attractive to many firms. For all these reasons, many workers who still have work to do in the enclosed docks can expect to continue using familiar techniques on familiar types of ship for some time to come.

The lighterage trade has also suffered a change of fortune over the last decade. The total amount of cargo carried on the river by lighters and barges has fallen from 13 million tons in 1963 to 4 million in 1973. This decline has resulted from increased unitization, particularly of the short sea trades, the growth of Tilbury which has never used much lighterage, the decline of the riverside wharves, and the great increase in road transport at the cost of river transport. Lightermen have been far more severely affected by recent changes than dock workers, though, like their colleagues in the docks, lightermen cannot be made redundant against their wishes.

The other source of change, the Devlin-inspired reforms of the institutional structure of the industry, are discussed more fully in the next chapter and elsewhere. One of the moving forces behind the committee's recommendations was the need to alter the attitudes and behaviour of managers and men, in order to pave the way for the other changes which were obviously about to affect the industry. The fundamental transformation occurred in 1967, when casual labour by the half-day, often for different employers on different days, was replaced by permanent employment for a single firm. The introduction of Phase 2 in London in 1970 was less dramatic in its consequences, and the package of reforms was a fairly conventional one which abolished piecework and protective practices and introduced flexible manning and shifts in return for a new wage agreement. The combined effects of Phases 1 and 2 on employment relations and the social structure of the docks have been immense. As far as most of the people who work in the industry are concerned, the era of the Devlin reforms has produced profound changes in their working lives. For dock workers, who are guaranteed employment and a high wage and are therefore insulated against the full effects of technical change, the Devlin Report has been more important than other developments.

Devlin also recommended a reduction in the number of employers in London's enclosed docks, from thirty-five to ten, in order to create firms which were sufficiently large to provide regular work for the new, permanent labour force and make adequate investment in equipment and staff. There were in fact numerous mergers throughout the middle and late nineteen-sixties and there were ten employers by the end of 1970. Since 1972, however, the worsening financial situation of several companies has led to a series of mergers and closures which has reduced the number to four major and fairly prosperous employers and two very small, specialized firms. Two aspects of the latest round of consolidation are noteworthy. The first is the almost complete withdrawal of shipowners from the business of stevedoring after years of domination in this sphere of port operation. The second is the movement of the Port of London Authority into stevedoring on a large scale for the first time (stevedoring operations are those which take place on board ship), as the result of its take-over of four stevedoring firms since 1972. Of the three stevedoring companies examined in this work, two are still independent and one has been taken over by the Authority.

The impact of these changes on the character of the industry, particularly on industrial relations and attitudes, is considered throughout the book and the changing nature of the docks is a major theme. However, although there have been major modifications of the traditional character of the industry, some of its core features have been retained so far. The essentially traditional nature of dock society has been maintained at the workplace in two particular aspects. The first is the continued existence of elements of a *gemeinschaft* society, so that primordial ties of kin, personal bonds between friends and a sense of moral obligation dominate the culture of the industry and its typical forms of organization. The docks do not totally differ from other industries nor are their methods of large-scale regulation completely different, because *gemeinschaft* elements are to be found in many areas of modern organization,[6] including both the professional and industrial, but these elements have been more important in the docks than else-

[6] An interesting discussion of this can be found in E. Shils, 'Primordial, Sacred and Civil Ties', *British Journal of Sociology*, 8, 1957, pp. 130–45.

where. The second is the preservation of an extremely effective system of administration which relies little on conventional bureaucratic or formal principles of organization, or on the regulative force of a set of organizational goals and an associated value system. The administration of dock work on conventional berths is largely in the hands of the men and their foremen, and the control exercised by these two groups is most unusual in modern industry; indeed, it is probably anachronistic in view of developments in managerial practice over the last half-century.

The continuation of casual employment was the main structural underpinning of these aspects of traditionalism. Casual employment was instituted and retained largely because dock employers thought that this was the most profitable form of organization in a situation where their demands for labour constantly fluctuated according to weather conditions, tides, seasonal variations and the state of the economy. Casual labour was responsible for many of the features of work practice and culture discussed in this book and had a significant impact on the internal organization of the dock companies. Casual labour also gave rise to the Dock Labour Scheme, designed to protect workers against the worst abuses of the employers' power, which placed many managerial functions in the joint control of men and management: joint control meant that dock workers could preserve certain aspects of dock traditionalism even after the end of the casual system, though the forces of change which are working on the industry may ultimately lead to the destruction of the remaining inheritances from the era of casual labour.

The London docks display a striking paradox between the traditional character of certain key features of social organization and the non-traditional character of the men who work there. The conventional stereotype of dock workers used to describe them as men who lived in closed and insular communities around the docks, isolated from the rest of society, and aggressively hostile towards their employers. This stereotype passed into sociology when dock workers were labelled as 'traditional workers'. These workers are thought to display a number of essential characteristics.[7] They have high degrees of job involvement, close attachments to primary work groups, high degrees of autonomy from technical and supervisory constraints and distinctive work cultures based on shared occupational experiences. Outside work, they continue their work associations into non-work life via friendship, kinship and close residence, so as to form occupational communities. Their characteristic outlook is collectivist and they have intense feelings of belonging to work-dominated social groups, while their communities are inward-looking and marked by a strong sense of class identity and consciousness.

[7] J. H. Goldthorpe, D. Lockwood et al., The Affluent Worker (Cambridge, 1968), vol. 2, pp. 74–5.

In London, the old docking communities were largely broken up by the massive rebuilding of the East End and the movement of the existing population out of the area in the two decades after the last war. The decline of the docks as a source of employment has further weakened old communities, while the widespread ownership of cars and the provision of public transport means that people often commute several miles to work in the docks. These changes, taken together with the evidence of dock workers' attitudes and behaviour presented in this book, suggest that most aspects of the working-class traditionalism just described have long since disappeared in this occupation. Indeed, one theme of the book is to show just how untraditional dock workers really are.

The Research

I spent nearly two years between the summer of 1969 and spring 1971 engaged in the field work on which this account is based. First I spent a total of three months with twelve foremen in order to observe what went on in the docks and to obtain some concrete information about what foremen themselves did during their working day. I recorded foremen's activities by using a method of activity analysis developed elsewhere,[8] but the real pay-off from this method was not so much the factual information as what I learned about the industry at the workplace level, and the contacts I made among the people working there. Then I interviewed 139 men and 93 foremen (93 per cent and 98 per cent respectively of the people I asked for interviews) to find out their views on a variety of subjects, many of which I regarded as important as the result of my earlier observations. When the interviewing was completed in late summer 1970, I continued to visit the docks periodically to chat to people about what was going on and to carry out further observations.

Most of the observation and interviewing was done in Tilbury and the West India/Millwall docks, chosen because of the contrasts between them. Tilbury was expanding rapidly and handled both conventional and unitized work. There were two container berths, two packaged timber and paper pulp berths and one roll-on/roll-off berth in operation for much of the time, while a third container and a third timber berth became operational after the interview stage had been completed. The West India/Millwall was more old-fashioned and handled conventional work of a traditional nature, though a modernization programme started while I was there. I also interviewed some foremen from the Royal Group of docks.

The private sector firms where I spent most of my time were small or

---

[8] K. E. Thurley and H. Wirdenius, *Supervision: A Reappraisal* (London, 1973), describe this method in detail.

medium-sized, with labour forces ranging from 500 to 3,000 manual employees. Most had branches in more than one dock, so the operating units were smaller than overall size would suggest: the largest Tilbury branch had 600 men and 30 foremen, the largest in the West India/ Millwall had 225 and 12 respectively. I also conducted observations of foremen in the P.L.A., but when these were completed and I had obtained the go-ahead from the shop stewards and the foremen's representatives to start interviewing, the P.L.A. management decided that it no longer wished to provide me with research facilities. The foremen in Tilbury offered to help me out by taking part in the inter- viewing programme after work in their homes, but this was not practicable with the much larger number of manual workers. Most of the account in this book therefore focuses on the private sector.

The private firms handled the operations on board ship when loading and on both ship and quay when discharging. The P.L.A. was a large bureaucracy which was only partly concerned with operational work in the docks. Its main tasks were to maintain the river and dock infra- structures, and in the early seventies its operational responsibilities were mainly confined to the warehouse or shed work associated with loading and discharging, together with the quay work on loading jobs. The P.L.A. was not at the time a large employer of labour in Tilbury, where much of the interviewing was conducted, so the loss was not too important. Appendix A contains a copy of the interview schedule, while Appendix B gives some more technical details about the research.

A number of assumptions lay behind the way I carried out the investigation. The first was the importance of studying foremen. As will become clear later in the book, foremen have been until recently the central group in the administration of the docks, with the freedom to run things at their own discretion. They have also been very important in the workplace and occupational social systems in which the men have been involved. Thus foremen play a significant role in any attempt to understand the traditional character of the industry and the attitudes and behaviour of the men.

Foremen were also assumed to be important for the understanding of social class, because of the ambiguity surrounding their position in the class structure and the difficulty of clearly assigning them to the working or middle classes. The common sociological tradition is to classify foremen as members of the working-class élite or labour aristocracy, along with skilled craftsmen, but this often leads to difficulties in specific cases, when foremen appear very marginally related to the working class. Jackson and Marsden, for example, found that, 'though the foreman is an aristocrat, he is like that other aristocrat, the policeman, separate and isolated from the working class'.[9] A study of the Manchester docks

[9] B. Jackson and D. Marsden, *Education and the Working Class* (London, 1961), pp. 71–2.

found that older foremen had lived in the docking community and regarded themselves as part of a local social élite, but younger foremen felt obliged to move out of the area on being promoted, in order to meet the expectations of their wives and managers.[10]

There is even ambiguity about the objective nature of the foreman's situation. His industrial role is normally defined by management theorists as forming the first line of management, though practising managers know that this definition has a hollow ring. On the other hand, the official classification, which takes the occupation of a person to be 'the kind of work he or she performs, due regard being paid to the conditions under which it is performed', assigns foremen who supervise manual workers of any skill status to the ranks of skilled manual work;[11] the problem here, of course, is that this classification often *ignores* the nature of the work foremen do and the conditions under which they do it. The foreman who performs non-manual tasks, exercises managerial authority and is office-based, but supervises manual workers, is classified along with these workers. Class position must appear problematic when even one of the objective bases of class placement is treated so peculiarly.

What is sometimes called the sociology of occupations was chosen as the mode of analysis. This is the 'study of those social roles which arise from the classification of men by the work they do',[12] which emphasizes the importance of people's location in the social division of labour: in particular, their work situation and their share in the power structures of their firms. It assumes that the correlates of classifying men by their work are fairly uniform for all those in a particular classification. Few sociologists would dispute that the job an individual does is crucial for his social existence, because this has always been one basic element of sociological definitions of social class. But in practice, recent sociology has too often treated workers as consumers and dealt with 'life styles' and the distributive aspects of modern capitalism, thus ignoring the significance of workers as producers. This account of docking is primarily concerned with the nature of the work people have to do, the conditions under which this is performed, and the social relations which result from the organization of production and the nature of the employment system: work and the social relations of

[10] University of Liverpool, Department of Social Science, *The Dock Worker* (Liverpool, 1954), pp. 45–6. (This will henceforth be referred to as *The Dock Worker*, without further reference to the author.) Whether this social marginality was the cause rather than the consequence of promotion cannot be ascertained, but there is no evidence in their book to dispute the authors' conclusions that it was the consequence. In my research I did not find any conclusive evidence on this issue either, though this makes little difference to the main themes of this book.

[11] Office of Population Censuses and Surveys, *Classification of Occupations* (London, 1970), pp. vii and xi.

[12] T. Caplow, *The Sociology of Work* (New York, 1964), p. 4.

production *must* be central interests in the study of occupations and social class.

Occupational sociologists usually distinguish between the objective and cultural aspects of occupational membership.[13] The first includes the analysis of work roles and people's places in the social division of labour at work. The second includes those features which give an occupation a social character, so that it forms a community or social system. Emphasis is placed on the occupational value system, which reflects and regulates the social relationships people find themselves involved in, and workplace analysis focuses on patterns of interaction between the various parties and the rules which guide interaction. Occupational culture also includes values and ideologies which have a wider reference, such as those defining occupational solidarity or those defining the skills and domain of the occupation. Sometimes the cultural aspect of occupations is so important that members come to define themselves in occupational terms, as expressed in a strong moral involvement in, and commitment to, the occupation: the occupational communities of traditional workers imply this sort of commitment. The extent to which there is an occupational culture among dock workers is one of the subjects discussed here.

Finally, a few comments should be made about the people I interviewed. Declining job opportunities and reduced recruitment have had an effect on the age structure of the ports, despite lucrative voluntary severance schemes, natural wastage and lowering the retirement age to 65 years in 1969. The average age in the industry was 45·7 years in 1965 and 44·5 years in 1971. Of the men interviewed here, 14 per cent were over 55 years old, 29 per cent were aged between 45 and 55, 33 per cent were aged between 35 and 45, and the rest between 21 and 35. Of the foremen, 36 per cent were over 55 years old, 41 per cent were between 45 and 55, and the rest were between 30 and 45.

The docks have always given people the chance of lifelong employment in the industry, though this was not always very meaningful during the casual era when there was no guarantee that a man would earn a living wage. But dock workers have taken advantage of this opportunity, despite the hazards of casual work. Seventy per cent of the men and 99 per cent of the foremen had worked in the industry for more than 11 years. Thirty-two per cent of the men and 74 per cent of the foremen had worked for more than 21 years, which are quite remarkable figures. Over 31 per cent of foremen had held their supervisory positions for 15 years or more, and a further 20 per cent had been foremen for more than ten years.

Because the minimum age limit at the time was twenty-one, everyone had previous work experience. The great majority had been in un-

---

[13] ibid., p. 101, distinguishes between the 'secular' and 'sacred' aspects of occupations.

skilled and semi-skilled work, though 20 per cent had been in skilled or supervisory work and 10 per cent had been in white-collar jobs.

Conditions of employment were not greatly different for foremen and men. The men's wages varied considerably according to the piece-work allowances granted, hours worked, and whether or not they were on unitized berths. The range of earnings among the people interviewed can be seen in table 1.3. Foremen at the time earned less than many of the men. There was a fall-back wage paid to the men when there was insufficient work to keep them in employment and a daily minimum when the men were working but piecework earnings fell below the minimum. Foremen were paid a weekly wage which covered the first ten hours of overtime, after which extra payments were made. The largest firm set the standards of pay for foremen in all companies. Pensions differed little between the two groups and the only real advantages foremen had were better sick pay schemes. Security of employment was remarkably high for everyone.

CHAPTER 2

The Employment Relationship

Some understanding of the nature of the employment relationship between dock workers and their employers, in particular the foremen who were the employers' agents, is basic to any understanding of the docks. The present-day situation is bound up with, and enormously influenced by, the old system of casual employment. This system of hiring individuals by the half-day when it suited the employer to do so was responsible for the growth of a variety of institutions and customs which have continued into the present, despite the abolition of casual employment. The products of the casual era, however, now bring very different consequences from those of earlier days. The point is not just that historical factors influence the contemporary situation, a contention which would hardly be disputed in many other industrial situations, but that the institutional and cultural structure of one distinct and unique system of employment relationships has been transposed into another. The attitudes and feelings of individual dock workers and managers, which were formed during the old days were carried over into the new as well, but these are probably less significant in the long term than the transposition of the institutions and culture.

The casual system of employment was abolished only in September 1967, two years before I began this research. Employment relationships in the docks had therefore been anachronistic for many decades in comparison with those in other industries. They had been severely criticized for well over three-quarters of a century, and even as early as 1851, in his account of London labour, Henry Mayhew gave special treatment to casual labour in the docks.[1] Late nineteenth- and early twentieth-century social reformers, notably Charles Booth and the Webbs, leading trade unionists and government inquiries, all condemned casual employment as degrading and exploitative.[2] Indeed, the idea of decasualizing labour was so well accepted and supported in establishment circles, that provisions were written into the 1908 Port of London Authority Act which required the newly established P.L.A. to introduce

---

[1] P. Quennell (ed.), *Mayhew's London* (London, 1969), p. 568.
[2] The best contemporary accounts are: E. C. P. Lascelles and S. S. Bullock, *Dock Labour and Decasualisation* (London, 1924); H. A. Mess, *Casual Labour at the Docks* (London, 1916); *Report Concerning Transport Workers' Wages* (London, 1920), Cmnd. 936–7 (Shaw Report).

14

permanent employment whenever possible in London. The maintenance of a pool of surplus, unemployed labour, in order to meet the full demands of the ports on their busiest days, created intense competition for work, while employers engaged men by the half-day according to their widely fluctuating labour requirements. In this situation, employers could easily exploit dock labour. Even when they treated the men reasonably, normal employment relations were absent:

> The system placed minimal obligations on the employer who virtually hired for each job by the piece, paying either for hours worked or tons removed. He took no responsibility for the welfare of men who sought a living from dock labour but were not actually in his employ, and yet he depended on a supply of men in excess of his average needs to cope with business peaks.[3]

Reform from within the docks, however, had achieved virtually nothing by 1940, apart from some voluntary schemes to register those eligible to work in the docks. During the war years, the rigours of the pure and unbridled casual system were moderated by the Minister of Labour and former dockers' leader, Ernest Bevin. He brought in a series of measures which were finally consolidated and extended by the post-war Labour government, of which Bevin was a member though no longer Minister of Labour, as the 1947 National Dock Labour Scheme. But permanent labour was still not established and the industry still showed little inclination to decasualize after the war. Although the employers were mainly responsible for preserving casual labour, which was an efficient system from their point of view, the men themselves were partly to blame. A sufficiently large proportion did well out of casual labour to split the rank-and-file on the subject of permanency, while the majority in any case accepted the employers' arguments about the need for a margin of surplus labour to be hired or fired according to fluctuations in trade. James Sexton, leader of one of the early dock unions and later a Member of Parliament sponsored by the Transport and General Workers Union, was typical when he claimed that, 'you cannot decasualize dock labour at all, you can relieve it but you cannot absolutely decasualize'.[4] Internal divisions and a fatalistic acceptance of the system partly explain the failure to abolish casual labour, particularly in the post-war conditions of full employment and under the protection of the Scheme when systematic and concerted action by organized labour might well have forced employers to accede.

It required the intervention of outside interests before anything realistic was done in the way of decasualization: the government's establishment of the Devlin committee of inquiry into the labour

[3] D. F. Wilson, *Dockers* (London, 1972), p. 17.
[4] *Royal Commission on the Poor Law* (London, 1909), Cmnd 4499, part 6, para. 276.

problems of the industry in the mid-sixties and the threat of legislation should the vested interests within the docks refuse to act upon the committee's recommendations. Devlin was concerned to alter the industrial relations of the industry, which many at the time considered to be unsatisfactory, and not with decasualization as such. However, the committee argued that there could be no change in the industrial relations without there first being structural alterations in the system of employment. It recommended that the dock workers' employment relationship should be brought into line with that prevailing elsewhere between employers and employees. Decasualization of the labour force was the first and immediate phase of reform recommended by Devlin, to be followed at some unspecified date by the productivity bargain which would constitute the second phase.

The Casual Situation

The employment situation of dock workers prior to 1967 was unusual in two respects: dock workers were the permanent employees of the various Labour Boards and not of the operating firms, and they were hired on a casual basis by these firms. The Labour Boards were established by the 1947 Scheme, in order to employ dock workers. But they were employers without any work for their employees to perform. In London, as in many other docks, the Board paid a guaranteed minimum wage when the worker could not find temporary employment with a company; the Board acted as the 'holding employer', while the companies or 'operational employers' made use of the men by the half-day.

The Board was jointly controlled by the port employers and the unions and was designed to give a semblance of security to the casual workers who made up the bulk of the labour force. To this end, all disciplinary proceedings were in the hands of the Board and no dock worker could be removed from the register of authorized labour without the joint action of management and the men's own representatives. This security was, however, minimal: although employers were unable to employ non-registered labour, or to sack or discipline the men, the Board could not guarantee that an employer would hire a man and could only provide a fall-back wage considerably lower than would have been earned actually working. Within these limits, the dock worker's position was legally protected by the Act of Parliament which set up the National Dock Labour Scheme (Dock Workers [Regulation of Employment] Act, 1946). London had a 'free call' procedure during the casual period, by which the men presented themselves to the employers directly and not through the allocation procedures of the Board: all the men wishing to work in a certain dock congregated 'on the stones' in a pound, where the permanently employed foremen of the various companies hired those whom they wished to employ.

The operating foremen were the key figures in the hiring system, not the managers of the operating companies. Management was content to place control of hiring, firing and payment, in addition to the normal technical and overseeing components of the supervisory role, in the hands of foremen and relied on them to produce a good quality labour force for each job. For the dock worker, the managers became shadowy figures who had little to do with his being employed or unemployed, whereas the foremen were vital. Indeed, the foremen were such important figures that many workers came to regard themselves as working for them rather than for the particular firms they represented. Comparable situations were common historically, particularly in craft industries where foremen acted effectively as sub-contractors,[5] but became increasingly rare as industry was bureaucratized and management emerged as a discrete function. The preservation of such a role into the second half of the twentieth century is most unusual, exceeding even what is found in the building industry.

Within this framework there were both variations and exceptions, however. An exception was the P.L.A., which inherited a tripartite system of employment from its forebears, the old nineteenth-century dock companies, of permanent employees retained on a weekly or longer basis, preference men hired from the casual 'pool' before others, and pure casuals hired when the first two groups were insufficient. The hiring agent for the second and third categories ('A' and 'B' men) was the labour foreman in each dock. Individual operating foremen were not responsible for hiring and received those allocated to them by this central hiring agency. Operating foremen were consulted, however, when vacancies occurred in the permanent or 'A' categories and their views about individuals were taken into account.

In the private sector, a few companies employed a small proportion of 'perms' (permanent men), though the labour force had resisted the introduction of this practice into Tilbury, but the basic hiring procedure took place via the operating foremen as described above. The amount of personal discretion which foremen had, however, varied from company to company and dock to dock. In the London and St. Katherine Docks the foremen had complete discretion to hire any individuals they wanted, and to make up the gangs from these men. Elsewhere, the gangs were often already in existence and the foreman's discretion was to choose between gangs not individuals, though he could often fill any vacancies with men of his own choice. Some firms limited the foreman's discretion to some extent by having a nucleus of gangs to which all their foremen were expected to give priority before hiring additional labour, although this was only a slight limitation

[5] K. E. Thurley and H. Wirdenius, *Supervision: A Reappraisal* (London, 1973), p. 6.

because the foremen could influence the choice of gangs for this nucleus quite easily.

However the men were selected for work, 84 per cent of the foremen interviewed for this book reported that they had some men who worked regularly with them on all jobs prior to decasualization.[6] Among the dock workers, 17 per cent reported that they had been 'perms' under the old system, 68 per cent that they had worked mainly for one company whenever possible, and 15 per cent that they had been unattached, i.e. 'floated' or 'drifted'. These figures compare with the Devlin estimate of 25 per cent 'perms' (which includes the P.L.A. 'perms' not represented in this sample), 25 per cent regulars, and 50 per cent 'floaters' or 'drifters'. The discrepancy between the two sets of figures for regulars and unattached is difficult to explain as Devlin does not give the basis on which his data are based, but the respondents' own perceptions in this survey seem valid for present purposes.

The consequence of this system was the unusually strong hold foremen had over those whom they supervised. There were two essential characteristics which gave foremen enormous personal power over their men. The first was the considerable personal discretion which the casual system gave foremen in all the methods of hiring save in the P.L.A. The second was the way in which casual labour placed individual dock workers in competition with each other for work, weakening their collective solidarity and strengthening the power of the foremen.

The most frequent complaint against the traditional hiring methods, which was voiced by the dock workers and has been expressed in writings about the industry, is that it opened the way to the preferential treatment of a minority of dock workers over the rest. In its most extreme form, this became known as the 'blue-eyed boy system'. Because of the virtual freedom of choice given to foremen in picking their labour, personal attributes were alleged to be more important in selection than the capacity to do the job; the situation is best described in the usual dock phrase 'who you know, not what you know'. All foremen were reputed to have their own nucleus of blue-eyes, or their 'shiny eight' in some areas, who could rely on what was in effect permanent employment throughout the year and who received preferential treatment both by being hired first and by receiving the best-paying jobs.

As described by dock workers, this was a purely ascriptive system, the three most common bases of ascription being nepotism, bribery, and ethno-religious origins:

In the London Dock there were ten brothers and cousins all in the same family—3 of them were shipworkers and the rest were in the

---

[6] 5 per cent of foremen had not been foremen during the casual era, so this question did not apply.

labour.[7] Well I mean to say, it was obvious who was going to get the cream wasn't it?

When I first started down the hold you had to buy your job off one of the shipworkers. Every night he used to go to the local and get his beer money off the barman—we all had to chip in a tanner and the barman kept a list of who'd paid. Any time you refused, you'd be on the stones next call looking for a job.

Take the Big Boot gang—got all the cream on those ferry boats at 34 Shed, but you had to be a green scarf[8] to get in there. Any time Father X (the local priest) found someone in trouble—you know, the kiddies without clothes or the wife sick—he told the shipworker and that man got a couple of days with the gang.

Figures on the number of blue-eyes are hard to come by, but the Devlin Committee estimated 25 per cent of the labour force; i.e. the 25 per cent in casual employment who worked regularly for one company. The Liverpool University study of the Manchester docks estimated 26 per cent of blue-eyed boys, but 45 per cent who worked as regulars. The figures from the present sample show that only 15 per cent report themselves as not having worked regularly with one company most of the time. From this, it would seem unwise to conclude that the number of blue-eyes can be estimated from the number regularly employed, or can be accurately estimated at all. During times of full employment, as was largely the case in London after the mid-1950s, regular work for one company was normal rather than exceptional; those who were unattached included a large number who chose not to work for one employer.

In fact, the blue-eyed system during these years was important for allocation to certain types of work rather than for being in work at all. A blue-eyed gang which was consistently given high-earning cargo could often work fewer turns, and thus appear to be less regularly employed, than a non-preference one. Yet it would still earn more money. The infamous Big Boot gang in Tilbury, referred to in a previous quotation, was a case in point: this gang always worked a large, well-designed hatch which carried a high-earning cargo which was easily unloaded; consequently, two or three days' work a week was sufficient to boost earnings and allow the men the rest of the week free.

The number of blue-eyes is obviously nearly impossible to estimate, nor does it seem particularly profitable to attempt this: the blue-eyed system appears to have been only the most extreme form of a type of social relationship that was inherent in dock work under the casual

---

[7] A 'shipworker' is the *foreman* who deals with operations aboard ship, not a dock worker.

[8] A 'green-scarf' is an Irish Catholic.

hiring system. It is appropriate to consider certain other aspects of the system and the men's reactions to it at this point. These illuminate the structural conditions which underpinned the relationship between foremen and men.

The casual system of hiring created a competitive situation from the dock workers' point of view: the workings of supply and demand meant that all dock workers were in a state of potential competition with each other, either for work at all during slack times or for the best-paying jobs during times of full employment. Competition was seen at its most intense when it was transformed into physical violence between dock workers during the labour calls. These occasions were rare, but most of the people I interviewed knew of incidents when violence had occurred. As one said:

> You stopped being a man and turned into an animal once you stepped on to the pound. It was like the law of the jungle on that call-stand—survival of the fittest was the only thing that counted. That's one reason why the pound never had any walls—to stop us trampling each other to death.

This competition was not completely unbridled, however, because various restrictions had been introduced over the years to make it fairer. The National Dock Labour Scheme was one institution which regulated competition, via the register of those allowed to work, but this was a minimal form of regulation: it limited competition to accredited men and ensured that the employers could not flood the labour market. The most important forms of regulation, however, were maintained by the men themselves, via their unions, and were frequently accepted by the employers.

The continuity rule was the main protective device. This was originally introduced by the employers in order to prevent the men leaving before a job had been completed, picking the best of the work and then moving to another job. The rule provided that a worker had to complete a job once he had started it. The job came to be defined very narrowly, referring to the hatch or hold worked, and not to the ship or quay as a whole. Jobs could not be started in the middle of a 'turn' (i.e. the half-day hiring period). From the men's point of view, however, the effect of this rule was to prevent too great an exploitation of the casual system by the foremen (acting for the employers) and to spread the work more evenly through the labour force by restricting the use of the blue-eyed boys. Blue-eyes could not be given just the cream of the work and none of the rest, nor could they be transferred from a ship nearing completion to start work on one just arrived, or from hatch to hatch on the same ship or from the ship to the quay. In this way, non-preference men were protected from constant under-employment and from being allocated only poor-earning cargoes when they were given work.

The overtime ban of the middle and late 1960s acted as a similar device. The ban was designed to supplement the continuity rule by preventing the blue-eyes from using overtime in order to finish one job so as to start another job the next day, a technique made necessary by the rule. It was also designed to ensure that all men had the chance of working and not only those who were willing to work overtime. Another device was 'excessive manning', though this was less specifically tied to the dock situation because it is a universal tactic of spreading employment. But it did have a particular relevance in the docks and was significant for reducing the inherent insecurity of casual labour.

The continuity rule and the overtime ban were protective devices, providing the individual with some protection not only from the foremen and employers but also from his co-workers. These two devices highlight one of the important characteristics of the employment situation in the docks prior to 1967: its divisive potential. The situation promoted individualism, setting one worker against another as previously described. It also fostered the formation of gangs, small groups which increased the individual's bargaining power and protected him against others. Even these were segmental forces, however, since they merely raised competition from the individual to the group level.

Nevertheless, dock workers have long had a reputation for striking displays of collective solidarity during any major industrial action, a paradoxical reputation in view of the true nature of casual labour. The study of Manchester dockers remarked on this paradox and explained solidarity as a psychological compensation for competition.[9] A recent description of dock workers has suggested that the traditional hostility of outsiders towards dockers has been another possible reason for this.[10] During my research for this book I found that the explanation appeared to reside in the sentiments of occupational identification and solidarity which were strongly held by respondents. These were the products of a common situation for the members of the occupation and served to unite dock workers at least on certain occasions. During the casual days, these sentiments appear to have been reinforced by an additional awareness that collective action was the only way to avoid the divide-and-rule policies of employers during major disputes at least, whatever competitiveness was manifest on smaller issues.

The continuity rule, the overtime ban and excessive manning were therefore elements of an occupational culture in the docks. They acted as norms which governed the conduct of occupational members in order to regulate the permanent tension of the casual system between individualism and solidarity.

The tension which the competitive employment situation created has in fact been a part of the ideology of docking until the present day.

[9] *The Dock Worker*, pp. 66–7.
[10] D. F. Wilson, op. cit., pp. 49–54.

Many of the descriptions of the call-stand would appear to have mythical overtones, possibly true at one time but not true of the post-war period: only a few dock workers claimed to have seen physical violence at first hand, but most mentioned indirectly experienced instances which formed part of the historical lore of docking or which their fathers and grandfathers had witnessed. These myths in fact revealed the potentiality of the call-stand and of the casual system generally, since they expressed the degrading nature of the system (which was directly experienced by all) and the fact that violence might emerge in certain conditions. Such an ideology provided an even greater commitment to those means which existed for regulating the competition to at least a limited extent. The regulative norms thus reflected certain fundamental values of docking. Indeed, the fear of competitive individualism continued after the advent of permanency: the policing of work-sharing agreements by the stewards and the move towards the equalization of wages were both designed to stop the individual benefiting at the cost of his mates and to prevent the emergence of a new blue-eyed stratum.

In the light of this situation, preferential hiring practices during the casual era can also be interpreted as one of the ways in which the individual introduced order into a hostile world, another way of bridling the competition of pure supply and demand. The large number reporting that they worked mainly for one company shows that some form of preference was not confined to the blue-eyed minority, but was in fact a normal relationship for many dock workers. The essence of this relationship, in the pure type, was the way in which it bound together people who interacted together on a personal, face-to-face basis. This was a dyadic tie, which linked together pairs of individuals and not groups.

This tie had four distinct variants, though they all overlapped in practice. These were kinship, friendship—which found their most corrupt forms in the nepotism and bribery alleged by dock workers—, the socio-religious community of the Irish Catholics, and patron-clientage.[11] Inherent in all of these was the exploitation of non-economic bonds for instrumental purposes at work. Given the inadequate institutions of employment, dock workers were obliged to seek informal structures which were interstitial and parallel to the formal ones. A system of personal bonds filled the 'functional gaps' which existed in the social structure of the docks, where the formal institutional framework was unable to protect the individual satisfactorily against chronic

[11] E. R. Wolf, 'Kinship, Friendship and Patron–Client Relations in Complex Societies', in M. P. Banton (ed.), *The Social Anthropology of Complex Societies* (London, 1966), pp. 1–22, discusses the various personal bonds which make up dyadic ties. *The Dock Worker*, p. 74, noted the importance of kinship, friendship and religion as the bases of gang recruitment in Manchester.

uncertainty. The most obvious sources of these informal structures were to be found in the ascriptive, specific and personal ties with foremen which existed before the employment relationship, rather than in the 'achievement' (performance)-oriented and diffuse ties which sociologists regard as characteristic of the modern, contractual institutions of employment which are typically found in developed industrial societies. (Though it has been suggested that interstitial relationships similar to those found in the docks are in reality quite common in all modern social structures, behind the formal institutional façades.[12]) In the docks, the personal bond was a solid, down-to-earth insurance policy.

In order to illustrate the nature of the tie between foremen and individual workers, some further discussion of the variety of hiring practices is required. This shows how the relationship could be modified by the incorporation of various collective elements in addition to the purely face-to-face ones. It shows also that the exploitative and corrupt nature of the casual employment relationship has perhaps been overstated and described in terms which are too simple and crude: reciprocity between men and foremen was always important and at the same time personal preference had to be modified by some consideration of achievement values. The amplification which follows is based on the views and justifications of the foremen, which are obviously self-interested but do serve as counterweights to the more common perceptions of casual labour, which in turn probably reflect some degree of self-interest on the part of other groups. The following analysis applies to the private sector unless stated to the contrary.

Reciprocity was an essential part of the link between foremen and their individual dock workers, because foremen saw the relationship as one of an exchange of favours. In return for employment the foremen expected hard work of a certain level of quality, because they themselves were dependent on the achievement of their labour force: any foreman whose dock workers consistently produced shoddy or slow work ran the risk of being sacked by the employer. Thus they reported that labour selection could never be on a purely ascriptive basis because their own employment depended on their employing a labour force of a certain level of competence. This was particularly true in the larger concerns. Nepotism and other forms of preferential treatment were openly admitted, but only if the subject of this preference could pull his weight in the gang: favouritism gave a man an edge over his equals but not over his superiors. (Nepotism was interestingly dismissed as a major source of corruption, on the grounds that all dock workers had relatives in some gang or other and so everyone was a potential beneficiary of the system.) At the same time, the men selected by a foreman were dependent for their earnings on the others he chose to work alongside

[12] E. R. Wolf, op. cit.

T.D.—2

them, and it was asserted that no gang would tolerate slackers kept on grounds of favouritism alone: the rest of the gang would sooner or later look for another foreman to follow.

Reciprocity was also expected by both sides in the allocation of work: foremen said that the greatest merit of the preferential system from their point of view was the way their men would take the bad with the good. This meant that the men would work as well and as fast on dirty, difficult, or generally low paying work as they would on the cream, because it was understood that they would get priority on the next good job. They further asserted that a foreman without a regular following would not be able to make up a gang for some types of work during periods of full employment. Foremen also justified the situation by claiming that regular gangs working for one shipworker or company learned the types of work usually handled and the shipworker's methods, and so could earn higher piecework wages.

Thus it was probably true that foremen were dependent on a reciprocal relationship with their labour force, to the extent that their own positions were dependent on the quality and speed of the cargo-handling allocated to them. How far foremen genuinely risked dismissal is unclear, given the inadequate records of most firms. There is little doubt that some foremen were dismissed for inadequate performance, but impressionistic evidence suggests that foremen exaggerated the risk in their recollections of the old situation. Nevertheless, to the extent that some reciprocity undoubtedly did exist, the picture of crude corruption and exploitation must be modified: ascriptive practices were inherent in dock work, but achievement norms formed some sort of counterweight.

The simplest variety of hiring process, and the one accepted as the paradigm of the employment contract under the casual system, was where the foreman chose thirteen individuals (the usual gang size) at the call and made them into a gang for the particular job. This clearly shows the foreman's great personal discretion and the power which this gave him. But it also demonstrates the personal nature of the relationship between the two parties: the employment contract was between the foreman and thirteen separate individuals, not between him and a collectivity nor between an inanimate company and employees. The foreman had complete control over whom he hired and how he allocated the individuals into gangs and hatches. So, in return, he expected loyalty to himself. This system was most common in the small docks in the upper sections of the river.

Downriver, including Tilbury, it was more usual for foremen to pick up ready-made gangs, over whose composition they had less control. These gangs were fairly coherent entities with their own leaders, who are commonly known as gangers or downhold foremen. However these leaders assumed their positions, whether by election or seniority in an established gang, or by breaking away and persuading others to join in a new one, they acted as sub-contractors of labour from the foreman's point of view: i.e. the foreman normally chose the ganger and got the individuals in the gang as a package deal.

From the dock workers' point of view, the crucial relationship was that between their ganger and the foreman: a ganger who had close personal ties with a foreman could ensure them work, whereas a ganger without these could do so less effectively. A ganger promoted the interests of his gang with foremen in a position to help it; he acted as their representative. The allegiance of the gang members was partly to the ganger as well as to the foreman, so that the relationship between foreman and dock workers might appear at times as one between an individual and a collectivity rather than between individuals. But even here personal ties and interaction were still important. The foreman could exert influence to place his own nominee in the gang, either when vacancies occurred or when the gang was being formed. Over a period of working regularly with one foreman, ties between the individual dock workers and the foreman developed and ensured continuing employment, while the hiring of a gang in the first place was commonly due to some shared bond between its members and the foreman and not only to that between the foreman and the ganger.

There was often, in fact, a tension between the gang as a form of collectivity and the assertion of individual relationships, and some gangs appeared to have resisted such pressures. In particular, an established gang with a good reputation, or a ganger with wide contacts, was able to switch allegiance from one foreman or company to another, using the market place to its own advantage. Two quotations illustrate the way the gang system could at times modify the customary relationship into an impersonal one based on collectivities, the first from a shop steward and the second from a stevedoring company director:

> The gang system was a device invented by the men in order to defend themselves against the insecurity of the casual days, as 13 men working together over several years provided a better service to the employers than 13 men picked up by the turn for a one-off job. It was also to defend themselves against the shipworkers by a show of collective solidarity—the shipworkers exploited the men by setting one man against the other on the principle of Divide and Rule, but the men saw through this and learned to present a united front.

> The basic unit of a capitalist system—a small group of men selling their labour to the highest bidder.

There was another possible variation which was compatible with either of the preceding ones. This was for the company rather than an individual foreman to have a small nucleus of quasi-permanent labour which all its foremen were expected to hire in preference to others. Collectively the foremen could influence the composition of this nucleus, but it was more difficult for an individual foreman to exercise his personal discretion. Achievement principles were more likely to count than ascriptive ones here, because the composition of this force was open to scrutiny by several foremen and the company's management as well. This variation appears to differ from the others, in that individual dock workers and gangers owed allegiance to several men rather than to one. In some cases, employment may even have been perceived as deriving from the inanimate entity of the company. However, individual dock workers still had to get on with individual foremen, even though this was with several rather than with one, and the foremen suggested that dyadic ties might assume importance even under this system: foremen still had some personal discretion in deciding who was in the nucleus.

In addition to the complexities of the hiring process and modifications of the basic tie, the preference or blue-eyed system was graded internally according to the nature of the gang: some blue-eyed gangs were more blue-eyed than others. Typically, this meant that most foremen or companies had some top gangs which got better work than the other preference gangs, or were guaranteed fuller employment than the others during periods of slack trade. Foremen justified this on the grounds that the top gangs were the best ones, and that this system kept everyone 'on his toes':

> It was a sort of promotion system really—the top gangs went to 2 and 4 holds, while the not so good ones went to 1, 3 and 5. If one of the top gangs was short, they would pick a good man from another hold to make up the numbers—this was how a good young 'un got spotted, and he could often get into that gang on a permanent basis. Sometimes we'd demote a top gang to 1, 3 or 5 holds, if it was 'sciving', so as to give 'em a shock, or we'd promote a new gang to see how it made out.[13]

With hindsight, foremen legitimized this arrangement as an achievement-oriented system. They argued that 2 and 4 holds on the average 5-hold ship were larger and so had more cargo (rather than better), but that in order to make the job pay it was necessary to work faster because the space was larger and more movement was required to maintain the same rate of output as in a smaller hold. (Hold No. 1 is always the smallest and in addition carries dirty or dangerous cargo.)

The foregoing demonstrates the variety of forms which the basic employment relationship could assume. Its formal structure was normally the individual tie between foremen and men. However, this description may have obscured the actual content of the relationship by

[13] *The Dock Worker*, p. 72, found a somewhat similar system of promotion.

overemphasizing foremen's views as counterweights to the men's. Elements of exchange did exist in the dealings between the two parties, and ascriptive ties did, therefore, have instrumental advantages for both sides. But the foundation of the relationship must ultimately have rested on power, given the foremen's position in the casual system. The maximization of the foremen's discretion gave them the right to decide who was allowed to work and how much he would earn. Even 'exchange' involved power elements, because the foremen alone decided who was to be allowed to enter into this relationship with them and what the terms of the exchange were to be. The other party had few rights in these decisions.

It is not entirely clear who benefited most. Dock workers probably had more to gain than the foremen, given their situation, because foremen enjoyed superior power and status and had a far more stable employment situation, despite their protestations that they could always be sacked. The contract between individual participants of differing status and power in situations of inadequate institutional development such as that found in the docks has been summarized by Wolf, as 'a lop-sided friendship, which provides instrumental advantages to both parties, but with an unequal distribution'.[14] The notion that subordinates benefit more in these cases is true in the docks, if attention is concentrated on the foremen to the exclusion of the companies which employed them. Foremen benefited less than the men so far as material rewards were concerned, although they enjoyed far more congenial working conditions and work tasks when they had power over the men than they did after decasualization. But the owners of the dock companies were the group to benefit most concretely: the good profits which resulted from high labour productivity and the low costs of administering a self-regulating labour force which required little supervision and no specialist personnel function were very tangible financial rewards.

When I asked people for their opinions and evaluations of the old system of employment there were predictable differences between the men and the foremen. Eighty-four per cent of the foremen stressed how important the men's loyalty to them had been in the old days, whereas less than five per cent of the men mentioned this aspect and 65 per cent emphasized the corruption and indignity of being beholden to the foremen. These differences show the very different meanings the two groups gave to the primary personal ties which underlay the employment system of casual work.

Foremen thought that affective elements were incorporated into the tie, this being one of the ways in which the relationship differed from coercion or pure contract in their eyes. The affect was not symmetrical, however, because it involved 'loyalty' on the part of dock workers but

14 E. R. Wolf, op. cit., p. 16.

did not necessarily presuppose affective sentiments on the part of foremen: the frequent reference to the shipworker's 'following' or 'followers' indicated where the emphasis was expected to lie and suggested the dependency underlying the tie. Dock workers, however, failed to emphasize affective elements and often indicated that the relationship had been entered into against their will. The ends of the relationship, rather than any other aspect, were what mattered: 95 per cent of those working regularly with one foreman prior to decasualization said that they had done so mainly for instrumental reasons.

There was potentially some tension between collective and individual principles of social organization on occasion. But in practice personal bonds and discretion intruded into nearly all relationships, even when the collective principle appeared to be important. Personalistic criteria were absent in only one instance, when achievement and contractual norms came to govern relations. This can be labelled the entrepreneurial case, which occurred when a particularly good gang exploited its position in a competitive market so as to create for itself the choice of foremen for whom to work. The intrusion of achievement norms into an otherwise ascriptive relationship, the result of the foremen's need for some reciprocity of benefits, opened the way for some notably high-achieving gangs to behave in this entrepreneurial manner. The exercise of choice in this fashion, selling to the highest bidder, was perhaps more similar to the impersonal and market-based contract of modern industrial societies, than to the more usual types of casual employment relationship in the docks.

There was a second source of supervisory control over the men, in addition to the actual employment relationship itself. This was the product of mechanisms internal to the labour force. The first was the position of the ganger or downhold foreman, as he has variously been called. As part of his split role as a type of labour sub-contractor and men's representative, he was entrusted with supervisory responsibilities by foremen. These included direction of work along with traditional labour control functions. Because all parties knew that the men's livelihood was at stake, foremen could delegate their operating responsibilities in the knowledge that gang and ganger would regulate themselves. Any decline in standards or speed of work would be remedied by expulsion of the offending individual from the gang.

The second of the internal mechanisms was the craft-like nature of dock work, particularly of stevedoring. Under a system of casual employment, traditional skills were an essential requisite, a form of insurance against unemployment, because good men stood more chance of work than bad. Ascriptive practices alone could not always guarantee employment. The inheritance of employment by one generation from another, often from father to son, has been a characteristic of docking throughout this century. In this instance, it served also to transmit traditional skills and pride in craftsmanship from generation to generation:

> I started out as a youngster working in my uncle's gang—all me mates did the same, 'cos that way you'd pick up stevedoring from the old hands. It was like an apprenticeship really—you kept on getting clouted until you could hold your own and the gang didn't have to carry you any more. You should've seen those old timers work—it was beautiful—they could shift 400 tons of cement from craft without sweating enough to take off their 'chokers', while we young 'uns were stripped. But that was how you learned the trade, and that's how you kept house and home together in those days.

Craft-like standards of discipline were also enforced by the National Amalgamated Stevedores and Dockers' Union, known historically as the 'blue' union after the colour of its membership cards, where foremen were members of the same branch as the men. The blue union originated as the organization of the highly skilled stevedores of the late nineteenth and early twentieth century, though it became representative of all dock workers in the early years of this century, and continued to maintain some aspects of what was effectively a craft mentality throughout the casual era. In particular, union rules made it an offence to behave in ways detrimental to the standards of the trade, and consequently foremen were able in certain circumstances to use branch meetings to enforce discipline if necessary. This reinforcement of internalized controls was not performed by the Transport and General Workers' Union (the 'whites') which historically had organized less skilled groups.

The Impact of Decasualization and Permanent Labour

The major impact of the decasualization of employment was on the traditional balance of power in the industry. The abolition of casual hiring resulted in the end of the old authority and exercise of control by the employers, and therefore by the foremen. But the new system of employment did not replace these with any equivalents, nor even with the same sort of power which most other present-day employers have over their workers. Permanent employment as it was introduced into the docks not only altered the old relationship between a worker and his company or its agent but, at least for a time, gave the dock workers a degree of security and power greater than is normally found in the employment situation of manual workers. The introduction of Phase 1 in 1967 and the failure to modify the old National Dock Labour Scheme at the same time explain how the shift to permanency could create such a dramatic alteration in the power of foremen and employers. The Scheme had originally been introduced in the casual context and worked in such a way as to limit the worst extremes of such a system, particularly its exploitation by the employers. But the Scheme had not encroached greatly on the power of the employer or his foremen because they could always refuse to hire a worker, their basic strength in dealings with labour. The continuation into permanency of the Scheme as a whole, particularly of the provisions regulating casual labour, produced completely unanticipated consequences for employers.

The role of the London Dock Labour Board under the Scheme has been significant during and after the transition from one employment system to another. At the change-over, the residual function of the Board as holding employer was to control the allocation of labour to the different companies, which removed hiring rights not only from the foremen but even from managers and owners. This allocation function has continued throughout the period since decasualization, as the men made redundant by the rapid and continuing contraction of employment in the upriver docks and wharves have been redeployed in the remaining dock system. In the early days, employers stated how many men they wished to employ and stated their preference for certain individuals. But it proved impossible always to match these preferences with those of the dock workers, who also had a choice, with the consequence that many companies had little control over whom they were allocated. Most local managements had to take on men who appeared merely as numbers on a page until they presented themselves for their first job. Thus the employers were able to decide how many men they wished to employ, but not choose the individuals who made up this allocation. (In the early 1970s, employers often found that they could no longer even control numbers and had to take on more men than they needed.)

Two other functions of the Board as a holding employer were retained after decasualization: control of the register of dock workers and control over discipline. Despite the greater security of permanency, the old legal protection of dock workers against the employment of outsiders and against dismissal from dock work was carried over into the new system. The register, which was designed to modify the abuses of an unrestrained casual system, was not abolished but continued to be supervised by the two sides of industry who jointly constituted the Dock Labour Board. Whereas previously the register in effect had protected only a man's right to *seek* work, permanency meant that the Board could now ensure that a man was given work on a regular basis. As a dock worker could only be removed from the register if he assaulted someone or committed a theft in the docks, this effectively amounted to guaranteed employment with no possibility of being sacked.

Moreover, the Board itself was responsible for all the other forms of discipline apart from removal from the register, and the employer had no rights in this area during Phase 1. This area of the Board's responsibility was extended by Devlin to include the men permanently employed by the companies prior to decasualization. The maximum penalty for any actions short of the two mentioned remained as it had been prior to decasualization: a three-day suspension. However, in view of the delays in hearing cases, the need to send representatives to the hearing, and the existence of equal numbers of union and employers' delegates on the Board's committee, employers were reluctant to use this machinery: they cited many instances where the lengthy and wasteful procedures were gone through, only to find that the union side prevented any effective disciplinary measures being taken. From the employers', and therefore the foremen's point of view, this mutation of the machinery designed to function under the casual system led to a total loss of power over the men. They possessed no disciplinary powers, had no right to sack their employees, could not in practice return an individual to the Board, and had no effective control over whom they were allocated in the first place, while the machinery set up by the Board was hamstrung from the outset by a balance of forces.

In theory, the Phase 2 agreement which the employers and unions jointly negotiated, and which was implemented in London in September 1970, gave employers more disciplinary powers in day-to-day affairs, although serious cases were still to go before the Board. Predictably, however, the men themselves have in practice resisted any real extension of managerial prerogative in this area. Managements have usually been unwilling to risk the disruption which would result if they were to force the issue in a systematic manner, and have by and large left the new powers in abeyance. (This has been true to date: it is of course possible that the situation may change in the employers' favour over time.)

It should be stressed at this point that the Scheme, and the system of Labour Boards which it established, has always been regarded by dock workers as one of the central institutions of docking.[15] The philosophy of joint regulation which it embodies is still unique in British industry, since no other arrangement has deliberately given the work force so much shared control over what are normally regarded as managerial functions.[16] The Scheme was undoubtedly the most successful attempt of the post-war Labour Government to provide for worker participation in industry, and the only case where the arrangements provided for more than a nominal participation of workers in management activity. Recruitment, dismissal, discipline, welfare and training are all jointly regulated by the men's representatives. This control has obviously given the men great security and some power over their employers, during permanency at least.

It has also had a major consequence for the occupation itself. Since recruitment was jointly controlled, the men were able to ensure that

[15] *Devlin Report*, para. 259.
[16] D. F. Wilson, op. cit., pp. 99–100.

docking continued to run in families long after other manual occupations were opened to outsiders. (Recruitment on the basis of kinship continued among professional occupations for far longer, of course, and is still an accepted practice in the medical profession today.) Each side nominated half the new recruits, which guaranteed that this proportion at least would be the close relatives of existing dock workers. In practice, managers observed conventional priorities, so that the sons and other relatives of dock workers have normally had preference in the employers' allocation as well.[17] The managers whom I interviewed said that one reason for this was the fact that they could reward foremen and loyal workers by putting forward their relatives as the employers' own nominees. The corollary of this was that the practice helped to build up loyal followings for the firms. The highly personal and ascriptive ethos of the docks is clearly shown in this convention: the idea that certain families produce 'good' employees and that a worker already employed will vouch for his kin. There was also the fact that, in the absence of proper training schemes, existing workers had to train new recruits and that kinsmen were more likely to be willing to do this than strangers.

It is worth mentioning here that occupational inheritance has, of course, created certain problems for the firms, mainly because it has fostered an historical perspective among dock workers. New recruits have knowledge of the industry which often stretches back two generations, even when they themselves are in their early twenties. Rochdale claimed that,

> few industries are so burdened with the legacy of the past. We have been struck by the extent to which many facets have to be understood against the background of history. Practices and attitudes can often be traced back a long way; old traditions die hard.[18]

This has been particularly significant in industrial relations, and foremen and managers are often confronted by events from the past. For example, one of the foremen whom I interviewed complained that he was still reminded of his father's actions twenty-five years previously, when his father (also a foreman) had treated the men particularly badly. During the interviewing, a further five people mentioned the famous dock strikes of 1911 and 1912 in the discussion of present-day unionism and industrial relations.

The changed structural conditions of permanency had a considerable effect on the relationship between foremen and dock workers, transforming what had been one of the most significant features of the casual system. After decades of power that was only loosely fettered, in the

---

[17] *Report of a Committee of Inquiry into the Major Ports of Great Britain* (London, 1962), Cmnd. 1824, para. 407. This will henceforth be referred to as *Rochdale Report* (1962), in order to distinguish it from a later report by Rochdale.

[18] ibid., para. 355.

private sector at least, foremen found themselves almost powerless after decasualization. The abolition of the right to hire and fire completely demolished their control over the labour force. They could no longer rely on that combination of favouritism and coercion which had been the foundation of supervisory authority and of the ties between men and foremen, while the men no longer found themselves the subordinate and dependent party in a highly personalized relationship of power.

Along with the loss of hiring and firing went the foremen's right to allocate men to the various holds. The Phase 1 agreement followed Devlin by laying down work-sharing requirements in order to abolish the preference system once and for all. Consequently, the allocation of work in all the companies studied was taken out of the foremen's hands and given usually to a senior member of the local management. The manager responsible arranged a rota in consultation with the shop stewards for each week's work and then met the stewards each morning to monitor the previous day's working, the rota being adjusted if necessary. Rotation was based normally on hatch numbers, so that everyone had an equal opportunity of working on the good and the bad ones.

This system went a long way towards the abolition of the blue-eyed boys, but it did not succeed in the equalization of payment between gangs which Devlin desired, because, under a piecework system, good gangs could earn significantly more than others in the course of a year (see table 1.3). Consequently, stewards in a local branch of one of the companies demanded a system of equalization of earnings: gangs which fell behind on piecework earnings were to be given a series of good jobs until their pay rose to the required level, while high-earning gangs were relegated to the worst hatches. This was introduced during Phase 1, and other firms began to adopt similar systems thereafter.

Decasualization led to a further and different kind of alteration in traditional relationships. The allocation of men at the time of the change-over, when individual workers stated which of the companies they would prefer to work for, and the continual redeployment of men since, following the contraction of the upper docks and the expansion of the lower ones, combined to destroy old social relationships forged during the casual days. Of the men, 53 per cent stated that they had worked regularly with a single foreman prior to Phase 1, but only 4 per cent of this number still work with the same man now with any degree of frequency. Equally, 79 per cent were members of a gang in the old days, but only 31 per cent of these men still work with the same gang now.

At the same time, foremen were prevented from building up new relationships with the new individuals and newly formed gangs with whom permanency brought them into contact. The work-sharing system mentioned above thus had a secondary consequence for foremen. Since work-sharing involves the rotation of gangs between ships and thus between different foremen, in all but the smallest companies it is now possible for a foreman to go for weeks or months before he is allocated the same men twice.

Foremen were asked for their views about the two methods of employment during the interviews. Despite their emphasis elsewhere on reciprocity and the exchange of favours, foremen were quite clear in response to this question that the basic underpinning of their old relationship with the men had been control over who could work. Sixty-five per cent of private sector foremen favoured casual employment for this reason. Foremen complained that their jobs had become much more difficult during permanency, because the pace and quality of the men's work had dropped, there was less co-operation in chasing cargo, and they had to increase supervision as a result. As one foreman said,

> Take the way the men work these days—I have to feel every man who comes aboard to see if he's still alive.

Indeed, they felt that the old power situation had been reversed: security of employment, work-sharing and ineffective disciplinary procedures meant that workers could ignore their foremen to all intents and purposes, if they chose to do so. The interviews showed that 60 per cent of foremen felt their own job satisfaction had declined and their prestige and personal pride were less after decasualization. As another complained,

> I could stand all the aggro' and blackmail from the men, if at the end of the day I could look down the hold and feel satisfied—you know, see it all neatly stowed and battened down and feel that I was responsible for it. But I get no satisfaction at all from the job now—it's a shambles from start to finish and the ship sails off with everything like a bollocking pigsty.

Not surprisingly, 91 per cent of the men preferred permanency, mainly because of the loss of self-respect and the corruption which the old system was seen to generate. More generally, they welcomed the end of casual employment because it had brought dependable employment, the end of the law of the survival of the fittest, and transferred the onus of finding work from the worker to the firm.

Decasualization also led to changes in the internal methods of control, gang and craft discipline. The importance of the ganger's role was bound up with the casual situation: while the men were partly dependent for employment on the ganger's ability to manipulate his range of contacts, and while it was important for the gang to be run efficiently and be internally self-regulating in order to provide a good service, the ganger was a strategic figure. However, the developments which eroded the foreman's position had the same effect on the ganger's. The advent of permanent employment and work-sharing, together with the end of any effective disciplinary controls, meant that the ganger lost his purpose from the men's point of view. This hit foremen and management, because it marked the end of the gang as a producing unit which could be left to its own devices and the end of the ganger as an individual who assumed some supervisory responsibilities for controlling the labour force.

Gangs were done away with on berths using unitized technologies during Phase 1, but continued elsewhere until the flexible manning agreements of Phase 2. The gang had long formed an important element of the culture and social organization of docking. But the value men placed on gangs followed situational factors, which in conditions of piecework and casual employment meant that gangs were primarily valued for their instrumental benefits: the security of employment and income they provided and the chance of maximizing earnings. The gang's security function was reduced as the result of the Phase 1 employment conditions, which in turn made it less salient to the men and eroded some of its power of social control. But the continuation of piecework payment during Phase 1 meant that gangs still had an instrumental use in maximizing earnings, because a regular team could move more cargo than one put together on an ad hoc basis. However, the subsequent abolition of piecework in Phase 2 destroyed even this rationale of gangs. Consequently the men agreed to abolish gangs when the employers negotiated reduced manning scales and more flexible manning arrangements. (Another protective device of the casual era, the continuity rule, also lost its purpose in the men's eyes once permanency was established and piecework abolished, and it too was given up as part of the Phase 2 deal. It had already been suspended on unitized berths which abolished piecework earlier.)

The old standards of work quality and discipline have declined over the last decade and a half, particularly after permanency. Traditional skills are no longer necessary as insurance against unemployment and the unions do not bother to enforce standards. Similarly, the introduction of a common register for all dock workers, in place of the old distinction between ship and shore work, has opened the more skilled ship work to all comers. The demarcation between the two types of work was given up as part of the price of decasualization. As this was followed by massive closures upriver, particularly among wharfingers, it led to the influx of men without the traditional skills and standards of self-discipline.

What happened in the years following decasualization was the collapse of a traditional system of power based on non-bureaucratic and personalistic relationships, and the growth of new social relationships at work. The old system and its transformation can be seen most clearly in the relationships between foremen and men. However, the new patterns of authority and administration were influenced by the inheritance from the casual era in such a way that bureaucratic principles and conventional employment relationships could not develop. This theme is elaborated at various points in succeeding chapters.

CHAPTER 3

Work

Modern sociologists have frequently neglected the tasks which people have to perform in their jobs and the immediate social and physical environments in which they work. This is a curious omission when one considers that over a century ago Marx regarded work and the conditions under which it was performed as sufficiently important for the analysis of capitalism to devote much of the first volume of *Capital* to the description and analysis of labour processes. The interest some people have shown recently in the impact of technology on attitudes to work has involved some discussion of work and working conditions, but this technological perspective has remained limited in scope. Yet there are good reasons for treating the work situation more thoroughly and extensively. An obvious reason is that firms are places where work gets done and that a minimum level of performance must be achieved by the individual. In addition, the work an individual does evidently has some meaning for himself, whether favourable or otherwise. More significantly, the individual's work situation is one of the basic elements of both his occupational and class positions.

Shared work helps to create a common structural position for those who do the tasks, while at the same time it marks them off from others who do different jobs. As the official classification of occupations states, 'the basic common factor of all groups is the kind of work done and the nature of the operation performed', due regard being paid also to the conditions under which it is done.[1] In social class analysis, both a Weberian multi-factor approach and a more narrowly defined, Marxist notion of productive and unproductive labour and relations to the means of production reach some common ground in the importance they give to work as a structural determinant of class position. Analysis of the work situation should therefore help to define the position of these dock workers and foremen.

Moreover, the precise character of an occupation and the typical attitudes and behaviour of its members reflect in part the reactions of individuals to their work situation. An occupation's social organization can be shaped by the way in which the work is organized, because the controls which the firms, the technology and the occupation itself

[1] Office of Population Censuses and Surveys, *Classification of Occupations* (London, 1970), p. vi.

37

exercise on work organization influence the nature and types of interaction which occur between occupational members at the workplace. At the same time, evidence suggests that those sorts of work which permit high ego-involvement, which are practised exclusively by certain groups, and which involve particular types of learning process are likely to foster sentiments of occupational identification among both manual and non-manual groups. In the manual area, craft work which has a high skill content and is intrinsically interesting, and which involves some process of craft socialization, has been shown to be particularly conducive to a strong identification and the growth of a sense of occupational community.[2]

In short, work tasks and the physical and social conditions of work are important objective features of employment, while people's reactions to these are subjective perceptions of considerable interest to industrial sociologists.

Foremen's Work

Very little is known about what foremen do in their jobs, although there is a considerable body of prescriptive information available on what commentators feel foremen ought to be doing. So one of the starting points of this study was to find out just what was involved in being a foreman in the docks. This was tackled by means of direct observation: I spent three months with twelve foremen, watching and recording what happened during the working day. Six foremen were drawn from the private-sector firms, all of them working on ships, and the rest from the P.L.A., two of whom were on container berths and four on conventional export shed work. Observation was structured by the adoption of a method of activity analysis which involved recording every two and a half minutes what the foreman was doing, classifying the activity under a variety of headings on pre-coded sheets.[3] Such a method cannot claim to be objective, because the observer is forced to interpret what the foreman is doing, but it has some rough and ready utility. The more familiar the observer is with the work and culture, the more useful the method.

More importantly, the indirect pay-off from this technique is particularly useful: three months of accompanying foremen provides knowledge and a 'feel' of an industrial situation which the use of interviews

[2] e.g. printing, which is discussed by I. C. Cannon, 'Ideology and Occupational Community: A Study of Compositors', *Sociology*, I, 1967, pp. 165–87, and R. Blauner, *Alienation and Freedom* (Chicago, 1964), pp. 40–57. G. Salaman, 'Some Sociological Determinants of Occupational Communities', *Sociological Review*, 19, 1971, pp. 53–77, discusses the general issues.

[3] Details of the method and the data which were obtained can be found in S. R. Hill, *A Comparative Occupational Analysis of Dock Foremen and Dock Workers in the Port of London* (University of London Doctoral Thesis, 1973).

alone cannot give. It meant in this case that informal contacts with men and management could also be developed, so that I became a fairly familiar figure prior to the actual interviewing. The fact that this technique involved me in tangible physical activity meant that I had a job of work to do and was not just wandering around watching all and sundry; in the docks, this helped to make legitimate the idea of social research in a culture which was hostile to academics and students.

There has traditionally been a tendency to study foremen as individuals rather than as the occupants of social roles in industry. This tendency has been most clearly expressed in the belief that the personality traits and leadership 'styles' of individual foremen are of crucial importance at the workplace and that training can ensure the most effective form of personality presentation. When the notion of role has been used, it has been assumed that the supervisory role has some clearly defined and universal function. This function is thought to be the supervision and leadership of men, so that the foreman acts as the linkage between management and labour.[4] Modern treatments developed in the European rather than the American context of the traditional accounts, however, assume that supervision must be explained in terms of industrial roles and also that the functions or purposes of such roles can be expected to vary from one industrial situation to another.[5] There is no single type of foreman role, because the actual patterns of behaviour in different jobs reveal a variety of supervisory functions. Dock foremen in this study behaved in ways which did not fit the older views, and supervision had purposes which were nothing to do with more conventional accounts of the foreman's job.

Detailed observation and discussion with foremen showed that the most important purpose of activity in the docks is to ensure an adequate flow of work. Work flow as the primary task means that the foreman's job is to get work out on time by easing bottle-necks and making sure that cargo is moving in the correct sequence and at the correct speed, whereas the popular view that foremen are continually involved in labour control activities, aiming to control the efforts of the workers by means of direct or indirect supervision, fails to hold good in the docks. Neither direct control in the sense of the foreman standing over the

[4] R. Likert, *New Patterns of Management* (New York, 1961), chapters 1–4, summarizes the literature on leadership and linkage themes.

[5] Two early contributions can be found in J. H. Goldthorpe, 'Technical Organisation as a Factor in Supervisor-Worker Conflict', *British Journal of Sociology*, 10, 1959, pp. 213–30, and T. Lupton, *On The Shop Floor* (London, 1963), pp. 184–5. The major theoretical and empirical contribution has been made by the Swedish Council for Personnel Administration and the London School of Economics' supervisory research project, summarized in K. E. Thurley and H. Wirdenius, *Supervision: A Reappraisal* (London, 1973), where supervision is conceptualized as a system of organizational roles and different systems have different characteristics, including different 'primary tasks'.

group of men nor indirect control in the sense of general supervision without direct contact are important parts of the foreman's role behaviour, accounting for a maximum of 5 per cent of any foreman's time. Other personnel functions, in addition to those connected with labour control, involve even less time.

There are two parts to work flow as the main area of the foreman's work tasks. The first is the co-ordination of the environment in which the actual handling of cargo takes place, while the second concerns the direction of the work itself. Both involve the foreman in mainly non-manual, administrative tasks. Manual and clerical tasks are rare, particularly among ship foremen. The first function is essentially a facilitating one which provides the correct environment in which the men can handle cargo most effectively. This means that the foreman maintains an adequate supply of work, equipment and labour in a co-ordinated system. Cargo arriving on time and in the correct sequence is particularly important, and here the foreman has to deal outside his own organization with other agencies concerned in the total movement of goods from point of origin to point of destination. From the dock workers' perspective, the foreman acts virtually in a service capacity in this instance, because he leaves the men alone to make their own decisions about the routine programming of their work and the methods to be used.[6]

The work tasks which result from the second part are more directly related to the on-going work flow. Here the foreman controls matters which concern the programming of work, production control, and work methods: he plans how the job is to be done, sets it up for the men, and monitors progress. Whereas the first function saw the foreman in a service capacity, the second sees him more directly concerned with production. Different mixes of the two parts can occur, all foremen spending a considerable amount of time on the first but varying amounts on the second. Private-sector ship foremen spend most on the second.[7]

Shed foremen allocate work to the gangs in the morning, and sometimes again in the afternoon, and then leave them alone for the rest of the day to deal with programming and work method decisions themselves. The foremen perform their primary function of co-ordinating the environment: getting lorries and rail trucks to the unloading bays in the right order, sorting them according to whether they carry heavy

---

[6] See J. H. Goldthorpe, op. cit., for historical parallels in coal mining.

[7] Ship foremen averaged 19 per cent of time in co-ordination activities (range 17–21 per cent) and 40 per cent on direction (range 36–42 per cent). Shed foremen averaged 16 and 14 per cent (ranges 14–18 and 10–18 per cent). The two container foremen spent 15 and 31 per cent of time on co-ordination, 23 and 23 per cent on direction. Shed foremen are underemployed and spend much of the day doing nothing, so their co-ordination and direction figures are relatively large as proportions of the foremen's active time.

or light cargo, arranging customs clearance, chasing missing items, and liaising with merchants, shippers, stevedore firms, and internal service departments.

The ship foreman has to consider this aspect of the job, but to a lesser extent since the shed foreman has already done part of the work for him. In theory, the public authority shed foreman should have done all this work, leaving the ship foreman merely to collect the cargo which the authority has delivered to the side of the ship, but this is rarely the case in practice. The work direction function involves the foreman in a series of decisions about the order in which cargo is to be loaded and the methods to be used if the cargo has any unusual qualities with which the men cannot cope, and a continual monitoring of the quality of the work done and the progress made. Should blockages occur, thien the foreman has to re-arrange the programme, give new orders to the men and then attempt to sort out the problem. The foreman spends about half his time on board the ship he is responsible for loading. He rarely descends into the individual holds where the gangs are handling the cargo, but remains on deck. In this position he can move so as to watch work in progress below him in the different holds or see what is happening on the quay and in the barges alongside, he can shout orders, and he is visible to the dock workers, his gangers and assistant, his superintendent, and the ship's officers, should any of these groups wish to consult him. The rest of the time is spent on the quay and in the sheds checking the cargo situation and resolving problems connected with the flow of work.

There were only two container berth foremen. In both cases, they were responsible for combined ship and shore operations. However, their job rarely took them on board ship (mainly because ship operations were vastly simplified) and most of their time was spent on the ground in the large container parks which stretched inland from the quayside or in their offices near the entrances to the parks. In principle, their job should have involved work direction only at certain times, giving the men instructions and leaving them alone until the work was completed, and some element of work co-ordination, ensuring that containers were where they were wanted at the right time. This necessitated contact with outside agencies. When work was running smoothly, there should in fact have been little for a foreman to do. However, the inadequate planning and design of early container operations, particularly the chronic unreliability of the machinery, meant that foremen were far more frequently involved in work direction than would normally have been the case.

Both private and public sector foremen have assistants. In the P.L.A. these are permanently attached to foremen, whereas in the private firms the practice has been to allocate those foremen without ships of their own in dock to act as temporary helpers of those with work. There was no noticeable division of labour between foremen and assistants and both did the same tasks. Gangers existed during Phase 1, but the supervisory element of their role was slight.

Information about the contacts foremen made with other people was also gathered. Personal contact, whether face-to-face or via telephone and radio, is extensive: ship foremen spend between 55 and 63 per cent of their time in interaction, shed foremen between 37 and 55 per cent, container foremen between 54 and 59 per cent.[8] The patterns of inter-action are interesting. Private-sector ship foremen spend just over a fifth of their time with the men they supervise (the average is 22 per cent and the range 12 to 26 per cent), which is relatively low, while shed foremen spend only about a tenth (the average is 11 per cent and the range 6 to 18 per cent).[9] All foremen have extensive contacts outside their own firms, shed foremen particularly, which shows how 'vertical' relations within the firms fail to control the work flow and how foremen need to call on 'horizontal' contacts with peers and 'diagonal' contacts with people of higher status outside the firm in order to do their jobs. Activity data also reinforce the view indicated by the analysis of the content of supervisory tasks, that the labour force is relatively un-important as a source of supervisory behaviour, contrary to popular views about the nature of supervision and the relationship between foremen and men.

In sum, the foremen's work when I was in the docks mainly involved administrative tasks which were neither manual nor routine clerical in nature. Foremen had to exercise their own initiative and discretion when taking decisions. Their work tasks did not appear to involve many 'traditional' supervisory functions connected with labour control or personnel management more generally. One would expect such tasks to give foremen greater work task satisfaction than would be found in many manual jobs, particularly machine-paced assembly operations.

In another aspect of the work, that is the share in the authority system, foremen were again more advantaged than most manual workers are known to be. In the first place, they appeared to share in the power system of the firm, occupying a position in the hierarchy which formally gave them authority over the dock workers at the bottom of the system. In the second, as already discussed, they had authority in the sense of discretion and control over work processes. Foremen acted fairly autonomously and were subject to little control from above, though this freedom was more apparent in the private firms than the public authority where jobs were rather more routine and circumscribed.

[8] The total contact time is similar to the data from other studies, summarized in J. Kelly, *Is Scientific Management Possible?* (London, 1968), p. 190.

[9] Shipworkers' interaction figures include non-work, social contacts during stoppages, which considerably reduce the amount of work-centred contact suggested by the data.

Dock Workers' Work

One might reasonably expect dock workers' work to differ from foremen's, because the men perform manual tasks and have little formal authority, unlike their supervisors. However, the issue is not resolved just by stating that dock workers are manual workers, and two things need to be clarified. The first is how far the manual tasks are skilled, because dock work has always been regarded as unskilled labour in occupational classifications, whereas foremen's jobs are invariably counted as skilled. The second is how much control dock workers have over their work, in particular the extent of their autonomy and their discretion to decide what they do, because control normally distinguishes middle-class occupations from working-class ones, though the amount of control can vary between different manual jobs.

I relied on observation of the men's work without attempting any activity analysis, because the use of watches and note-books was too reminiscent of work study to be acceptable to the shop stewards. I was particularly interested in the impact of technology, because some sociologists have argued that the production hardware and materials determine people's tasks and skills, and in this way their job satisfaction, while others have argued that technology relates one job to another and so determines the possibility of social interaction between workers. Both arguments emphasize the crucial importance of the man–hardware relationship and both assume that different people share the same personality needs which technology fulfils or frustrates.[10]

There is a more moderate and less deterministic perspective which emphasizes that the work organization, which relates to each other those who carry out the necessary tasks, is partly independent of the technical system and interacts with it. The notion of a socio-technical system suggests that the manner in which work is divided up and co-ordinated owes as much to decisions taken by managers and workers as it does to technology in many cases.[11] Work organization and technology may correspond, as when a specific work flow has been designed into the hardware, but the division of labour and the flow of work may often be independent of technical considerations. The key issue is to find how the work organization is structured in any given case. In the docks there was little technological structuring of the immediate work organization, nor was there much structuring by managers. Over the years, dock workers have largely established their *own* control, at least on conventional operations.

[10] e.g. R. Blauner, op. cit., pp. 33–4, and E. L. Trist and K. W. Bamforth, 'Some Social and Psychological Consequences of the Longwall Method of Coal Getting', *Human Relations*, 4, 1951, pp. 3–38.

[11] Indeed, because production hardware is consciously designed, any determining influence which it may have on work organization is *in turn* the product of the definitions of appropriate work organization held by the designer and management.

Docking retains a predominantly hand-work system of production, except on the advanced technology operations which deal with unitized cargoes.[12] It consists of transfer operations, moving cargo from one place to another, which are performed manually with some machine assistance. The extent of machine assistance varies, the limitations of the physical infrastructure of the docks and ships preventing much mechanization in many cases: sheds, quays and holds were largely designed before the advent of, or without reference to, modern handling devices such as fork-lift trucks. Fork-lifts and motorized trollies are used on a small scale in most shed and quay operations, but only in purpose-built structures such as can be found in the modern section of Tilbury are these simple mechanical devices used extensively. Sheds designed without internal pillars or other obstructions and with wide and high openings, and quaysides which are wide and flush-surfaced are essential for extensive machine assistance.

The combination of modern facilities and pre-palletized cargo which was found at Tilbury during the period of study made it possible for shed workers to split into pairs, one fork-lift to each pair, so that one man drove while the other guided and performed the simple manual operations which were needed. On board ship, however, mechanization was rarely found except for the quayside cranes. The confined spaces, low ceilings and uneven floors made holds unsuitable for mechanical devices on most ships. The palletization of cargo on board ship proceeded slowly throughout the sixties and lagged far behind the palletization of shore operations. This was particularly noticeable at Tilbury, where several of the berths were of an advanced design but goods had to be de-palletized after their transfer from quayside to ship's hold, because the ship could not cope with palletized units. When such units can be manoeuvred in the hold, they have simplified the stowage and the handling operations performed by the men. While I was in the docks there was a handful of new vessels with interiors which were designed to accept a small fork-lift in part of the working area. Newly-built conventional cargo ships have increasingly incorporated this facility for part of the hold space. The partial mechanization of hand work by means of simple mechanical aids will increase in future and the palletization of many cargoes may become more common.

One set of demands which work tasks make on the worker comprises attention requirements. These include the extent to which the worker's hand movements have become customary and habituated, the length and repetitiveness of the operation cycles, the degree of mental or cognitive involvement which is required in the performance of tasks,

[12] M. Meissner, *Technology and the Worker* (San Francisco, 1969), passim, has formulated a useful set of categories by means of which to analyse the relationship between technology and worker; his classification and terminology are used throughout this section.

and the location of the worker's visual focus. In conventional, un-mechanized work these requirements can best be described as low. There need be only a loose focus on the hands, on tools when these are used (crow-bars and hooks mainly), on the pieces of work handled, and on the work performed by others nearby. Hand movements are partly habituated, since the basic movements which make up the subsidiary sequences are relatively automatic even though the complete sequences can be unique. High mental involvement in thinking through the work process and in planning may occur when the job is being set up, after foremen have done the basic planning, but is only intermittent there-after. Some concentration is needed throughout, however, in order to avoid accidents. Planning and setting-up rely heavily on customary experience and on the skills of the foreman and ganger. Operating cycles vary according to the cargo handled. Long runs of identical goods, mainly 'bag work' cargoes such as cement, can have short and repetitive cycles, the handling movements being few and simple and the same set of actions being repeated time after time. But most com-modities differ from each other and do not allow regular cycles to develop, because of constant variations in size, weight and ease of handling.

This schematic description of dock work on conventional operations indicates that the direct relationship of the individual to his work tasks does not make the sort of demands on the dock worker that machine minders in more mechanized technologies experience. The production hardware and the nature of the raw materials do not exercise those sorts of constraints on the individual, coercive and possibly alienative, which are known to be characteristic of assembly lines or other machine-dominated systems. Within dock work, the tasks involved in ship work normally require considerably greater physical exertion when moving, lifting and bedding-down cargo than in shore work. This is the result of the low level of mechanization, the constrained layout of the holds, and the need to stack cargo on top of other cargo already loaded (or vice versa if unloading). The work is made even more fatiguing by the heat and damp which are always found in a ship's hold. Somewhat greater cognitive involvement in planning, more discretion in work processes, and greater manual dexterity and co-ordination are also required. Taken together, these mean that ship work is usually regarded as being more arduous and skilled than work on the quay or in the shed.

It might be expected of a predominantly hand-work system that the work organization would be more significant for the individual than the technology and hardware. It is true, of course, that physical constraints limit the possible ways of organizing production, because the nature of ships and cargoes limits the range of handling methods used. But these are broad limits and, within them, decisions taken with regard to the organization of production, how it is to be divided and how the work flow is programmed, are more significant for the job an individual does than the direct relationship of the individual to hardware.

The overall work flow can best be described as sequential, in that cargo movement is through successive work locations rather than to and from each one separately. Goods arrive by lorry at the shed, are placed into the shed to await the loading of the ship, are then moved onto the quay alongside the ship, and finally are moved from the quay into the hold where they are stowed. This flow also involves the functional dependence of the work stations and workers, since a second job can normally only be undertaken once the first is completed. For example, when loading a ship from sheds, those members of the ship gangs who work on the quay, attaching the cargo to the cranes, cannot do their job unless the P.L.A. 'shipping-off' gangs have produced the cargo from the shed, while the crane is dependent on the quay hands, and the men in the hold are dependent on the crane. Dependence can be reduced, but not eliminated, by stockpiling cargo at various stages in order to even out fluctuations in supply. But this strategy requires stockpiling space which is often not available; moreover some types of cargo cannot be stockpiled in this way.

The categorization of the overall work flow and the dependency which the organization of production has created between the various stages in the process is fairly straightforward. Description and categorization are not so simple when the focus of attention is the micro-level of the processes internal to the gang, particularly a gang engaged in ship work. Gangs are normally thirteen-handed, though the size can vary. Each gang has a crane driver and a hatchway man, who stands on deck guiding the driver with hand signals (since the edge of the hold prevents the driver from seeing where he is placing the cargo). The rest of the gang do not normally specialize in any function, and are interchangeable between the two different work locations of the ship's hold and quay side (or on board the barge when lighterage is used). Individuals on the quay attach cargo to the crane, either by slings or in nets fixed to the slings, or detach it when discharging, while the men in the hold remove the cargo from the crane and stow it aboard ship. The job of hatchway man frequently goes to the ganger, since it alone has a vantage point to view quay, crane, and hold. However, since the job is physically less arduous than most, as are the two or three jobs on the quay, there is a tendency for both hatchway and quay hands to be old or infirm workers if the gang contains any. One of the ways in which the occupation protects its weaker members is by providing such jobs.

The relations of dependence and independence which the flow of work creates among the down-hold section of the gang are however variable. They are partly influenced by the nature of the cargo and also by its location in the hold. Heavy or large commodities may require the whole gang to co-operate in manhandling an article into position, the work organization being based on teamwork. Crane driver and hatchway man can be involved in the team since the crane often has to be used to help move very heavy articles across the hold. Dependence is thus high, but not sequential in nature since it involves simultaneous co-operation.

Position in the ship's hold is also important. The hold is divided into a number of separate horizontal floors. Running through these is a vertical, square-section shaft, open at deck level where it forms the hatch, which provides the opening through which cargo passes. Loading starts at the lowest level of the ship and works from the extremities of the hold towards the open shaft. When the whole of one level is full, the shaft is boarded over flush with the steel floor and loading starts at the next level. Thus, if any article is to be placed in the central square section at any level the crane can do this accurately, with the consequence that manual handling is cut to a minimum and involves merely detaching the cargo from the slings. This reduces the number of men and the degree of co-operation required: in most cases, two men can deal with anything in the central square. There has been a trend over the past decade to build ships with much wider hatches and central shafts than was customary in the past. This has greatly simplified and expedited cargo-handling within the ship's hold. Indeed, wide hatches are more common and probably more labour-saving than mechanization which uses fork-lift trucks and other aids actually within the hold.

When cargo has to be moved sideways outside the square, underneath the floors, then fuller teamwork is needed when loading or discharging because more individuals are involved and more complex tasks are performed. One common method is to swing the crane's cable like a pendulum and to use the steel floor above as a fulcrum, so that the cargo swings in an arc under the floor, and the cable is given more slack at the crucial moment so that the cargo drops into the correct position. This involves crane driver, hatchway men and some members of the down-hold gang. Alternatively, since this method is officially banned as dangerous, cargo is dropped into the square and manhandled into position by the whole gang. If the hold can take a fork-lift truck, then it can be used to move quite a range of different cargoes from the square. Manhandling is still normally required for final placement.

The gang splits into smaller units for other articles, such as bag work or small, cased goods. The size of the unit varies according to the cargo and the way chosen to handle it, but is never smaller than a pair. The pair is the basic unit of dock work, and most individuals have their own regular mates. The units are normally independent of each other, but relations of dependence usually exist between the men themselves within each unit. Internal dependence is normally simultaneous: both men haul or shove together on the same piece of cargo. But it can be sequential at times, as is sometimes the case when the men choose to make the work flow from one individual to another on some types of bag work: one man may stand in the square and pass bags to his mate for stacking. There is no fixed work location within the hold, so spatial constraints on interaction scarcely exist.

The physical 'demands' of the organization of production on dock workers therefore appear to be flexible. Constraints exist, but wide ranges of behaviour are possible. The physical characteristics of production, the cargo and the spaces into which it fits, vary widely between jobs and even on the same job: the organization of work changes with variations in the cargo handled and as the hold changes shape (as it becomes fuller or emptier).

The work organization, in fact, owes as much to decisions about how the work is done as to any physical elements of the job. Variety depends largely on the decisions of those people involved in production, whether directly or indirectly. The overall division of labour in the port is one factor influencing the organization of production and the breakdown of tasks between operations. Within this framework, other decisions are taken. Foremen, in conjunction with ships' officers or their own super-intendents, decide broadly where and in what order cargo is to be stowed on loading jobs. On discharging jobs, these decisions have largely been pre-empted by the way in which those who originally loaded the ship decided to plan the stowage, but some discretion remains. Foremen have some influence over the methods of working, particularly if the cargo is unusual so that the gang needs technical advice.

Once the job has been set up and the broad planning decisions taken, however, gangs have a free hand to do more detailed planning, to decide on work methods and to allocate individual workers to the various parts of the job. In some gangs the ganger takes the decisions, in others they are taken by all the members together, depending on the nature of personal relationships within the group. These decisions concern the nature of the work flow, the degree of dependence, the extent of differentiation and the length and regularity of cycles which are to be adopted.

Such decisions about the organization of work are properly part of the control system of a firm. To the extent that work organization is independent of technical constraint, decisions regarding this organiza-tion are normally made by management and form part of the system of control which regulates both production and the people engaged in producing. Structuring the work organization is one of two methods open to management in order to control the labour force: such structuring prescribes both the relationships between workers and the tasks an individual has to perform. It is an indirect and impersonal method of managerial control. The alternative, the use of the authority system and supervision, is more direct and personal, although it has an impersonal variant in the use of payment schemes as controls.[13] In the docks, there is considerable freedom to structure work within very broad physical limits on conventional operations, but it is the workers themselves who command the organization of work. They control the constraints which derive from the way work is organized. The combination of those work skills which historically have meant that managers and foremen could rely on the men to organize themselves in a manner satisfactory to management, and of the new strength of the men after Phase 1, has ensured for the labour force an unusually effective command of its work.

Those constraints which are often regarded as important aspects of the manual worker's situation are thus fairly slight in both the technical hardware and management control system contexts. Within any group of men at one work location, such as that formed by the gang members in the hold, on the quay, or in the barge, there are few barriers to the formation of those 'informal' social bonds and primary groups which have traditionally been of concern to industrial sociologists. An individual has freedom to choose with whom he talks, for how long and on what subject. He can extend this choice to purely work-centred activities, since he can choose his own immediate work mate and his wider contacts within the gang, at least when less than the full gang is required for a job. He can choose, or influence the group's decision, where he works, on the ship or the quay, and his position in either location.

Actions thus have a large voluntary content with low constraint. Indeed, within the group of workers at any work location the conventional distinction between voluntary and constrained social behaviour makes little sense, because the range of choices left open by the technology and worker control of the decisions made within this range means that most social behaviour is in a sense voluntary, even when it appears to be required by work organization. That is to say, gang members have chosen to work in this way. Social behaviour involves communication and co-operation, both of which are voluntary. Between groups or sub-units in different workplaces, on the other hand, co-operation is required and obligatory rather than voluntary because it is governed by the work flow from shed to hold, or vice versa. Communication may also be non-existent, as happens when men are separated into quay and down-hold units, because of the physical separation of the work locations. Given the excess manning of most jobs, however, interaction of a voluntary nature between members of groups in different workplaces is feasible; but this is in no sense work-

---

[13] This classification of the types of control system is taken from T. Kynaston Reeves and Joan Woodward, 'The Study of Managerial Control', in Joan Woodward (ed.), *Industrial Organization: Behaviour and Control* (London, 1970), p. 39.

related because it occurs outside the work relationship, unlike the social interaction within the groups at particular work locations.

On this subject of the social interaction which occurs at work, another aspect of the working conditions allows sociability to extend beyond the immediate gang or sub-unit of the gang. The erratic rhythm of dock work, periods of intense activity followed by complete idleness, means that each day there is a lot of free time. This can often stretch to several hours. One survey, conducted in the late 1960s on behalf of the London employers, found that up to a third of the working day was lost as the result of the weather, lack of facilities, the failure of other agencies, equipment malfunctions, poor time-keeping and disputes.[14] This survey was carried out in the summer months, with the result that only nine per cent of the time lost was due to poor weather. In the winter months, the weather causes far longer stoppages, often of several hours' duration.

It is common in these circumstances for all the gangs on a ship, sometimes the shed workers as well, to congregate in the ship or shed in order to kill time together. If the stoppage is widespread and lengthy, as when weather prevents work, then men from the different ships being worked may meet in the canteens. (This also occurs during the official breaks, of course.) In this way the work on occasion throws dock workers together into groups which are more extensive than the immediate work group or gang, and which may counteract any tendency of the organization of production to split up the occupation. Interestingly, many foremen return to their own foremen's messes if the stoppage is of any length, preferring the company of their colleagues to that of the men.

These observations do not apply to container and packaged timber berths, however. Dock workers here have their own canteen facilities and rarely use those in the older parts of the docks. Thus the two or three dozen men found at each of these berths are split off from the rest of the labour force. This was found at Tilbury to be partly the result of the distances between the new berths and the old dock area where most men worked, which meant a twenty-minute walk from one to the other, and partly the result also of the different hours the men on the new operations often worked. The isolation of the men on unitized berths from the majority of dock workers was most noticeable during the observational research. It was also something which the shop stewards feared, lest the physical isolation of container operatives led them to feel separated from the concerns of the main body of dock workers.

For many workers there is thus something of a social system at the

---

[14] This survey is quoted in D. F. Wilson, *Dockers* (London, 1972), p. 253. In addition to the actual stoppages, it was claimed that more time was effectively 'lost' as the result of wasteful practices while working. The result was that only 46·5 per cent of the working day was fully productive.

workplace in which they can choose to participate if they wish. There are patterns of personal interaction which build up primary social groups in the form of gangs. There is also the possibility of joining wider social groupings which can link together collections of individuals who are not related to each other on the basis of shared tasks: the typical working day allows an individual to transcend the limitations of his immediate work group, should he wish to do so.[15]

In sum, the work situation on conventional operations gives the dock worker as an individual or as a member of a gang, a high degree of autonomy, discretion and freedom from the conventional constraints on manual workers. This applies to the man–hardware relationship and to the nature of the work more generally. This freedom has two sources: the relative lack of physical constraints and worker rather than management control of aspects of the work organization.

Brief mention of what workers do on mechanized operations and on cranes is appropriate, though a detailed account is unnecessary since only a minority of men do these types of work. In both cases, the work involves a more direct man–machine relationship, less control over work organization, and reduced social interaction when compared with conventional work.

Driving cranes and some other machines makes demands on the individual which differ from those of manual work. Attention requirements are externally focused, in the sense that individuals must observe the production process and be aware of events taking place at other workplaces, which is not a requirement of hand work. Hand movements are habituated. Cognitive involvement in the sense of concentration is high and continuous, if only to avoid accidents. Involvement in the sense of thinking through processes occurs less frequently and varies with the amount of variety in the cargo being handled since each reprogramming requires this type of involvement, whereas repetitive operations only need thinking through at the beginning. Container berths have mainly standardized and repetitive operations, whereas crane driving on conventional berths has to cope with frequent variations. Operation cycles are constant where standardized cargo is handled, as on container and other unitized systems, but irregular where cargo varies, as on conventional operations.

Crane driving on both conventional and unitized operations is highly dependent on the performance of other groups, being part of a sequential work flow. It is also highly differentiated, in that very little interchangeability is possible between cranes, and few dock workers have the skill to replace a crane driver. Control over work speed and

[15] For a similar analysis of interaction and the social system of an occupation at the workplace, see R. K. Brown, P. Brannen, J. M. Cousins, M. Samphier, 'Leisure in Work', in M. A. Smith et al. (eds.), Society and Leisure in Britain (London, 1973), pp. 97–110.

over production organization is low, since the dependence of crane driving on other operations takes work speed out of their hands, while work organization is largely determined by the foremen and the rest of the gang on conventional work. On unitized work, organization is determined to a greater extent than on conventional work by the design of facilities and by the orders of the shippers, who exercise more control on these berths than elsewhere. Personal contact with others is limited to what is required by technical and work organization design, since the marked physical separation of crane driving from other operations and the high dependence on the work flow act as constraints preventing 'informal' social interaction of a voluntary nature. Required communication and co-operation tend not to be social in the normal sense, since they are governed by hand signals between crane driver and the men 50 feet below and not verbally.

Apart from cranes, the mechanical handling devices on most unitized systems require a low dependence on others, because the organization of work has been so designed that individual machines can work independently at most stages in the operating cycle. Work flow tends not to be sequential between work locations once a stockpile of cargo has been built up. The speed of work is thus individually controlled by machine operators. On the container berths operating at Tilbury at the time of my research, the machines were straddle-carriers. A straddle-carrier is a vehicle approximately 35 feet high, with three legs per side, each leg having a driven wheel at the end, which lifts and transports a container by first straddling it and lowering a frame which clamps to the top of the container, and then raising the whole assembly and driving to wherever the container is required. Containers are moved from lorries to the container park and subsequently to the crane at the ship's side, or vice versa on discharge operations.

An alternative system of moving the same containers was awaiting the removal of the ban on new unitized work before moving from trial to operational status at the time of my research. This berth used the same sort of quay crane as in the previous cases, but had a second crane inland and a shuttle service of conventional lorries running between the two in place of straddle-carriers. The very different design philosophy which created this system involved a far greater sequential flow and dependence than the systems already operating, despite the identical nature of the steel boxes being moved. (This system was abandoned in favour of straddle-carriers, because it lacked flexibility to cope with containers which were stowed in the wrong order.) On the packaged timber and paper pulp berths the shore machines were heavy duty fork-lifts with purpose-built forks and powered clamps, cranage being provided by the ships' own gantries.

Work organization on unitized berths is determined by the people who designed the layouts of the berths and the machinery employed there, and by decisions taken by the managements of the employing companies and the shippers. Dock workers therefore have very little control over work organization. Indeed, the managers of the steve-doring firms themselves do not have much more control, because the design of machines and the physical layouts has normally rested in the hands of the shipping companies renting the berths. These companies have tended to import systems from North America or to design their own without much reference to the managers of the operating com-panies. Social interaction on the job is very low and constrained, since machines are operated by single operators who do not need to co-operate between themselves and who work at great distances from each other. Conversation between operators would in any case be impossible, due to the noise. However, the manning arrangements negotiated by the men's representatives are such that nearly half the working day can be spent off the job, usually in the rest room attached to the berth. Therefore, social interaction between members of the berth crew is possible and occurs frequently but not on the job itself.

This description of work in the docks indicates that dock workers on conventional operations, the vast majority during my research, enjoy conditions very different from those of factory workers, particularly machine-dominated workers. The oppressive control of either tech-nology or management is notably absent, placing dock workers in an extremely favourable position in comparison with what we know about the bulk of working-class jobs and work experience. Printing, building, agriculture, lorry driving and possibly mining offer similar but less extensive freedoms, most of these being non-factory occupations like docking. But even in these trades, the introduction of potentially coercive forms of mechanization and work organization has already occurred, in much the same way that the new unitized dock systems which limit the traditional independence of dock work are spreading with increasing rapidity.

Foremen and men can be distinguished from each other by the performance of manual or non-manual tasks, which is conventionally regarded as a basic source of social division though one which is ambiguous and possibly blurred at the level of intermediate groups such as foremen. The differences between the work of men and foremen are easy to describe but more difficult to evaluate, because both types of work are unusual with regard to what is found elsewhere. However, the descriptions of work indicate that of the two, foremen do have the more advantageous situation. The differences are fundamental if it is assumed that manual and non-manual tasks are the bases of funda-mental cleavages. If, however, the important differences are thought to be the amount of control over tasks and the work environment and the de facto possession of power, then the differences are matters of degree rather than of fundamental substance.

Both groups performed tasks which were relatively free of technical constraints, and the physical aspects of production acted as a boundary within which a wide range of choice was available. The conventional production system within which most of the two groups worked was itself mainly the product of social rather than technical determinants, as will be demonstrated later when the historical evolution of the London docks is discussed. The production system of unitized berths was also influenced by non-technical factors, though the design of a berth was the result of conscious choice rather than of the vagaries of evolution.

Within the very broad constraints of the production system, both groups possessed considerable control over their work. The origins of the foremen's control will be discussed in greater detail in Chapter 5, where control will be seen to depend on the foremen's own expertise in managing a complex and unco-ordinated system of production. It was possible for the men to exercise control because the labour force had taken charge of the work organization, which ought properly to have been part of the organizational control system. In work which has comparatively few technical constraints the organization of work assumes greater importance for structuring shop-floor behaviour and determining work tasks. Thus worker control of this particular function was of central importance for the freedom and autonomy characteristic of dock work. The underpinnings of this control were studied in the previous chapter, and later sections of the book will trace some of the additional consequences.

Both sets of work tasks involved some degree of skill, manual as well as of other sorts. Foremen had to possess the technical and manipulative skills associated with the manual tasks, so that they could give advice to the men if this was necessary. The major area of the foreman's work, however, required organizational competence and knowledge of the overall port operation in order to co-ordinate a complex division of labour. The ability to plan the loading of a ship was of equal importance in this major area of the work role. The skilled nature of supervisory work roles is well recognized, and in this case the skills are largely managerial. The managerial component is probably greater than is normally the case, however.

Dock work, particularly aboard ship, is skilled in ways which are largely unrecognized outside the dock industry itself. Observation showed that the work required a certain level of manipulative skill which involved both manual dexterity and knowledge of the most efficacious procedures. There was also a need for more conceptual skills, because the men controlled the organization of work and had to plan work sequences and methods, including re-programming when necessary. These skills were all necessary if high outputs were to be maintained, if cargo was to be stowed in a way which was economical of expensive hold space, and if provision were to be made for the safety of the ship at sea and those working on her in port. Any unskilled labourer could perform many of the purely manual operations after a fashion: slowly, dangerously, and at financial loss to himself and his employer. But to do the work as well as an experienced dock worker required skill, while the planning element of the job and some of the more complicated manoeuvres could not have been performed at all by an untrained man.

These skills may not be equivalent to those of the recognized crafts, because they are traditional in nature and have been passed down through generations of occupational members rather than by apprenticeships or other formal training. There are also signs that the skills may have become somewhat less important recently with the spread of unitized operations and the gradual palletization and partial mechanization even of conventional work. However, it is a questionable assumption that a craft apprenticeship or its non-manual equivalent in professional training indicates that an occupation is in fact skilled, because craft and professional control may often rest on the historical nature of an occupation's tasks which were once skilled but have since been 'de-skilled' by various changes. It can be argued that once craft or professional control has been established, then the perpetuation of an illusion of skill is easy, particularly where there is an effective occupational body such as a trade union or professional association to preserve the occupation's special status even after its special expertise is no longer so noticeable.

The control which the men and foremen had over their work gave both groups considerable freedom for social interaction and the choice of patterns of sociability. The rhythm of dock work, with periods of intense activity interspersed by periods of complete inactivity, allowed social relationships to transcend the boundaries of the immediate workplace and to encompass all who worked in the same ship or shed, or on the same quay, and on occasion to encompass people from all over the dock. This sort of freedom of sociability has in other industries constituted one of the structural underpinnings of an occupationally-based social 'community' at work.[16] In the docks there were elements of activity (and sentiment) which reflected the community idea, though these should not be overestimated in the way many other occupational studies have done in their search for such communities.

---

[16] See ibid. for shipbuilding; I. C. Cannon, op. cit., and R. Blauner, op. cit., for printing; G. Salaman, op. cit., for two other examples. The 'traditional' worker theory makes a similar point: J. H. Goldthorpe, D. Lockwood et al., The Affluent Worker (Cambridge, 1968), vol. 2, pp. 74–5.

CHAPTER 4

Reactions to Work

Perceptions of Work

To the outsider, a most noticeable characteristic of work in the docks was the relative absence of those 'alienating' features which are to be found to varying degrees in all industrial jobs. The use of the 'alienation' concept in industrial sociology tends to be shallow in comparison with the deeper meaning given it by Marxists, for whom it means vastly more than dissatisfaction at work. So the terms preferred here are those of job satisfaction and dissatisfaction.[1] The combination of freedom from constraints and the skills involved in dock work meant that the work situation had the potential of being experienced as relatively satisfying by both men and foremen.

One of my aims was to find out what in fact people's reactions were to the structure of tasks and work organization. I made a distinction between the work itself, the content and the tasks performed, and its other aspects, such as the nature of the social relationships which the work fosters or permits. This corresponds to the conventional distinction between the 'intrinsic' and other aspects of work. Studies of other groups of workers have attempted to show the main considerations which enter into people's evaluations of their work. The most important considerations are often thought to be those deriving from the man-hardware relationship, but they should in fact include those originating in the organizational control system, when this acts as a constraint via supervision or payment schemes. Six broad aspects of work have been identified: variety of tasks and actions, autonomy and discretion in choice of methods and sequences, skill requirements, responsibility, and both required and permitted interaction.[2] Provided a sufficient

---

[1] Both R. Blauner, *Alienation and Freedom* (Chicago, 1964), and A. Touraine *et al.*, *Workers' Attitudes to Technical Change* (Paris, 1965), talk about alienation at work when they in fact mean job dissatisfaction. It is quite possible that alienation is not a concept which can be made operationable in empirical sociology.

[2] These are the aspects identified by R. Blauner, op. cit., pp. 16–34, and A. N. Turner and P. Lawrence, *Industrial Jobs and the Worker* (Cambridge, Mass., 1966), p. 22.

level of generality is used, these categories would appear to be applicable to both manual work, on which they are based, and to non-manual.[3] It is in fact of considerable interest to see what differences or similarities exist between the work experiences of the two groups in this research.

Taking the two groups together, the results are much as one would have expected from the previous description of the situation. Both groups experience their work as something which incorporates few constraints or pressures, allows them to retain some control over its organization, is fairly interesting, extends the capabilities of many of the respondents and involves some degree of skill. In nearly every case, foremen are even more likely to stress these qualities of the work than are the men. Foremen are also more likely to perceive their work as skilled and exclusive. Those dissatisfying characteristics of industrial work tasks which are notoriously typical of many factory jobs were markedly absent from the foremen's jobs, while even the manual dock workers perceived their work as being relatively free from most of these sources of deprivation.

In more detail, table 4.1 shows the responses to the questions on the nature of work. Both men and foremen reported that they felt a sense of control over aspects of their work. Pressure was not something which was felt on a widespread scale, because few remarked that the pace of work was too fast or that they did not have freedom to control their own speed.[4] When complaints did occur, these centred mainly on piece-work as a source of constraint among the men while among the foremen they centred on the men's speed. Foremen complained that their work was too slow, not that they felt compelled to work too quickly. Neither group saw the technology as a constraint on either conventional or mechanized work. The men did not often regard supervision as a constraining pressure, though some did complain of pressure from the gang itself. Supervision and piecework payment are both varieties of organizational control. The dock workers' perceptions of these controls suggest that they are regarded as no more significant than technology as sources of pressure. Excessive fatigue, which is usually

[3] Trahair, for instance, has developed a similar set of job characteristics to be used in the analysis of both types of work: R. C. S. Trahair, 'The Workers' Judgement of Their Job as a Variable in Work Role Analysis', *Human Relations*, 21, 1968, pp. 141–62.

[4] Control over the rate of working has long been regarded as an important element of job satisfaction. Comparative figures are 33 per cent for Blauner's auto workers and 10 per cent for printers; 31 per cent for the total Luton sample and 11 per cent for craftsmen, using a less strongly worded question: R. Blauner, op. cit., p. 200; J. H. Goldthorpe, D. Lockwood *et al.*, *The Affluent Worker* (Cambridge, 1968), vol. 1, p. 18. Working at one's own speed seems to be the crucial element of control for manual workers. Complaints about the pace being too fast are probably of lesser importance in the docks, because here the individual controls his own speed either himself or collectively with his mates.

interpreted as evidence of the presence of uncontrolled pressures on the individual, was mentioned by a small minority.[5]

Feelings about control over work pressure were matched by feelings about control over the way work was done, the organization of work. Both groups felt that they enjoyed considerable amounts of discretion and responsibility. The men's perceptions of these two characteristics were similar to those of craftsmen in one study and mid-way between craftsmen and assembly-line operatives in another.[6] Foremen, however, were noticeably different both from dock workers and from the men in other studies in their evaluations of how far their work allowed them to decide how the job was to be done and of the scope they had to try out their own ideas. The men complained about the planning of work, by which they meant those areas controlled by the foremen and managers, whereas the foremen thought that this was satisfactory.

Few people in either group found the work to be monotonous or boring, particularly in comparison with the data available from other studies.[7] Most found that there was sufficient variety and that the work required maintained concentration.[8] The work therefore appeared to be fairly interesting to those involved. A fair number of men also felt that the work allowed them to try out their own ideas about how it was to be done, one aspect of the notion of personal growth or creativity in work. Nearly a third of the men, however, stated that the work was in fact too simple for the full use of their abilities, a proportion which appears to be fairly high.[9] For these people, dock work may be reasonably interesting but is not a job which provides a challenge to the full range of their abilities. Foremen were far more likely to regard work as using their abilities.

The question of skill is relevant here. The great majority of men thought that their work was skilled or semi-skilled, and only about one-fifth perceived the job as unskilled. The skills involved in docking were seen largely as the products of long experience on the job rather than formal training or short periods of familiarization (see table 4.2). The learning cycle was seen in terms of years, given the transmission of skills from old-timers to young recruits which was the normal way in which the job was learned. Blauner's description of traditional skill as cumulative, which 'increases with experience in the trade and

[5] Comparative figures are 12 per cent for printers and 34 per cent for auto workers in Blauner's study, op. cit., p. 200.

[6] Dorothy Wedderburn and Rosemary Crompton, *Workers' Attitudes and Technology* (Cambridge, 1972), p. 52; R. Blauner, op. cit., p. 201.

[7] Comparative figures are 8 per cent for printers and 68 per cent for Blauner's auto workers, op. cit., p. 204; 41 per cent for J. H. Goldthorpe, D. Lockwood *et al.*'s sample, op. cit., vol. I, p. 18; 13 and 21 per cent for craft and general workers in Dorothy Wedderburn and Rosemary Crompton, op. cit., p. 51.

[8] Only Blauner's printers gave as high scores, op. cit., p. 205.

[9] Nearly as high as Blauner's auto workers, ibid., p. 205.

constitutes a kind of lore which is taught and passed on through the generations',[10] fits fairly well the views of these dock workers. Foremen were even more likely to regard their work as skilled. They were also considerably more likely to emphasize the exclusivity of the work, because most of them denied that everyone who had a knowledge of dock work could do their job. The learning process involved was seen to require long experience on the job.

Finally, dock workers tended to regard freedom of movement and opportunities for social interaction as characteristics of their work. Constraints on sociable groupings were negligible. Foremen and men were very similar in their replies here. Taking all the different aspects of the work together, it is hardly surprising that nine-tenths of the men should report liking the work itself, and that foremen should tend to opt for replies of greater intensity on a fixed-choice scale.

The same categories of analysis proved capable of describing both the manual and the supervisory perceptions of work and showed up differences between the two. The differences were not always large, and they had been expected to be greater, since one job involved manual work tasks whereas the other did not. The manual versus non-manual division may be somewhat blurred in this instance, of course, because these dock workers appeared to experience few of the constraints to which manual work frequently gives rise, and seemed to feel that the nature of the work was fairly interesting. However, the differences on the subject of using one's abilities in work indicate that many dock workers perceived at least one aspect of their work very differently from foremen.

This last point provides further confirmation of the fact which has occasionally been noted in other studies, namely that work which can be experienced as creative and demanding is associated with occupational status and class position.[11] That is to say, the lower down the occupational hierarchy a group is placed, the more likely its members are to experience work as something which is meaningless and lacks the capacity to provide positive satisfaction of their needs and desires, as something which is truly 'alienating'. It can be argued that this is one of the most fundamental aspects of the social inequality of modern society. Conversely, the higher the occupational and class position of the group, the more work is likely to be found to be meaningful, stimulating and satisfying.

It is appropriate to discuss mechanized work here, because both the working conditions and the men's subjective perceptions differ on these operations. The main sample of dock workers produced few people working on mechanized operations because there were com-

[10] ibid., p. 37.
[11] See R. Blauner, 'Work Satisfaction and Industrial Trends in Modern Society', in W. Galenson and S. M. Lipset (eds.), *Labor and Trade Unionism* (New York, 1960), pp. 339–60, for a review of the relevant evidence.

paratively few individuals engaged upon this type of work. Therefore, an extra sample of machine operatives was taken for the purposes of comparing reactions to the work. These individuals were not included in other sections of the interview schedule, since their inclusion would have severely biased the sample. It was not possible to do the same with foremen, since the total number on mechanized systems was too small to make a reasonable unit of analysis. The men were taken from the modern, unitized systems, where they more frequently drove vehicles than cranes, and from the crane drivers on the conventional operations.[12]

Both groups of mechanized workers reacted similarly to hand workers with regard to the pace of work and the freedom to work at their own speed. Few respondents felt that they were greatly constrained in this area of job control. Mechanized workers, in addition, reported less fatigue than had those on conventional operations, which probably indicates that machinery had a beneficial effect on this aspect of the work at least. Very small proportions of the two mechanized groups reported excessive tiredness as the result of the work. Thus the impact of mechanization, if any, on this aspect of the individual's control can be described as largely beneficial. The reason, of course, is that the machines in the docks are operator-controlled, so that the individual is not machine-paced, while the physical effort is reduced.

Control over the other aspects of the work was reported less frequently than among the conventional workers. With regard to the organization of work, neither group of mechanized workers reported much control over how the work was to be done or that the work allowed them to try out their own ideas. On this second point, machine drivers on unitized berths differed significantly from crane drivers, the latter reporting the least use of ideas. The men, therefore, thought they had considerably less control over the selection of methods and sequences than did workers employed on conventional hand work. Drivers on unitized berths tended to cite the organizational control system as the reason for their low control in this area. This was because the managers themselves exercised greater control over the work organization, and because the berths had deliberately been designed so as to programme work flow. Crane drivers were more likely to feel constrained by the decisions taken by the gang. Drivers on unitized systems thought that the work was well planned, whereas crane drivers shared the hand workers' contempt for the way in which jobs were set up. Unitized work was simpler and more rationally designed than conventional and this allowed more efficient planning.

Mechanized work involved other differences as well. Both groups found their work more boring and less varied than did those on conventional jobs, while crane drivers scored particularly low on variety.

---

[12] The revised sample contained 30 container operatives, 25 crane drivers and 113 conventional hand workers. The figures in the original sample were 12, 14 and 113.

Concentration or cognitive involvement was high among drivers on unitized operations, but crane drivers reported about the same level as hand workers. While unitized and conventional hand workers generally did not find the work too simple for their abilities, crane drivers gave the reverse pattern of replies and only a minority felt that the work was not too simple. There were, however, no statistically significant differences between any of the groups about the levels of skill involved in their respective jobs. To sum up, in comparison with hand workers, both groups of mechanized workers experienced certain aspects of the intrinsic work content differently: there was in particular a greater sense of the routine character of tasks than on hand work. Crane drivers, in addition, complained that the work failed to tax their abilities.

The impact of age on experience of work was also considered in the data analysis, because other studies have found it a significant variable. There was a wide range of age groups among the men interviewed while the foremen varied less but had a higher average age. It seemed possible that the evaluations of the content of work, particularly of the physical and mental characteristics and the demands work made on the individual, might vary with age. In the first place, there may have been differences related to age within each group. In the second, those differences which existed between men and foremen may in fact have been due to the different age distributions rather than to other differences in the situations of the two groups.

Information is presented for those above and below the age of 45 years. I chose this dividing point because it corresponded to the average age of the men in the London docks, because it divided the sample of dock workers into fairly even sub-groups, and because any lower age limit would have produced very few foremen below the dividing line. (A different age division is used where relevant.) The noticeable finding, however, is how little importance age has had in this research. Tables 4.3 and 4.4 present any differences of more than 5 per cent, from which it can be seen that comparatively few items are affected by age, and that the differences which do occur are usually slight (though the small numbers in each group make the statistical analysis difficult).

I had expected the older men to report greater pressures and constraints than the younger ones on the subjects of pace of work and freedom, but there was no difference by age within the dock worker group. Among foremen there were differences, but in the opposite direction to what one might have anticipated: the younger group was more likely to find the pace of work too fast, while the older one was more likely to complain of not working at their own speed (the speed of the men being too slow).

Age had a greater impact on the evaluation of the mental demands of the work than of the physical, but not overly so. The first finding was that young men and foremen were more likely to feel that the work was too simple and less likely to feel that it required concentration. Fewer young dock workers than old perceived the work as involving the use of ideas, though the foremen were not divided by age on this subject. The second finding was that the impact of these age differences on the original distinctions between men and foremen was statistically significant in only one case: on the subject of the freedom to work at one's own speed, young dock workers and foremen no longer differed whereas overall the men and foremen had. Thus age was fairly unimportant so far as people's perceptions of work demands were concerned, and did not explain the differences between men and foremen.

This last finding brings us to the impact of age on perceptions of skill. Here there are age-related differences within groups and, more importantly, the overall differences between men and foremen are modified. The distinction was made between those who described their work as skilled rather than semi- or unskilled, which is a more demanding criterion than the skilled and semi-skilled versus unskilled categorization which was used earlier. Among the men, the main division occurred at the 35-year-old line: less than 40 per cent of those below that age limit described their work as skilled, whereas approximately 70 per cent of those over this age thought that it was. Among foremen, there is some difference between the groups aged above or below 45 years, but it is not statistically significant. Controlling for age, there is now no longer any significant difference between men and foremen in the over 45 years age range; this suggests that the difference originally noted between the perceptions of the men and foremen can be attributed partly to age as well as to the factors associated with the differing status of the two groups (differing types of work, for instance).

The less favourable evaluation of the skill requirements of the job among the younger group, which is more noticeable among the men than among foremen, deserves further scrutiny. There are in fact three possible explanations of this phenomenon, though choice between them is extremely difficult. There may have been a real change in the nature of the work over the last twenty years on conventional as well as unitized operations. So far as ships' gangs are concerned, the slow development of methods of packaging (including pallets) which are designed to facilitate handling and modern holds which are easier to work in, and the greater use of shore cranes rather than ships' gear, may have reduced the skill requirements of conventional dock work in comparison with earlier periods. In that case, it can be claimed that the younger men realistically appraise the nature of the work, while the older ones remember work as it used to be and fail to appreciate the changes. A second possible explanation is either that the aspirations of younger workers are greater than those of their elders or that younger workers have greater knowledge of the tasks performed in other occupations, particularly in those generally acknowledged as skilled trades. If that is so, the lower evaluation of the skill content of docking may reflect changes in the frames of reference and comparison which are commonly used by dock workers, rather than major changes in the nature of dock work itself. A third possibility is that the perception of the skill of one's work is something which normally increases with advancing years as part of the process of ageing. This process has been noted among other groups of workers. If this is the case in the docks, then the younger respondents may come to perceive their work as more skilled as they themselves grow older. It is not at all clear which of these three possible explanations is more likely to be correct in this instance.

The real significance of a decline in the evaluation of the skilled nature of the trade lies in the repercussion which this has on the occupation itself, particularly on occupational consciousness and identity. Belief in the skilled nature of its work is often part of an occupation's self-justificatory ideology, which is used in such a way as to distinguish the occupation from others, to win acceptance of its claims to have an exclusive sphere of competence, and to foster the identification of members with the occupation. Such a belief forms an essential element of what has been called the 'sacred' realm of an occupation: that collection of myths, values and norms which constitutes the distinct culture of the trade or profession, and which both binds the members to the occupation and controls their activity.[13]

However, the evidence for such a decline is not clear-cut in the docks, given the difficulty of choosing between the three explanations above. In particular, the third of the possible explanations would suggest that no decline had taken place. Few respondents in any group regarded the work as being totally without skill, while the age groups in which less than half the people regarded the work as being skilled constituted small proportions of all the men and foremen interviewed. Overall, well over half of all the remaining respondents still thought that the work was skilled, rather than semi- or unskilled.

One objection which could be made to the tenor of the preceding pages is that the work elements under discussion were not particularly important for the men and foremen, even though respondents gave the pattern of answers which one would have expected from people doing such work. (This expectation was based on the evidence of other studies.) The argument is that we need to know what people expect of work before we can assess the meaning of their reactions to their work situations. I therefore asked the men and foremen what they thought were the main advantages of dock work over other types of work, in order to throw some light on the nature of subjective meanings. From their replies it was quite apparent that they did in fact evaluate their immediate work situations in terms similar to those used in the previous discussion and in other studies.

[13] T. Caplow, *The Sociology of Work* (New York, 1964), p. 101.

Most people in each group listed advantages which were associated with the intrinsic character of the work. One particular attribute of the work was singled out by 98 per cent of the men and 83 per cent of foremen, namely the freedom which docking allowed the individual at work. When these replies were followed up in greater detail, it became apparent that this category of freedom embraced a complex of specific work attributes for most people. The freedoms referred to were freedom of movement, of time-keeping and speech, freedom from supervision or discipline, and freedom to work autonomously (with some degree of initiative). A second attribute of work, its variety, was also singled out by 27 per cent of the men and 37 per cent of foremen. Indeed, only 13 and 14 per cent respectively of the two groups failed to emphasize at least one intrinsic aspect of the work. Interestingly, only 8 and 5 per cent respectively of men and foremen cited the nature of social relationships with work mates, these being of far less importance than the intrinsic aspects of the work. These results demonstrate the appropriateness of the concepts and explanations used so far in this chapter and the similarities between the attitudes of those who work in the docks and the people cited in other investigations. They further demonstrate the inherently satisfying nature of at least certain aspects of dock work.[14]

Expectations of Work

In recent years there have been several attempts to demonstrate that different groups of workers expect markedly different things from their jobs. A simple and fundamental distinction between those expectations concerned with extrinsic rewards and those concerned with intrinsic ones underlies the most common classifications of 'orientations to work', to use the current terminology.[15] The concern with extrinsic factors is expressed in highly favourable evaluations of pay and security (often classified as the 'instrumental' reasons for working), whereas a concern with intrinsic factors is thought to comprise evaluations of the nature of the work tasks, control over the work and the quality of the human relations at the workplace.

Current usage of the 'orientations' concept has not passed unchallenged, however. There are two main foci of argument: that current usage oversimplifies what are in fact highly complex phenomena, and that they ignore the impact of work experience and socialization on individuals' expectations. It is argued that people cannot be divided on such simple criteria, because they are always in fact vitally concerned with both the extrinsic and intrinsic aspects of work. It is further

[14] Money was also mentioned by 27 per cent of the men and 24 per cent of foremen.
[15] For a comprehensive summary of the literature on orientations see R. K. Brown, 'Sources of Objectives in Work and Employment', in J. Child (ed.), *Man and Organization* (London, 1973), pp. 17–38.

argued that different emphasis will be given to the different aspects at different times, depending on the situations in which people find themselves: for example, in a context of bargaining between men and management workpeople may tend to emphasize extrinsic and instrumental expectations, whereas they become more concerned with the intrinsic aspects of work when the bargaining is over.[16] The second argument is that the use of the 'orientations' concept causes the sociologist to over-emphasize the relatively unchanging nature of expectations and to attribute their origin to social mechanisms which are prior to, or outside of, work. This therefore devalues the role which the experience of work has for the formation and subsequent change of expectations.[17]

Consequently, there are powerful arguments against the acceptance of the extreme claims made by some proponents of the 'orientations' approach to the analysis of work attitudes and behaviour. However, the notion of expectations is not discredited by the revelation that particular usages and interpretations have a limited explanatory value. It certainly seemed important in the docks to find out what sorts of expectations the two groups had of work, without making any judgement as to how or where these originated, because it was apparent that the expectations which were characteristically held helped to explain other aspects of docking.

In order to find out what people wanted out of work, I compiled a list of seventeen job attributes on the basis of Herzberg's summary and typology of the job satisfaction literature, which is the most complete discussion of the available evidence.[18] The people interviewed were asked to imagine that they were looking for a new job, outside the docks, and to rank each item in terms of the importance which they would attach to it in their perfect job. A rating scale was used to give some idea of the degree of importance of each item. (The items and scale can be found in section D of the interview schedule.) The advantage of this method is that the various aspects of work are isolated in advance, while the person being interviewed is not forced to choose between items and can give high scores to as many as he wishes. An alternative was also used, which was to ask the respondent to choose in order the three *most* important items of the ideal job from the list of seventeen, forcing him to rank one item against another. The data are presented in tables 4.5, 4.6 and 4.7.

Taken together, the results of these two questions suggest that both

[16] W. W. Daniel, 'Understanding Employee Behaviour in its Context: Illustrations from Productivity Bargaining', in J. Child (ed.), op. cit., pp. 39–62.

[17] R. K. Brown, op. cit.

[18] F. Herzberg et al., *Job Attitudes: Review of Research and Opinion* (Pittsburgh, 1957), passim; and F. Herzberg et al., *The Motivation to Work* (New York, 1959), pp. 143–8.

men and foremen rate highly a wide range of items, when they are not forced to choose between them. The range includes the extrinsic categories which have an instrumental meaning, such as security, company efficiency and high pay, aspects of the intrinsic content of the work itself and certain types of social relationship. The first set of items is concerned with instrumentalism. ('High pay' was chosen in preference to 'pay', in order to maximize the instrumental, reward-centred meaning of the item.) The scores for these attributes show that security is placed first, while efficiency and high pay are placed ahead of most other factors in table 4.5. The data on security and high pay, which are the more important categories of instrumentalism, do not conceal a situation in which a sizeable group gives both items and inflates the total score, because 71 per cent of foremen and 73 per cent of dock workers gave one or other of the two main items. The second set of items shows a concern with the intrinsic attributes of work. Both groups regard the relationship between an individual and his work tasks as a significant element of his job. The third set properly belongs in the extrinsic category, because social relations form part of the context of work and are not determined by the work. This wide range of highly evaluated items means, of course, that neither group shows any tendency to view work in mutually exclusive categories. Thus the concern with the extrinsic rewards of work co-exists with an interest in the intrinsic. Two other results stand out: that men and foremen share similar expectations; and that differences between age groups are not large.

It is noteworthy that local communities do not appear to have any impact on orientations. The 'traditional worker' theory has argued that the society outside work has a major impact on orientations, particularly the local community in isolated, single-occupation areas, and that solidaristic ties are more important than instrumental rewards in traditional communities. If such communities exist near the docks, then one would anticipate that the work expectations of community members would differ from those of people who live outside the dockland area. The evidence of this research shows that there are no variations either by area of residence or distance from the dock gates and that instrumentality is *not* related to local communities in the predicted way.

It is scarcely surprising that such a pattern of expectations should result from the series of questions presented to respondents. People were not asked to make a trade-off between the various elements of work, but to state how they would evaluate these elements in a world without constraints. It has been claimed that most semi- and unskilled manual workers are forced in reality to choose between work which is highly paid and that which is intrinsically satisfying, and that the choice an individual makes in this situation indicates the priority of his work expectations.[19] Now one may object to such a formulation, on the grounds that less skilled manual jobs infrequently present such a clear choice between extrinsic and intrinsic satisfaction (intrinsic rewards rarely being particularly high in any of these manual jobs), that most individuals cannot choose their jobs because they are constrained by local labour markets, or that few individuals know enough about the content of the available jobs to make a realistic decision. Nevertheless, the fact remains that few manual jobs provide both types of reward and many provide only small amounts of either. Thus the men and foremen interviewed in the docks were presented with forced-choice questions in order to see what sorts of priorities they held. The answers to these questions in fact reveal that extrinsic and instrumental expectations have primacy in this situation also, followed by a concern with certain intrinsic aspects of work, particularly those which provide a sense of achievement, while the nature of social relationships takes third place.

In reality, of course, neither dock workers nor foremen are placed in the situation of having to choose between the maximization of pay and security at the cost of intrinsic work satisfaction. Docking in recent years has been an occupation which has allowed comparatively high extrinsic and intrinsic rewards to co-exist. In comparison with many other manual jobs the work tasks would appear to be reasonably satisfying, though the extent and nature of this satisfaction ought not to be exaggerated for a sizeable minority of the men. At the same time, the combination of the Scheme, decasualization and a powerful labour movement means that dock work is now highly attractive for instrumental reasons as well. Only 5 per cent thought they would earn more outside the industry.

When an ordering of priorities does occur, however, then the two groups do place greater weight on the extrinsic or instrumental factors of security and pay than on others. The concern with high pay indicates the importance of calculative elements in people's orientations in the docks. 53 per cent of the men and 27 per cent of foremen thought that they could earn more in another dock company than they were currently receiving, though the Scheme and the general lack of recruitment tied them to their existing firms. I was interested to see what the consequences of these unrealized financial aspirations might be, given the argument that different expectations create different types of attachment to employment.[20] In reply to a question about leaving, 38 per cent of dock workers and 6 per cent of foremen said that they had considered leaving their firms. These replies were then correlated with their views about earning more elsewhere, which showed that there was a definite but fairly small association between the two subjects so far as the men

[19] J. H. Goldthorpe, D. Lockwood et al., op. cit., vol. 3 (1969), pp. 54–64.
[20] ibid., vol. 1, pp. 38–42.

were concerned.[21] Too few foremen had considered leaving to make the calculation worthwhile. People who considered that they could earn more gave significantly greater weight to what might be called the 'negative' reasons for staying where they were (inertia, age, the impossibility of moving firms, the fact that other firms were really none too different), than to 'positive' ones (such as the quality of human relations in the firm and sentiments of satisfaction and identification). The associations were definite for both groups, fairly small in the men's case but moderate in the foremen's.[22]

These findings clearly demonstrate the importance of the concern with instrumental rewards at work: feelings of satisfaction or dissatisfaction with payment, relative to what are perceived as possible earnings elsewhere, are demonstrably associated with certain feelings about present employment. Dissatisfied people are more likely to consider leaving and to minimize their feelings of attachment or their response to the 'positive' aspects of a company.[23]

Gangs and Work Groups

Neither men nor foremen mentioned the quality of social relationships with others as a major advantage of docking over other occupations, and both gave relationships a fairly low evaluation in the various tests of expectations. Yet conventional dock work, to judge by its observable characteristics and the perceptions of those involved, placed few obstacles in the way of work group formation. Indeed, the organization of production was centred on the work group, because the gang was the basic unit until Phase 2 in theory introduced more flexible manning arrangements. The arguments of those who uphold the tenets of the human relations school, that all workers seek supportive sociability within groups, and of those who believe that a 'solidaristic' orientation which values the social community of work mates is characteristic of occupations such as docking, must seriously be questioned by the failure of those engaged in dock work to respond to such a favourable milieu. The potential of the work organization for the creation of strong social bonds among those working on common tasks was not fulfilled, because of the low valuation people placed on this aspect of work. The importance of sociable groupings in the docks would appear to have been exaggerated, and the bases of groupings to have been misconstrued.

[21] $\Phi = \cdot 28$ at the 0·01 level.
[22] $\Phi = \cdot 32$ and ·49 respectively, both at the 0·05 level.
[23] There is no association between people's *actual* earnings and their replies concerning the importance of instrumental factors in the perfect job, earning more elsewhere or thinking of leaving their present job. The category of 'moral involvement' as a source of positive attachment is discussed more fully in Chapter 6.

The gang of twelve or thirteen men has been regarded as a classic case of the human-relations-style work group. The study of Manchester dock workers saw gangs as semi-permanent institutions, nearly 70 per cent of members having belonged to them for more than a year and nearly a quarter over five years.[24] The relationships between gang members were regarded as voluntary and co-operative, because the gang was not an officially constituted unit imposed on the men by foremen or managements. Gangs were seen to constitute a form of social community for the members, providing supportive social relationships which included protection of the elderly. The study did note, however, that not all gangs were characterized by affective relationships, and also that most individuals in its sample were not, in fact, gang members.[25] In the London docks, given the earlier description of casual labour, the purely voluntary nature of the associations between gang members and between the gang and the foreman might have been disputed prior to 1967. But the potentially coercive elements of the casual system disappeared with the introduction of Phase 1, so that real freedom of choice was possible when I carried out the research. Individuals came together to form voluntary associations, gangs, which usually owed little to any managerial initiative. Moreover, managers found it difficult to refuse to recognize gangs, however undesirable they found some combinations of individuals, because the right to form a gang was a fairly well established custom, though the shop stewards recognized that managers also had rights in the deployment of the labour force and would negotiate on the subject of gang formation. Several comments can be made about the gang system in this period.

Three-quarters of the sample of dock workers were working regularly as gang members,[26] the rest being unattached men, who made up vacancies on a temporary basis, or men temporarily on light duties. The gangs themselves, however, were of comparatively recent origin, given that only about a third of the men who had been in gangs prior to Phase 1 were still working with the same people at the time of the research. The process of change-over from casual employment to a permanent attachment to one firm split many gangs, because individuals went their own ways, while the closure of the upriver docks during Phase 1 led to labour migration throughout the period. This destruction of established gangs was not necessarily imposed upon the men, because it was frequently possible for gangs to remain intact if their members

[24] *The Dock Worker*, p. 75.

[25] ibid., pp. 61–83.

[26] This includes members of berth crews on unitized operations. These crews differ in size from gangs. They are normally formed by management, whereas gangs are voluntary associations of men over whose composition management has little control.

wished, particularly during the transition to permanency. What appeared to happen, however, was that individuals made personal choices based on which firms and which docks best suited them individually.

76 per cent of the men I interviewed preferred to work in a regular gang, 21 per cent did not, while the rest did not have a preference. But gangs were in fact rarely valued as a source of supportive or solidary social relationships at the workplace, and most people gave a highly instrumental meaning to the gang unit. 64 per cent of those favouring gangs did so because gangs developed teamwork, with the result that the work was done more speedily and efficiently by a regular group than by a collection of individuals brought together on a one-off basis. The traditional piecework payment system meant that teamwork was necessary in order to maximize earnings, which was the evaluation most respondents made. A subsidiary benefit of working in a gang was to make the job a safer one, since teamwork reduced accident risks. 11 per cent of the men mentioned social relationships, while a further 24 per cent mentioned both sociability and teamwork. Paradoxically, many of the men in this study who objected to working in gangs gave human relations reasons in reverse, as it were: 87 per cent of those who disliked gangs complained of the boredom of working always with the same people and of the way in which gang members exploited each other. The study of Manchester dock workers provided evidence that the various instrumental benefits of membership were in fact important for that group of workers as well, despite the study's efforts to fit gangs into the human relations mould. Manchester dock workers gave security, safety, financial reward and physical ease as reasons for gang membership. Many gangs were notable for the feelings of antipathy between their members.[27]

The relative unimportance of the gang as the source of feelings of group 'belongingness' is further demonstrated in the replies to other questions. When asked how upset they would be if they were moved to another job, similar to their present one but away from the people they normally worked with, 78 per cent of dock workers reported that they would hardly be concerned at all. This is a higher figure even than that found in *The Affluent Worker* studies, where the question was used in order to measure the extent of people's 'affective involvement' in work groups.[28] A second indicator of such involvement, the extent to which the people one works with are also friends outside work, produced a similarly low involvement: only 23 per cent reported seeing something of work mates outside work.

The foremen's work did not put them in groups in the same way as did the men's. The system of gangs rotating between different foremen

[27] *The Dock Worker*, pp. 70–6.
[28] J. H. Goldthorpe, D. Lockwood *et al.*, op. cit., vol. 1, pp. 50–1.

prevented the foremen from participating in the men's work groups. Foremen did have frequent contact with others in the course of their work, but this was with a wide range of different individuals only some of whom were seen often enough for social relationships to develop. Foremen were no more likely than the men to continue friendships from the workplace in their non-work lives. However, they were considerably more likely than the men to be upset at moving jobs away from their present work mates. 47 per cent said they would be upset to move. Most foremen referred to the other foremen in the firm as their work mates (though these were not properly speaking work mates because contact normally occurred off the job in the staff mess room), and to a few of the superintendents. It is noticeable that, among foremen, age was associated with feelings of 'affective involvement' and that the older foremen were significantly more likely to report that they would be upset than the younger. See table 4.8. This contrasts with the sample of men, for whom age was unimportant. Thus the foremen appeared to place a greater value on social relationships than the men, even though a majority of foremen still did not care about these. However, those who did care did not cite relationships which were occasioned by the work situation, so much as those brought about by a common employment and status situation in the same firm.

An obvious explanation of the low value given to work groups as sources of social interaction is that dock workers do not regard work as an area of life in which sociability is of much importance. It might be argued that the instrumental view of work overrides all other considerations, as was held to be the case with engineering workers in Luton. This would be a somewhat over-simplified view, however, since social relationships were included among the priorities of work expectations, although lower down the scale. While the significance of social relationships has indeed been exaggerated in the docks there is nevertheless evidence of some desire for sociability. However, this desire can be met by contacts made outside the immediate work group nearly as easily as by those inside. The description of the work showed how social contacts outside the gang were possible, because of the frequent delays which were characteristic of conventional work. These could stretch into several hours a day, particularly during poor weather. Observation indicated that a few gang members used these stoppages, plus the official breaks, to maintain friendships with other individuals who were valued in an 'affective' way. Therefore, some cliques and friendship groups formed which were not co-extensive with work groups or even with the firms for which individuals worked.

Indeed, the strong attachment to the work group which various academic theories attribute to dock workers could well be a socially divisive force in the docks. The study of industrial relations in Britain and the U.S. over the last twenty years has demonstrated that, under certain conditions, work groups can develop into sectional phenomena which split labour forces and occupations into smaller sub-units.[29] These groups become introverted and selfish, acting in response to narrow conceptions of self-interest which frequently place the groups into conflict with each other as well as with management. Work group bargaining, which increased in importance during the 1960s and has been hailed by some commentators as the major dynamic of contemporary British industrial relations,[30] is a classic example of the sectionalism which results from certain forms of group attachment. Different groups negotiate directly with management in order to maximize their own advantage, such advantage often being defined in relation to the relative position of other groups in the firm. Thus the idea put forward by the 'traditional worker' theorists, that a strong sense of attachment to the group is the basic unit of wider loyalties of a class type, would certainly not appear to have been borne out in recent British industrial relations.

In the context of earnings, there was in fact a tension between work group sectionalism and loyalty to the wider occupational community. This was because piecework created inequalities of reward between the more and less efficient gangs. However, such pressures towards sectionalism were reasonably well contained by the action of shop stewards who generalized any special awards won by individual gangs and insisted on equitable work-sharing. Gangs rarely displayed those introverted and solidaristic characteristics which would have accentuated any inclination towards a social divisiveness based on groups. (This theme is developed more fully in the later discussion of piecework and industrial relations in the docks.)

Dock workers frequently had good friendships with others in the industry, though not to the exclusion of outsiders. However, the origin of common bonds is not the work group, but the fact of occupational membership in combination with factors based on the outside community.[31] This complements the remark made by a few dock workers,

---

[29] See L. R. Sayles, *The Behaviour of Industrial Work Groups: Prediction and Control* (New York, 1958), passim; J. W. Kuhn, *Bargaining in Grievance Settlement* (New York, 1961), passim; A. Flanders, *Management and Unions* (London, 1970), pp. 155–211; and A. Fox and A. Flanders, 'The Reform of Collective Bargaining: From Donovan to Durkheim', *British Journal of Industrial Relations*, 7, 1969, pp. 151–80. A summary of the available evidence and an evaluation of the usefulness of the work group concept can be found in S. R. Hill, 'Norms, Groups and Power: The Sociology of Workplace Industrial Relations', *British Journal of Industrial Relations*, 12, 1974, pp. 213–35.

[30] This analysis underlay Donovan's description and recommended reforms of British industrial relations in the late 1960s: see *Royal Commission on Trade Unions and Employers Associations* (London, 1968), Cmnd. 3623. The most coherent statement of this analysis, which also attempts to conceptualize the evidence of this commission, is to be found in A. Fox and A. Flanders, op. cit.

[31] Chapter 9 gives details of the origin of friendships.

to the effect that moving away from one set of mates would not be a cause of upset because all dock workers were potential mates; i.e. they all had a sufficient amount in common for an individual to feel at home wherever he worked.

Reactions to Technical Change

The long-term trends towards the greater unitization of all break-bulk cargoes and the associated growth of new cargo-handling technologies are bound to have a major impact on the dock worker's working conditions and his perceptions of work. Description of unitized berths and the perceptions of those involved in working on them has indicated the major changes involved: rationalization and simplification of the production process have facilitated greater managerial control and a greater integration of work organization into the physical layout of the production system; the redesigned cargo packages and the new berths have facilitated the introduction of machinery which replaces manual labour. In view of the nature of conventional hand work and the feelings of satisfaction which this gives most men and foremen, what were the reactions of the two groups to the changes which the new methods promised to bring?

The job satisfaction of those who were actually working on the new technologies when I did the interviewing was high, but there are good reasons for supposing that the response of these individuals would not necessarily be typical of all other workers. In the first place, those working on the new systems were largely self-selected at that time: less than 10 per cent of any company's labour force was involved and all the men had volunteered to work on the new methods. The largest firm included in my research had several unitized operations which were to start immediately the union ban was lifted and therefore kept a list of all those who wanted to work on them, but no more than 20 per cent of all its employees had volunteered (despite a potential earnings level which was up to 50 per cent more than on conventional work at the time). In the second place, the combination of the comparatively recent origin of all the new operations with the stewards' policies of labour rotation meant that no one in the sample had been able to work on unitized systems for much over twelve months, and many had worked for less. It may be the case that nobody had worked long enough fully to appreciate what the work involved.

One would have expected the new technologies to have provoked opposition, for reasons connected with the nature of conventional dock work if for no other. The traditional skills of dock workers and foremen represent the cumulative wisdom of the occupation which has been transmitted from one generation to another, often from father to son. As was shown in the description of conventional work, the content of this occupational expertise included both the manipulative, manual skills of the physical tasks and the cognitive ones involved in controlling the work organization. The unitized systems had no place for such skills, however. Machinery replaced the manipulative skills, while the rationalization of production replaced the experience of foremen and men with standardized procedures. Unitization and new techniques would thus appear to have led to the 'de-skilling' of conventional occupational tasks. The discrete body of techniques and knowledge which docking traditionally embraced was no longer required on the modern systems.

Driving skills and the new ways of organizing work were no longer part of the traditional exclusive expertise of dock work, the 'property' of the occupation, but the product of formal training by the employer or the dock training agencies. Indeed, there was little alternative once the decision to introduce a new technology had been made, because the occupational skills of traditional dock work had little relevance to the modern type of work, and there would have been nothing to replace these traditional techniques had not management intervened with more formalized procedures. Foremen did manage to retain control over some of their old organizing role, of course, because the inevitable teething problems and failures allowed them to develop a direct operating knowledge which others did not possess. But even here, the fund of expertise which they alone possessed was not of the same order as before.

In view of these fundamental alterations to the nature of dock work, one might reasonably have anticipated that many workers and foremen would have objected to the new methods on the grounds that they destroyed what were customary and valued tasks.[32] It is a commonplace in the sociology of work that skills which derive from the nature of the work frequently constitute part of the culture or belief system of an occupation. Such an occupational culture places value on the elements of work which define the nature of the occupation and its essential tasks, distinguish the occupation from any others, and justify the position of the occupation to a wider public.[33] Furthermore, this culture may be internalized by individual members to form part of their own self-images, which are thus defined in occupational terms. One consequence is that changes in the nature of the tasks performed by members, when these changes are in the direction of a less discrete and exclusive job content and when they also lead to what can be regarded in occupa-

[32] This is a separate issue from that of redundancy. Objections to the manpower implications of the new methods may of course have been expected as well, if the two groups were concerned about the possibility of redundancies.

[33] This idea has been developed by E. Krauze, *The Sociology of Occupations* (Boston, 1971), p. 88, and, in the context of professional work, by E. C. Hughes, *Men and Their Work* (Glencoe, 1958), p. 121.

tional terms as 'de-skilling', will be perceived as attacking the basis of both the occupational culture and the self-images of the individual members. This compounds the loss of intrinsic satisfaction which might be felt by anyone who moves to relatively less skilled work. In fact, the idea of technological change was considerably more popular among the two groups than had been anticipated. Remarkably little opposition was voiced against the introduction of the new unitized systems, and few complained of the possibly deleterious consequences of such systems either for the occupation or for the individuals concerned. Indeed, it appears that these two groups saw the impact of technical change as being potentially beneficial in both aspects.

People were asked whether they would prefer to work on the new systems rather than the old ones they were on at the time, while those who were already on the modern berths were asked whether they preferred the conventional work which they had left behind. In the first group, 70 per cent of the men and 59 per cent of foremen said that they would prefer to be on the modern, unitized systems, while in the second, the vast majority preferred the new work. In both groups, the bulk of the reasons given for this preference centred on the greater physical ease of the new methods in comparison with the arduous nature of conventional hand work. This idea of physical ease normally included reference to the effects of conventional manual work on health and safety. (83 per cent of the men and 61 per cent of foremen on conventional work had previously complained that accident risks were too great on that type of work.) A sizeable minority of the men was also attracted by the financial rewards then available on unitized work.

In addition to questions which were designed to ascertain how individuals felt about the new types of work, both groups were asked about the impact of the new methods on the occupation as a whole. They were asked whether they thought that the new methods of cargo-handling were 'good things' for dock workers and foremen as a whole. 86 per cent of the men and 94 per cent of foremen thought that the new technologies were in their best interests. Once again, reasons centred on the easiness of the work. A sizeable minority also mentioned approvingly that the new methods were more modern and efficient than the old, and were therefore better for the occupation.

Technical change was not seen as an unmixed blessing, however, because the respondents were well aware of possible disadvantages. It was just that the benefits were thought to outweigh the disadvantages. 50 per cent of both the men and foremen, when asked what reservations they had about the new methods, stated that one cost of unitization would be more boring work: i.e. they were well aware that the intrinsic interest and satisfaction of their work would decline with modernization and the changing nature of the occupational tasks. But the old tasks were seen to involve costs in terms of physical effort, health and safety, which made them less attractive to preserve. There were no differences by age in either sample's receptivity to technical change: the older dock workers and foremen were no more likely to feel that unitization was a bad thing, to prefer conventional work, nor to express reservations about the new methods.

The fact that both samples welcomed the idea of technological change, if not the subsequent practice, and thought that they would like to work on the unitized systems, reflects on their previously mentioned conceptions of conventional work. The most highly valued aspects of conventional work were the freedom and the variety, rather than the specific skills of the work tasks. Indeed, a number of the men had thought that the work did not fully utilize their capabilities and a number had not described the work as being skilled, though these were both minority responses. More foremen were likely to mention the demands and skill of their work, but they still saw the freedom and variety as the main advantages of dock work. Conventional work also had severe costs associated with it, notably the problems of physical exertion and accident risks. It seems, therefore, that the commitment to specific occupational tasks and the skills associated with these was not very great among the manual workers at least, though there was some degree of commitment among the foremen. Certainly, the benefits of unitization were thought to outweigh the costs in this context. Undoubtedly, those reservations which were mentioned in the context of changing to unitization centred on the loss of variety and the fears of boredom, and not on 'de-skilling' as such. However, the freedom of dock work, which was one of the major sources of gratification, was not regarded as being in danger.

Rather than new technology being perceived as an attack on occupational skills and values, it was welcomed as a way of raising the status and prestige of docking in the eyes of the dock workers and foremen themselves: rather than threatening his self-image it allowed the individual to have an even greater pride in his job. It was also felt that technological change would enhance the status of docking in the eyes of the outside world: 91 per cent of men and 95 per cent of foremen said the occupation's status and prestige would be enhanced. Technology was regarded by men and foremen as a legitimating force, because unitization was thought to symbolize modernity and thus the incorporation of dock work into contemporary society.[34] Dock workers have traditionally been accorded a very low social status in the eyes of the public, being stigmatized as loutish and unskilled labourers. This public image dates at least from the nineteenth century and has been confirmed in a more recent occupational prestige scale which placed dockers twenty-ninth

[34] A similar idea can be found in D. Pécaut, 'The Worker and the Community', in A. Touraine et al., op. cit., pp. 133 and 137.

out of thirty, just above road sweepers.[35] The study of Manchester dock workers showed that outsiders, particularly those living in the same neighbourhoods as dockers, had a low evaluation of docking.[36]

Therefore, technical change was appreciated as the means of enhancing the occupation. In particular, given the presence of a dominant social ethic which places value on technical rationality,[37] an ethic which these dock workers shared, unitization was regarded both as an event which ought not to be opposed in principle and as an event which would place docking in the ranks of the modern, high-prestige occupations. Unitization was the symbol of progress which allowed dock workers to claim the title of contemporary men rather than traditional workers.

This perception of the situation was probably only possible because of the protective function of the Scheme, which defined dock work and reserved it for registered workers. The Scheme protected docking from the competition of other occupations, which might have been a consequence of changing the exclusivity of dock tasks, and protected the individual against redundancy or competition for his job. The Scheme defined dock work and reserved it for registered dock workers. In this way, the handling of unitized cargo inside the existing Scheme ports was defined as dock work, which meant that the new tasks could still be regarded as the property of the occupation. Consequently, technical change was not perceived as destroying the basis of differentiation between the occupational tasks and others, but merely as re-defining what these occupational tasks involved. This meant that occupational tasks and skills did not have to act in such a way as to mark off the occupation from the competition of others: the definition of the nature of the occupation and its essential work, and the delineation of the occupation from others, was ensured by Act of Parliament. Specific tasks and skills might still be valued, but their symbolic importance did not need to be as great as it was in less protected occupations.

In the same way, occupational commitment and identity could be promoted by a range of factors other than valued skills. These included the enormous symbolic importance of the Scheme and registration, which was central to the occupational culture, the hostility of the public towards dock workers, the existence of some sort of occupational community outside work, and the danger of the work.[38] Moreover, the protection apparently afforded by the Scheme meant that the new working methods could be regarded as an updating of occupational skills, rather than as the destruction of the exclusivity of dock work and the conse-

[35] J. Hall and D. Caradog Jones, 'Social Grading of Occupations', *British Journal of Sociology*, 1, 1950, pp. 31–55.

[36] *The Dock Worker*, pp. 50–4.

[37] J. Habermas, *Toward a Rational Society* (London, 1971), pp. 105–22.

[38] These factors have been identified respectively by the *Devlin Report*, para. 241; D. F. Wilson, *Dockers* (London, 1972), p. 53; *The Dock Worker*, p. 79; and J. Lovell, *Stevedores and Dockers* (London, 1969), pp. 39–40.

quent opening up of the occupation to competition from other groups. 'Re-skilling' rather than 'de-skilling' was thought to be the effect of technological change.

The fact that the distinction between docking and other occupations was blurred by the changing nature of tasks and skills was either not realized or it was not seen as important, because the Scheme protected dock work of the old and new varieties equally: this meant that dock workers could still regard themselves as practising a distinct and exclusive occupational role. The registration provisions of the Scheme prevented the employment of outsiders in those ports covered by it, while guaranteeing employment for registered workers. There was thus no great reason to fear at this time that drivers would be recruited for the new machines from outside the docks, for example, or that registered workers would be made redundant. For instance, the two-year ban on the introduction of additional unitized systems, which was lifted in September 1970, was neither caused nor maintained by fears for employment nor by resistance to the idea of modernization. It was created simply as a bargaining counter in order to win better pay and conditions for all workers throughout the port. (As such, it worked quite effectively.)

There were some fears expressed during the interviews, however, that technical change might not be entirely in the dock workers' best interests. 27 per cent of the men had reservations which centred on the possibilities of redundancy. In a few cases, these reservations were sufficiently strong for people to oppose technical change entirely. It was during this period that the unions and employers in London set up a private inquiry into the definition of dock work, after a company had threatened to withdraw from the port area and to continue most of its work outside the jurisdiction of the Scheme. The Bristow committee was in fact set up to consider the general problem of re-defining dock work, but it soon became apparent that this problem could not be treated in isolation from the growth of unitization. Indeed, by the time I finished the field work for this book, the problem of possible unemployment resulting from the new technologies had become of greater concern to dock workers, as had the question of the definition of dock work.

The very rapid unitization of conventional work, which followed Phase 2 and the lifting of the ban on the special manning arrangements required by unitized operators, has made no dock worker unemployed in the strict sense. The Scheme guarantees a fairly high fall-back wage whether a man actually has work or not, since dock workers surplus to the requirements of employers are maintained on a temporarily unattached register and paid out of a levy on all employers. However, the fall-back is not as good a wage as could be earned in proper employment, so dock workers' livelihoods have been affected by the presence of surplus labour. Moreover, the existence of a large pool of temporarily unattached workers obviously leads employers to put pressure on the Scheme, and dock workers sometimes fear that the legal protection which they have enjoyed for a quarter of a century might be abolished as the result of these pressures. The threat of redundancy is a major concern, though this threat has yet to become an actuality.

The expansion of the previously small ports outside the Scheme has added to these fears. These ports are not subject to the restrictions on managerial prerogative nor to the financial levies of the Scheme ports, and have offered better and cheaper services. Much of their new competitiveness can be traced to the simplification of dock work which has followed from unitization: the manipulative and organizational skills of traditional dock workers and foremen are not so important on unitized systems, so that the traditional advantages of ports like London no longer hold good.

The argument that much of the work connected with unitized cargo systems is no longer dock work in the strict sense, has been accepted by the courts. Dock work has been legally defined by Parliament for the purposes of the Scheme, and is one of the very few legal definitions of an occupation's work. But the definition was originally made in an ambiguous and ad hoc fashion. Consequently, the use of new methods of cargo-handling outside the actual dock area has been judged to fall outside the scope of the legal definitions.[39] This has been particularly important for the growth of container groupage depots and meat cold stores, work on which might be argued by those in the dock industry to be dock work. This argument has been employed with considerable force by the dock workers when employers of dock labour have closed down their warehouses in the dock area, only to re-open outside the dock gates and carry on businesses similar to those of their old establishments. Indeed the joint union-employer Bristow committee recommended that all container work within a five-mile corridor on either side of the Thames should be handled by registered dock workers. This followed the successful American precedent which guaranteed dockers all container work within fifty miles of a port.

At the time of my research for this book, the reduced labour requirements of unitized operations were very apparent to dock workers but caused little opposition to the new methods, because it was assumed that the Scheme would protect the interests of the occupation and individuals. Various reports made it quite clear at this time that the demand for labour would decline. What dock workers had not anticipated, however, was the growth of the non-Scheme ports and the restricted definition of dock work which the courts would apply. The definitional problems had been anticipated, but it had been assumed that a solution on Bristow's lines of a 'corridor' alongside the Thames, inside which dock work would be established, would be upheld. Indeed,

[39] See D. F. Wilson, op. cit., pp. 135–54, for a discussion of the legal definitions.

the mere fact of technical change has not threatened the continued existence of docking as a discrete occupation in anything like the way in which these two other developments have done. A situation has been created whereby dock workers are established in ports which have large, declining sections, while anyone can work in the growing ports or perform the activities which dock workers regard as the modern version of their work, outside the docks altogether.

In sum, the reactions to changing technology suggested that commitment to the established tasks of traditional dock work was not great. The commitment to the freedom which the work situation provided was strong, but this freedom was not thought to be compromised merely by a change of technical artefacts. The variety of traditional work was seen to be threatened, however, and people were concerned about this. A weak commitment to traditional tasks was understandable, because the Scheme meant that the work did not have to be invested with any practical or symbolic significance as defining the domain of the occupation and people could judge tasks on their intrinsic merits. Therefore, it was possible to interpret the principle of technical modernization as being mainly advantageous to those concerned. Regarded in another way, however, the contraction of the industry's manpower needs, which has resulted from the new methods of cargo-handling, is obviously disadvantageous to the occupation in the sense of its long-term numerical decline, even though actual redundancies are most unlikely. Were dock workers and foremen to be interviewed now, it is possible that the principle of technical change might be treated with greater reservations, though it is clear that other changes have had far more deleterious consequences for docking than the mere fact of introducing new techniques.

CHAPTER 5

Foremen's Roles

It is quite evident that the men and foremen had unusually great freedom to control their work. Both groups were noticeably unrestricted in what they did and how they behaved at work. For dock workers, this lack of restriction could be explained partly in terms of the Scheme, the custom-based nature of the work organization dating from the casual era, and a strong rank-and-file labour movement which took advantage of the possibilities inherent in both. But the freedom enjoyed by the foremen was more remarkable, given that neither the Scheme nor the labour movement advanced their interests in the same way as the men's, though customary work arrangements did favour both groups. While observational and survey data revealed this apparent freedom from external constraints, it also established that different foremen displayed similar patterns of behaviour: i.e. it appeared that supervisory behaviour conformed to some definite pattern despite the freedom of individual foremen. The apparent freedom of individuals to control their work and the structuring of behaviour which actually occurred deserve further scrutiny.

Any discussion of the nature and origin of the foremen's control at work must involve a wide-ranging appraisal of the port industry and the dock companies: the historical growth of the London dock system, in particular its extreme and illogical division of labour, the structure and character of the dock companies, and the significance of the occupation itself are the three elements of this appraisal. The focus of attention is the role of foremen, in order to clarify how freedom and constraint co-exist. The discussion has much wider implications, however, since it helps explain how the occupational culture makes its influence so strongly felt at all levels of the docks and so provides a more rounded picture of the industry.

Technology and the Industrial Division of Labour

The description of the foremen's daily work suggests systematic differences between foremen's jobs on the different types of operation (shed, ship and container operations). These differences indicate that the technology of the various operations may have a dominant influence on the foremen's roles and the consequent patterns of activity. It was shown earlier that the direct man–hardware constraints were unimportant for foremen, but there is a popular alternative argument, put forward by Joan Woodward and Perrow,[1] that technology influences the structure and functioning of organizations and thus determines the nature of organizational roles. I tried to interpret the role behaviour of foremen in this way and found little evidence of role structuring via the technical system, although the analysis of technology did highlight the industry's division of labour, the product of social rather than technical forces, which had a significant influence on foremen.

There was obviously little direct link between technology and the organizational role of supervision, because behaviour was often similar in different technologies and dissimilar within a single one: container foremen had similarities with ship workers, while the latter often differed from shed foremen who were engaged in the same unit production process and worked with the same hardware. The idea that the amount of variation in machines and raw materials causes uncertainty which has to be solved, and is thus the indirect link between technology and roles, also proved unsatisfactory in the analysis of foremen's roles, because of the difficulty of defining, let alone measuring, uncertainty: neither I nor the foremen could really distinguish routine variations which created little uncertainty and were covered by fairly standard operating procedures from non-routine variations which involved foremen in working out new solutions, though this distinction is supposed to be a vital one in the analysis of variation and uncertainty.[2] Since variety is normal, any exception might have a precedent in a foreman's own job history. At the same time, because operating programmes are flexible and lack formalization, being based on informal norms and past experience rather than explicit rules, every exception can be regarded as fitting a known rule or precedent, whether or not it 'really' fits these.

Only on container berths was technology of any obvious importance, when observation of the variations which led to stoppages showed that machinery failure was a major problem on these operations. Raw materials were standardized into two or three basic sizes of box. These were of varying weights, but this variability was unimportant since all machinery could cope with the different weights. The theory of containerized operations is that all operating cycles are standardized and repetitive because all items of cargo are the same. However, the lack of mechanical reliability meant that nearly 20 per cent of the two

---

[1] Joan Woodward, *Industrial Organization: Theory and Practice* (London, 1965), and *idem* (ed.), *Industrial Organization: Behaviour and Control* (London, 1970); C. Perrow, 'A Framework for the Comparative Analysis of Organizations', *American Sociological Review*, 32, 1967, pp. 194–208, and *Organizational Analysis: A Sociological View* (London, 1970).

[2] C. Perrow, op. cit. (1967), and *idem*, op. cit. (1970), pp. 75–80.

container foremen's time was spent coping with machinery variation. This involved considerable re-scheduling of production and other work flow functions, which ought to have been virtually non-existent on a container berth and was due to the experimental nature of the equipment. There was thus a fairly direct link between technology and certain aspects of behaviour, though it was not one which was mediated via the organizational structure and it would disappear once the machinery problems were solved.

Some physical aspects of production were obviously of some concern to foremen, for instance the shape of the ship's hold. But they were not of great substantive interest, because in most cases they acted only as loose constraints on behaviour and the supervisory role-system.[3] The point is that the system of production did have an effect on the supervisory role, but this had little to do with the technological characteristics of production. Rather, the emphasis on easing bottlenecks and ensuring cargo flow should be attributed to the division of labour and responsibility in the dock industry, particularly in London. This in turn reflects the historical development of the port and the fact that organizational forms persist over time.

The physical flow of goods from manufacturer or despatcher to ship's hold has four distinct phases on conventional cargo operations: transport to the docks by road and rail hauliers; unloading and storage in the sheds by the P.L.A.; shipping-off from the shed on to the quay by the P.L.A.; transference from the quay into the hold where stowage is carried out by the stevedore companies. There are two occasional variations on this usual process. Direct delivery bypasses the P.L.A. stages completely, so that stevedores load the ship directly from lorries; this only occurs when cargoes are too bulky or dangerous to be stowed in the shed. Overside delivery, which was fairly common but is becoming less so, occurs when the goods are transhipped into lighters upriver and brought alongside by lightermen to be transferred by stevedores. There are numbers of servicing functions related to these operations, such as clerical procedures and documentation at each stage, and customs inspections, which further add to the complexity.

Co-ordination of this fragmented system is vital, as the last major inquiry into the ports recognized: 'the greater the number of different bodies involved in port operation the greater the premium to be placed on liaison and co-operation'.[4] This is largely how the foremen themselves perceived their role. Foremen acted on the basis of shared definitions of necessary behaviour which placed a high value on work flow

---

[3] F. C. Mann and L. Hoffman, *Automation and the Worker: Social Change in Power Plants* (New York, 1960), pp. 149–51, provide an interesting example of how supervisory roles can be manipulated without reference to technology or physical constraints.

[4] *Rochdale Report* (1962), para. 71.

functions, in particular co-ordination. In this way, the fragmented system could be made to work. But foremen at the end of this chain of activities are vulnerable, since failures are inevitable given the extended and complex nature of the chain.

Views on the importance of the division of labour varied, and private sector foremen cited it more frequently as a major obstacle than public sector foremen: 51 per cent of all the obstacles private sector foremen mentioned concerned lack of co-operation with other agencies against 9 per cent for the public sector.[5] Private sector foremen probably experienced these obstacles more intensely for a variety of reasons. Ship foremen were at the end of the chain, so that the potential number of failures earlier in the system was at its greatest for this group. This was particularly true when the P.L.A. failed to fulfil its obligations to consolidate and deliver cargo to the ship's side. Equally, the vagaries of lighterage, tally clerks and customs' officers hit ship operations more than any other. Secondly, ship operations had tighter time limits than shed ones. Thirdly, the ability of P.L.A. foremen to insulate themselves from criticisms originating either outside or inside the organization, in the way typical of groups in many bureaucracies, made their failures to cope with problems less threatening or salient.

Lack of articulation between operational stages was one major problem. But it was compounded by the fact that divisions into stages coincided with divisions between different firms. Divisions were not based on production or technological logic; indeed, they were basically arbitrary and incompatible with efficient working, since they did not coincide with logical discontinuities between processes.[6] Rather, they coincided with organizational boundaries. This was especially true of the ship and quay versus shed operations, where one natural process was divided into two and handled by different organizations.

The consequences for foremen were two-fold. On the one hand they had to bridge these artificial discontinuities. But, on the other, they had no control over those responsible for the related activities in the other organization. For example, P.L.A. foremen withdrew from the shipping-off operations in the shed and allowed ship foremen to deal with the authority's labour, so that some co-ordination could be achieved. But the P.L.A. dockers refused to accept a ship foreman's orders as binding, since he had no authority over them. Likewise, both public and private foremen were dependent on customs' officers and tally clerks, yet neither had any control over the way these two groups did their work.

---

[5] The next major category concerned the men's failure to co-operate, accounting for 29 per cent of obstacles in the private sector and 22 per cent in the public. Public sector foremen complained most about poor gear and facilities: 34 per cent of all obstacles given.

[6] E. J. Miller and A. K. Rice, *Systems of Organization* (London, 1967), pp. 8 and 36, show the importance of having discontinuities based on production logic rather than any other.

Thus foremen were dependent on the integration of a work flow process which had no central or single control, and in which co-ordination could not be enforced.

Unitized systems on purpose-built berths were not beset by these problems to the same extent. The ship–shore discontinuity was abolished, since only one agency was responsible for cargo-handling on container and packaged timber operations. Documentation and the co-ordination of transport were simplified, since individual berths were controlled by single companies or consortia, which ensured that there was tighter control over the stages in the cargo flow preceding handling in the docks. Foremen were provided with a continuous and steady flow of cargo which merely required loading. The absence of overside work and direct deliveries, and the simplified customs and tallying procedures, further contributed to the rationalization. The simplification and rationalization on these berths has, in fact, altered the basic nature of the dock operation; rather than representing a major halt in the flow of cargo, at which a complex series of activities are co-ordinated and synthesized, it has become merely one stage among several in the total through-put. The dock is now merely a point of interchange between modes of transport rather than the terminus of the process.[7]

Two aspects of the situation just described are peculiar to Londoi and the way in which its dock system grew up.[8] These are the marked disjunction between ship and shore operations, and the great reliance placed on lighterage (though overside work has been declining in recent years). London docks were developed by groups of merchants in the various overseas trades in the early and mid-nineteenth century. Parliament invested these merchant companies with privileges to develop the dock system and certain excise concessions, and mercantile interests dominated the port until the early twentieth century. London's trade pattern by the mid-nineteenth century was based on imports and transhipments, while its physical structure was based on the growth of massive warehousing facilities.[9] For most of the latter half of the century, there was a running battle between the dock companies, who needed to keep their warehouses in full use, and the shipowners, who objected to the near-monopolistic control of dock facilities. The dispute centred on the stevedoring operations in particular, because

[7] This point is made by McKinsey and Co., *Containerisation: the key to Low-cost Transport* (British Transport Docks Board, 1967), p. 6.

[8] The early history of the Port of London is documented by J. Broodbank, *History of the Port of London* (London, 1921), Vol. 1, and C. Capper, *The Port and Trade of London* (London, 1862), on whose works the following two paragraphs are based.

[9] The move to open new docks downstream, first the Royal group and then Tilbury, was the result of the need to keep control of the transit trade and maintain the supply of goods to the warehouses of the upper docks when ships grew larger and could not navigate the upper river; R. B. Oram, *The Dockers' Tragedy* (London, 1970), p. 95.

the dock companies insisted on controlling all discharging in order to provide trade to their warehouses.[10] They were happy to let exports be loaded by shipowners or their stevedore contractors, since these cargoes required less warehousing than imports and transhipments. Shipowners complained that they could discharge more cheaply and efficiently than the dock companies, particularly since their labour forces often performed the more difficult job of loading.

In the early 1890s, the shipowners won their argument. The poor financial position of the dock companies and the conviction, after the 1889 strike, that employing labour was too troublesome, led to a reallocation of functions. All discharging and loading was to be the shipowners' preserve, except in certain upriver docks where the companies retained the right because of the physical constraints on separation. But the companies continued to control the shore and warehousing operations. This created the divided system which has continued through to the present day, and which was formalized by the establishment of the P.L.A. in 1908 to take over from the old companies. The 1908 Act perpetuated the status quo, and made certain that any attempt to change the situation would come to nothing by giving port users (shipowners, stevedores, lightermen, wharfingers) the majority representation on the board.

The 1908 Act also perpetuated the 'free water' rights which exempted lighterage from any charges made by the old dock companies. These traditional water rights, which had existed prior to the creation of an enclosed dock system, gave lighters and the associated wharfingers competitive advantages over other forms of transport. This is the major reason for the unique importance of this method of cargo movement in the London dock system.[11]

The situation in the London docks, therefore, has been unique in terms of the role given to competing private companies, the nature of the ship-shore division and the importance of lighterage. Many of the present differences between British ports can be explained by reference to the differing patterns of growth, in particular the ways in which vested interests have become established and have resisted change in existing arrangements. Such interests prevent the reorganization of the ports except under duress. The consequence had been virtually to fix port organization until the early 1970s on the basis of the legacy from the late nineteenth century.[12]

The inefficiencies which result from the complex division of re-

[10] J. Broodbank, op. cit., p. 258.

[11] *Rochdale Report* (1962), para. 75.

[12] This analysis of vested interests is put forward by the *Rochdale Report* (1962), paras 70 and 71. This illustrates the argument that the way an organization is shaped historically and the strength of its vested interests are vitally important for explaining its present structure: see A. L. Stinchcombe, 'Social Structure and Organization', in J. G. Marsh (ed.), *Handbook of Organizations* (New York, 1965), pp. 142–69.

sponsibilities in London and elsewhere have long been recognized by practising managers and even by the various official bodies inquiring into the state of the industry over the last decades. As was noted above, the Rochdale inquiry emphasized the need for co-ordination but showed how rarely this was achieved. The proposals of the Labour government in the late 1960s to nationalize the ports were in turn justified partly on the basis of the greater efficiency which would result from an integrated industry.[13] Progress towards integration has been painfully slow, but two developments of the last few years have fostered some increase in the pace.

The advent of new technologies has led to the abolition of the old divisions on those berths which have been modernized. There is no intrinsic reason connected with the nature of these technologies why the organization of work should be simpler. Rather, the high capital costs of unitization and the legitimating functions of technological change have created a climate of opinion in which the various vested interests in the port have allowed the simplification of the division of labour to take place, in order that the new systems might be utilized most effectively. The second development has been the expansion of the P.L.A. into stevedoring after 1972. This expansion has resulted from the financial difficulties of several private sector firms and the decision of the authority to buy up these ailing companies. As a consequence of this development, the P.L.A. now works an integrated operation on conventional ships in certain parts of the port. Though this integration is not complete, to the extent that certain men and staff still specialize in the different areas of dock work, it means that both sides of the major division are under a single direction and authority.

Role Definition

It has been implied so far that the supervisory role in the docks is clearly defined and that foremen act out this role in a fairly faithful fashion. It has further been assumed that the foremen's organizational role is the crucial one. The first assumption repeats a commonplace of organizational analysis, that members of industrial organizations have fairly clear role specifications which guide their work-relevant activities, though the extent of compliance with these specifications may vary in different cases. The second assumption follows from the convention of placing foremen in 'the first line of management' and the belief that foremen are important for implementing the plans of more senior managers: the literature customarily regards the supervisory role as one which is crucial for the attainment of organizational objectives. In order to examine the processes connected with the definitions of the foremen's roles, I decided to gather material on this subject

[13] *The Reorganisation of the Ports* (London, 1969), Cmnd. 3903.

T.D.—4

in a systematic fashion at both the observational and interview stages.

Two broad approaches to the concept of the role have been distinguished: the processual and the conformist, to borrow Turner's terminology.[14] The first emphasizes the definition of the social act in a processual manner, the uniqueness of the individual act, and the analysis of social interaction in terms of the actors and their actions, while the second lays stress on the determination of systems of inter-action in terms of conformity to reasonably well-defined and persisting social structures. These two approaches ultimately reflect different views about the nature of social reality,[15] but at the level of competing role definitions either approach can use elements of the other in its ex-planations. The second approach was the one preferred here, for the following reason. If an individual's roles are in any sense determined, then this is most likely to occur in highly structured social systems such as formal organizations, even though one might not wish to make this assumption about other role systems. Organizations in theory have clearly defined goals and authority systems, which can be expected to structure behaviour more rigorously than in other areas of social life. This would appear to be particularly true with regard to task roles, which are of interest here. Members of the processual school have indeed upheld this view on occasion.[16]

Most empirical analyses of role assume, explicitly or implicitly, that overt behaviour reflects role pressures. These pressures are expressed in terms which allow for the operationalization of the concept, as emanating from specific individuals. Together, these individuals form the role set of the focal role. The first concern here is to see how far foremen's behaviour is explicable in terms of pressures from specific individuals comprising a role set.

The study of role sets was mainly confined to the foremen's im-mediate superiors and was not concerned with subordinates, peers, senior managers or outsiders. The most intensive study of organiza-tional roles has suggested that immediate superiors are of overwhelming importance in comparison with other groups.[17] This was also the impression I gained during my preliminary observation in the docks, when I found that foremen rarely had contact with any specific individuals other than their immediate bosses over any length of time, because of the way in which work was organized (e.g. the labour force rotated after each job and outside agencies had numerous different

[14] R. H. Turner, 'Role Taking: Process versus Conformity', in A. M. Rose (ed.), *Human Behaviour and Social Processes* (Boston, 1962), pp. 20–40.

[15] J. Urry, 'Role Analysis and The Sociological Enterprise', *The Sociological Review*, 18, 1970, pp. 351–63.

[16] e.g. R. H. Turner, op. cit., p. 22, says of bureaucratic behaviour in formal organizations: 'The formal regulation system restricts the free operation of the role-making process, limiting its repertoire and making role boundaries rigid.'

[17] R. L. Kahn *et al.*, *Organizational Stress* (New York, 1964), Chapter 11.

representatives). These findings also agree with organization theory which traditionally holds that role pressures and definitions flow from the top downwards. For these reasons, most attention was focused on the foremen and their immediate bosses.[18] Several aspects of role definition and behaviour were considered.

The extent to which both managers and foremen knew what foremen did in their jobs was examined first, because knowledge of performance has rarely been discussed in the literature on roles,[19] and what is widely known about behaviour in organizations shows that the knowledge which superiors have of their subordinates' activities is often extremely defective. At the same time, role studies normally rely on hypothetical and reported rather than actual and observed behaviour, whereas common sense suggests that people, when faced with hypothetical situations presented in questionnaires, may report various patterns of behaviour which, often unwittingly, do not correspond to their patterns of behaviour in real situations.

The managers and foremen involved in the observational research were asked to assess the proportions of time the foremen spent on the various functional areas of their jobs, in order to cover the routine, day-to-day aspects of the supervisory role rather than the critical incidents.[20] See table 5.1 for the relevant data on this subject. The foremen were fairly accurate in their assessments (any discrepancy of less than 10 per cent ought to be ignored) and displayed a better knowledge of their own jobs than was found among a comparable group described in other research,[21] whereas the managers were mainly inaccurate in assessing actual activity, and moreover, were often in disagreement with the foremen's self-assessments. In other words, managers displayed imperfect knowledge of what their foremen did and also of what their foremen thought they were doing.[22] Public authority managers appeared to know less than their private sector colleagues.[23] Evidence on the openness of communication between

[18] Superiors above the level of immediate boss were ignored because contact with them was so rare.

[19] Though R. K. Merton, *Social Theory and Social Structure* (New York, 1949), Chapter 9, does discuss 'visibility' as a variable.

[20] Critical incidents are normally used by those who study role conflict. However, if role analysis is to provide useful explanations of behaviour, it should presumably be applicable to everyday work routine as well as to the unusual and non-routine.

[21] J. Kelly, *Is Scientific Management Possible?* (London, 1966), p. 191.

[22] Some discrepancies are greater than others, but the trend is consistent across all six items, which adds weight to this conclusion (i.e. even when the differences are not statistically significant, the relationship remains the same and has substantive significance).

[23] There are systematic differences between the two sectors: public sector foremen feel less sure about the role pressures from above, feel that the managers have less knowledge of the foreman's job, and feel less assured about management's role evaluations than do foremen in the private sector.

foremen and managers which was collected in the survey considerably reinforces these conclusions. See table 5.2. Specifically role-relevant communication was reported to be much less open than other types in both sectors, while P.L.A. foremen reported worse communications than their colleagues in the private firms.

Thus the ability of members of the role set to evaluate role performance cannot be taken for granted. In this case, managers seem to have defective knowledge of what their foremen do, which means they are not always likely to know when foremen act in ways of which they disapprove. This type of ignorance is hardly surprising as it is probably a very common feature of superior–subordinate relationships in industry, and it has certain consequences for the activities of subordinates. In particular, if the boss is unable satisfactorily to evaluate the role performance of his subordinates then the constraining force of his expectations on his subordinates becomes less effective: subordinates realize that they have some freedom to ignore or resist unwelcome role pressures without fear of sanctions.

There were, in fact, systematic discrepancies within the observational sample between the perceptions of the two parties about the content of the supervisory role. This in turn raises the question of how far the managements put pressure on their foremen concerning the allocation of time and how far the foremen were aware of such pressures. Most empirical analyses of roles have relied on the focal person's perceptions of pressure and have not looked at the pressure itself. Yet it has been shown elsewhere that those people who occupy role positions frequently mistake pressures or are unaware of pressures which are directed at them from role definers in power positions.[24] Therefore, I asked dock managers whether they were happy with the way foremen allocated their time or whether they wanted their foremen to make changes. (I asked for this information in the context of the managers' estimates of the actual amount of time foremen spent in various activities.) The foremen were then asked whether they felt their bosses were happy with the amounts of time the foremen had reported, or whether they felt any pressure for change from those above them.

I presented managers with a list of six aspects of the foremen's job and asked whether they wanted their own foreman to change the amount of time he spent on them. Managers wanted change in 39 per cent of cases: public sector managers wanted change in 53 per cent of cases, private sector in 25 per cent. Foremen thought that their managers wanted change in at most 11 per cent of cases. This information shows how foremen fail to perceive their managers' expectations of change in supervisory behaviour. Moreover, of the 28 actual changes which managers desired, foremen *correctly* perceived only 3 (all of

[24] J. J. Preiss and H. J. Ehrlich, *An Examination of Role Theory: The Case of The State Police* (Lincoln, Nebraska, 1966), pp. 110–18.

which were in the private sector). If it can be assumed that these desires concerning the allocation of time are expressed in some form of transmitted pressure, then foremen misperceive these pressures.

If we look at this same information in another way, the gap between the parties is even more marked. The pressure for change was not particularly great, especially among the private sector managers, because managers were satisfied that *their* estimates reflected the real situation, while the foremen, by and large, felt that their *own* assessments corresponded in fact with what managers demanded of them. Yet the earlier data have demonstrated how dissimilar the assessments of the two parties can be, a gap of which neither party appears to be aware.

Thus the managers' knowledge of the foremen's role performance and the foremen's perceptions of the managers' role pressures are both somewhat faulty in this instance. These two characteristics of the supervisory role have fairly obvious consequences for dock foremen. So far as everyday routine is concerned, the consequences appear to be that foremen have considerable freedom to act independently of the prescribed role behaviours which originate in the authority structures of their firms, while the difficulties managers face in evaluating the role performance of their foremen hinder them in applying sanctions designed to ensure conformity.

Thus foremen have an area of discretion in which they can 'role make' vis-à-vis their firms and in which they are not circumscribed by their organizational roles. Later evidence shows that managers are important in some specific situations, while common sense suggests that organizational rules must act to limit the scope of role-making to some extent, particularly in the bureaucratic public authority. Nevertheless, it is necessary to appreciate the low salience of the organization and the extent of the discretion available to foremen, in order to understand the situation in which both foremen and dock workers work and the content of the supervisory role.

The freedom to create roles in the context of the organization should be regarded as 'role-taking' or the acting out of prescribed behaviour in another context, that of docking as an occupation. The fact that role creation did not lead to random, individual definitions of the situation but to activity patterns which were fairly consistent indicates that some structuring of the foremen's behaviour exists. There are obvious reasons to doubt the influence of technology or the organization, and what emerges from the evidence of the observation and the survey is the significance of the occupation. Indeed, the occupation would appear to be the major source of role behaviour while the firm has a lesser influence, particularly in the private sector. In this context, the docking culture, which is shared by men and foremen alike, provides a set of generalized expectations or norms of behaviour for certain areas of the supervisory role. In the mainly technical functions, the specific occupational sub-group of foremen is primarily significant rather than the occupation as a whole. The occupational context cuts across the organizational one, so that the horizontal stratum within several vertically structured companies is of more significance than the various discrete and vertical lines of authority, though in the docks the occupational and organizational determinants of role behaviour are frequently compatible, given certain circumstances. Where they are not formally compatible, then informal accommodation takes place within the organization.

The crucial processes in the formation of the occupational role are job socialization and the internalization of occupational values. The result of these processes is that foremen internalize the appropriate definitions of correct behaviour so well that the definitions appear to them as parts of their own conceptions of the job and not really as impositions from the outside. So far as empirical research is concerned, this situation creates two practical problems. Traditional role analysis, which identifies the role pressures transmitted by specific individuals in the focal person's role set and studies this person's responses, cannot be used when internalized norms guide behaviour. At the same time, the specifications of behaviour which are contained in cultural norms are obviously of a somewhat general nature and thus difficult to define precisely, while the level of generality and the loose sanctions available to occupational members mean that even the occupational constraints on behaviour are matters of degree which allow the individual some areas of freedom to modify and create.

Dock foremen originally learned much of what they had to do in their jobs from other foremen. At the time of my research, provisions for the formal training of people who were promoted to supervisory posts were non-existent and all firms relied on what was, in effect, the apprenticing of trainees to more experienced foremen. Some foremen attended courses organized by the National Ports Council, but these normally came several years after appointment and, moreover, were not regarded as being especially relevant to dock work. 78 per cent of foremen in the private sector and 100 per cent in the public sector gave fellow foremen as the major source of job learning when asked how they learned their jobs, whether by means of prior knowledge based on experience in the labour force, formal company training, interaction with the immediate boss, or learning from fellow foremen. Even when experience in the labour force, or management were mentioned, foremen were coupled with them. It is clear from preceding discussions of the nature of dock work that this makes inevitable a pattern of socialization which is based on the handing down of skills from one generation of the occupation to another: the inherent complexity of dock work and the consequent lack of formalized and standardized procedures place a premium on experience and traditional skills, in both the technical and the social aspects of the job. The earlier discussions of the manual workers' jobs indicated that the same pattern of job learning and work socialization holds good for dock workers as well. This would in fact appear to be true of traditional occupations which display craft characteristics.

In the public authority at the time of my research, a future foreman was recruited from the lower level of the clerical staff and attached to a foreman as his assistant. Assistant foremen had no prior, direct experience of production because they had never been manual workers in the docks. Promotion from assistant to foreman was by seniority and the length of time spent as an assistant varied greatly. In the sample this was between two and ten years (though the career prospects of present-day assistants are considerably less favourable because of the large number of young foremen created in the late 1950s and early 1960s, and because of the number of foremen being relocated as the upstream docks are closed). In addition, all the sample of public sector foremen had rotated among several foremen while acting as assistants, and ten had also worked in other docks. One obvious consequence of this pattern was that definitions of appropriate behaviour were generated and reinforced through the community of foremen, by means of the control over the job socialization of new recruits.

In the private companies, new foremen also acted initially as assistants to experienced foremen, but for a shorter period, about six months in most cases. This was a sufficient period of time, because a foreman could always request help from others after the introductory period and because of the common practice of allocating those foremen temporarily without ships of their own in dock to act as temporary assistants to others. This latter custom keeps each individual foreman in constant interaction with his peers throughout his career as a foreman. Unlike public sector foremen, those in the private sector all had experience in the labour force, and over 80 per cent of the sample as leaders of their own gangs. Most felt that the experience was a useful one which helped foremen to know what to do, but that it was a limited experience which only went part of the way in teaching foremen their job: 'In the "slave" you don't know what's going on outside of your hatch, but a shipworker's got to know what's happening in the whole ship . . . as a hatchwayman you only see the one side of it, but now I can see all sides. It's much more difficult than I ever thought.'

The aspects of the supervisory role which a man had actually to learn when he started out as a foreman were probably picked up from others in the manner described. The organizational skills needed to keep the work flowing smoothly, i.e. planning the layout and timing of work, co-ordinating the gangs and the outside agencies, were learned from other foremen. In learning these skills, foremen learned those aspects of their roles which were concerned with the co-ordination of the environment. These were the job elements to which foremen referred during the interviews. But the other technical skills, such as those connected with the handling of cargo in the most efficient manner, were learned prior to promotion in the case of private sector foremen, as the result of experience in the labour force.

Beyond the technical area, definitions were much more widely based. For instance, the norms of appropriate behaviour governing relations between foremen and men were embodied in an occupational culture which both parties shared, as indeed did many managers. This culture left the foremen some freedom of action, but there were fairly clear expectations about what foremen were allowed to do; these were enforced by the men and tolerated by management. The earlier discussion of aspects of the interactions between men and foremen in the periods before and after the decasualization of employment showed clearly how these were firmly grounded in a shared and custom-based culture. A later chapter discusses the nature of the relationship between men and foremen in more depth and again demonstrates the importance of cultural expectations. Private sector foremen had internalized this culture as the result both of spending their working lives almost entirely in the docks, first as dock workers then as foremen, and of anticipatory socialization from their docking kin prior to entry into the industry.[25] (In this context, it is relevant that over half had kin who had also been foremen.) Public authority foremen had no direct labour experience, but they too had numerous docking kin and had spent most of their working lives in the industry, with the result that they were steeped in the dock culture in much the same way as their counterparts in the private firms.

The way in which these role definitions can successfully structure behaviour is partly explained by the types of organization within which foremen work, because these are remarkably well suited to the incorporation of occupational roles. During my observational research it became obvious that all the private sector firms had similar management structures, simple ones with few hierarchical levels and little functional specialization. The hierarchy in every case was that of foreman, superintendent, local dock manager and board of directors. So far as foremen were concerned, the local management structure had only the two levels of superintendent and dock manager. There was little division of labour among supervisory and managerial staff, mainly because the operations of stevedoring firms were so simple: the supply of labour and little else. The fact that the P.L.A. was responsible for investment in the dock infrastructure and also took the lead in the purchase of new operating machinery, while the Dock Labour Board controlled many personnel functions, helped to keep operations simple. The possibilities

[25] Data on the occupations of kinsfolk are presented and discussed in Chapter 9.

of functional division were further limited by the primitiveness of stevedoring firms with regard to modern management techniques: for example, personnel specialists were non-existent, accounting techniques were simple and marketing was governed by tradition.

This situation has been bound up with the skills of traditional docking. Foremen are regarded as skilled craftsmen fully conversant with traditional and well-proven techniques, on conventional ships at least, working with labour of a calibre similar to their own. Management is based on the assumption that foremen and the gangs can be left to work without the need for control or direction. Until permanency, foremen had in a sense acted as sub-contractors, even though regular employees of one firm, and were responsible for virtually the whole job, planning and executing the work, hiring and firing the labour, while the employment situation of casual labour meant that the men assumed many production responsibilities and that personnel problems were few. The discussion of the work situations of the two groups showed the control and responsibility which both were given.

Permanency and technical change have undermined the structural conditions which made this situation possible, as has already been discussed, but the old attitudes and behaviour continued during the period of my research. By virtue of his control of so many functions, many of which are normally divided among management specialists in other industries, the foreman of traditional dock work has a multi-functional role similar to that of a manufacturing foreman in earlier times.[26] This role means that complex management systems have no place here, because foremen and men act in place of management. In the private sector this role substitutes customary technical and administrative expertise for bureaucratic rules and procedures. The organization is run on non-bureaucratic, 'craft principles of administration', which place great reliance on the skills of foremen and men alike for the routine administration of the company's work.[27]

The distinction between 'craft' and 'bureaucratic' organizations is a fundamental one in the development of industry, and is often recognized in organization theory though the terminology may vary. 'Craft' principles of administration assume that firms can be run by people with certain types of capabilities which are based on specialized knowledge, and that there is no need to reduce the dependence on such skilled people. If the idea of 'craft' is extended to all occupational groups with specialized technical knowledge analogous to the craft type, such as

[26] E. V. Schneider, *Industrial Sociology*, 2nd ed. (New York, 1969), pp. 167–75, and The National Institute of Industrial Psychology, *The Foreman* (London, 1957), document the traditional role.

[27] The notion of craft versus bureaucratic principles of production is borrowed from A. L. Stinchcombe, 'Bureaucratic and Craft Administration of Production: A Comparative Study', *Administrative Science Quarterly*, 4, 1959–60, pp. 168–87.

many modern professional groups, then organizational forms such as the 'organic' administration found in high technology fields can be classified in the same basic category. Bureaucratic principles, however, assume that tasks must be specialized so as to reduce activities to simple routines which can be performed by anyone, given some training and practice, and co-ordination of activities is maintained by specialist groups (managers) and by formalized rules and procedures. The first type of organization usually relies on occupationally generated capabilities, whether those of manual craftsmen or of white-collar professionals, whereas the second devalues these external sources of capability, in order to reduce the power which occupational members achieve over their organization by virtue of their specialized knowledge.

The way in which managers are recruited and trained in the private sector reflects and reinforces this reliance on the capabilities of the lower-level employees, and helps to make clear why firms allow foremen so much freedom. Over 95 per cent of superintendents in private firms have been recruited from the ranks of merchant navy officers (though many firms intend in future to recruit about 20 per cent from the ranks of their own foremen). The seafaring experience which these ex-officers possess may be useful for one aspect of dock work, planning stowages to ensure correct trim at sea, but it does not usually qualify them in other technical areas nor in the managerial and social aspects of the job. Given the importance of custom and practice and traditional skills, new managers are barely qualified for their jobs. Nor have the companies provided any formal training for their new superintendents apart from attaching them to a more experienced man for a brief period, because it has been assumed that the sea-training is sufficient. Not surprisingly, managers have been forced to rely on their foremen, in the past at least, for most of their knowledge about their own jobs and the docks. 77 per cent of foremen claimed that they had been responsible for training their superintendents because the latter lacked the relevant expertise. In support of this claim, many cited the great age and experience differential between themselves and the superintendents; whereas foremen tended to be in the older age groups in the docks and had normally worked in the industry from their late teens or early twenties, the superintendents were much younger and usually had only a few years' experience in the docks.

Even if the claim is treated with a pinch of salt, it still contains an element of truth, given the nature of dock work, the primitive managerial techniques of the firms and the obvious reliance on the men and foremen for routine administration. Adding together the comments made above, certain consequences are readily apparent. Foremen are fairly free to define their roles and persuade managers to accept these definitions. Managers internalize the prevailing culture and customs of the industry, and come to regard them as normal and appropriate in the dock setting: thus they usually accept the control which all the lower-level employees have over their work. Nor is it surprising that managers should accept their subordinates' definition of managerial roles and relationships with other groups, when the firms which employ the superintendents rely on craft principles of administration, when superintendents are given no formal training and have to pick up their jobs and the work culture from foremen, and when they have no managerial experience outside the industry. Rather than the normal line of vertical relationships, whereby job definitions in theory proceed from the top downwards, private sector dock firms have an alternative arrangement, whereby workers and foremen largely define their own positions and succeed in imposing these definitions on the higher strata.

There is more evidence available from the survey which supports and extends the above argument, clarifying the precise nature of the private dock companies and the position of foremen within them. This evidence concerns the nature and extent of role ambiguity and conflict in the firms. Discussion of ambiguity and conflict incidents complements the analysis of role definition and socialization, given that these incidents deal with events which occur after the basic role elements have been learned and so reflect an analytically and temporally distinct dimension of role analysis.

Table 5.3 shows how many foremen felt that there was some ambiguity surrounding their expected role behaviour and that this centred on the lack of information available for effective task performance. In his classic study of ambiguity and conflict in organizations, of which I partly used the questionnaire in my research, Kahn found that large ambiguity scores occurred in two other job areas, namely ambiguity about others' expectations of one's behaviour and ambiguity about the scope and responsibilities of the job.[28] Dock foremen do not experience either of these common types of ambiguity strongly, which is what one would expect in view of the way foremen's roles are defined with little reference to the organization and are internalized over a lifetime in the docks. But given the problems of the division of labour in the port transport industry, the emphasis on the uncertainties concerning information relevant to the technical side of task performance is not at all surprising. Foremen attribute these uncertainties to other agencies and the overall division of labour rather than to sources within their own firms.

Feelings of role conflict were widespread among the foremen, which appears to support the common view that supervisory roles are extremely stressful. The data presented in table 5.4 show that 44 per cent saw themselves in the sorts of conflict situations which are common

[28] R. L. Khan *et al.*, op. cit., p. 74: technical information = 38 per cent; others' expectations = 29 per cent; scope and responsibility = 35 per cent.

in the studies of the subject, where two or more sets of people demand incompatible things (inter-sender conflict). Another 32 per cent spoke of situations where they were one of the two parties involved (intra-sender conflict), despite the phrasing of the question which was designed to involve other people only. The sources of conflict are normally managers and outsiders, and the men are scarcely mentioned. Conflicts centre on the task aspects of the job, the planning and execution of work, rather than any other.

However, the manner in which these conflicts are resolved is of greater significance than evidence which proves the existence of conflict. One needs to ask whether foremen merely respond to pressures from their own superiors against those of status superiors outside the organization or against their own conceptions of appropriate behaviour, which is what those who emphasize the importance of formal power processes in organizations would predict, or whether they have other courses of action open to them, as was suggested in the preceding analysis. The survey showed that this had to be answered with reference to specific situations, because different cases have different outcomes.

There were two typical situations in the private sector firms. The first was a case of intra-sender conflict, when the foreman was in conflict with his immediate boss or with the firm's client (the latter situation was rare). The second was inter-sender conflict, when a foreman received conflicting demands from his boss and the client. When foremen described their courses of action, it became apparent that other aspects of the foremen's situation reduced the amount of conflict actually experienced in these two instances. In particular, the expertise and resulting authority with which foremen were accredited and the relationships between private sector firms and their customers were crucial.

The nature of dock work and the manner of job learning means that foremen possess considerable skill and can claim to be treated as experts. They expect to be consulted rather than given arbitrary commands, and they expect their views to be accepted in the first type of role-conflict situation. They claim to be successful in enforcing this definition of their role on clients and management. Thus expertise enables those at the bottom of the organizational hierarchy to have legitimized authority over those who possess formal power over them. In this way it acts as a variable which mediates conflicting pressures.

Two aspects of the relationship between the stevedore firm and the customer are important. The economics of shipping are such that the speed and efficiency with which dock workers load a ship can be as important for shipowners' final costs as the direct charges quoted by the stevedoring firm. Time spent in port involves the shipowner in daily port charges and loss of earnings while his large capital investment and his crew are idle. Rochdale has estimated the average conventional, break-bulk, dry cargo ship spends 60 per cent of the year in port, and that two-thirds of all operating costs are directly or indirectly incurred in port, while the direct charges for cargo-handling do not exceed one quarter of total operating costs.[29] The quality of the stowing also has an effect on the ship's earnings, because efficient stowage maximizes carrying capacity and reduces discharge times at the port of destination. Thus, the actual price of the stevedoring operation is not the ship-owner's only concern: the quality of the service is also extremely significant. Hence the premium that stevedoring firms place on expertise, particularly on that of their men and foremen, because this expertise is what these firms are selling. Even when it is owned by a consortium of shipping companies, a firm still has to provide a service which is reasonably competitive with that of other companies.

The relationships between stevedoring and shipping firms tend, in addition, to be relatively long-standing. A shipping company prefers not to change its stevedore too frequently, because one regular firm can build up a working knowledge of the shipper's vessels and cargoes, which helps improve the speed and quality of the port operations. When the shipper is part of a consortium which owns a stevedoring company, then the pressures to remain with this company are even greater. Strong bonds develop between individuals at all levels in the two firms and close working relationships grow up as the result of their fairly enduring ties. The emphasis on providing a good service to customers, which foremen accept, the customers' reciprocal recognition of the foremen's expertise and the close personal ties combine to reduce the significance of conflicts of the second type. Give-and-take between the firms, with the presumption ultimately that the customer is right, allows an easy resolution of any potential conflict, because foremen act in accord with the customers' wishes.

The organization of the public authority is structured very differently, which in theory allows far less scope to extra-organizational definitions of role or to role creation, nor does the relationship between the authority and its clients favour foremen as it does in the private sector. The public authority, in fact, fits the prescriptions of classical manage-ment and bureaucratic theorists, because role definitions proceed from the top downwards via an official hierarchy of authority which is exercised impersonally and impartially, and due respect is paid at the same time to an official, standardized and impersonal body of rules.

The authority is noticeably more bureaucratic in its administration. There are more levels of management above the men and foremen, normally four grades of manager within each dock and two or three above these in head office below board level, in comparison with the

[29] *Report of the Committee of Inquiry Into Shipping* (London, 1970), Cmnd. 4337, paras 345, 618, 620; figures relate to conventional 'break-bulk' ships (general cargo ships).

shallow management hierarchy of the private firms. There has always been a complex and extensive division of labour, based partly on the far greater scope of the authority's activities (maintenance of the river and port infrastructure and services in addition to the cargo-handling operations) and partly on traditional views about the virtues of specialization even within one activity such as cargo-handling. The Rochdale Report recommended that the P.L.A. become more commercially minded,[30] which led the authority to set up internal costing and profit points during the late 1960s. But this reform has made little difference to the bureaucratic nature of the organization, and has further added to the organizational complexity.

Given this description of the P.L.A., it is not surprising that it should have an extensive, formal and clear-cut body of rules which is supposed to regulate people's conduct in their jobs. The foreman's role is officially defined for him by these rules and his conduct is constrained by the regulative force of such written instructions. Traffic Officers (the equivalent of private sector superintendents) received a lengthy and systematic formal training which provides them with definitions both of their own and their foremen's roles. These definitions reflect the content of the bureaucratic rules which lay down the duties and authority of the various strata; they are thus generated by the organization and not by the foremen.

But equally, given the bureaucratic nature of the P.L.A., it is hardly surprising that the authority should display a variety of those informal characteristics which past research has shown to be inherent in such types of organization. The detailed role analysis conducted with the observational sample reveals a wider divergence between the perceptions of foremen and managers, a greater pressure for change and a greater likelihood that foremen will misperceive this pressure in the public authority than in the private sector firms. The data on openness of communication and role definition taken from the main survey (table 5.2) indicate a far greater blockage of communication in the authority than elsewhere.[31] These findings suggest that the P.L.A. displays that separation of hierarchical levels into isolated strata, between which communication is inadequate and contact rare, which is characteristic of many large bureaucracies.[32]

Predictably, this situation is exploited to avoid formal role prescriptions. But there remains a tension between the formal requirements of the organization and the informal behaviour which frequently

[30] *Rochdale Report* (1962), pp. 218–22.

[31] The questions designed to test openness of communication have been taken from P. Jackson, *Operational Change and Supervisory Effectiveness* (unpublished Ph.D. thesis, London University, 1970).

[32] These characteristics are well developed in M. Crozier, *The Bureaucratic Phenomenon* (London, 1964), pp. 175–212.

occurs. Various pieces of information show what actually happens. Public foremen normally report conflicts of the inter-sender type rather than any other. Such conflict involves contradictory expectations from Traffic Officers (T.O.s) and clients. How the conflict is resolved depends on the extent to which the foreman can conceal the problem and his actions from his superiors: provided he agrees with the client, he will act contrary to the organization's rules or his T.O.'s known and anticipated expectations if he feels that he can conceal what is happening from the T.O. By preventing information concerning role performance or relevant issues reaching management, that is by blocking communication, foremen attempt to maximize their discretion.

As the result of the new commercial emphasis within the P.L.A., which replaced the traditional corporate ethic of providing a loss-making service, such situations of conflict became increasingly frequent during the period of my research: T.O.s were compelled to adopt profit criteria when dealing with clients whereas foremen preferred to use the criteria of the services customarily provided in the past. In such circumstances, when higher management decided to break with the sixty years of custom and practice which had governed the relationships between customers and the organization, and demanded that customers pay more for the same or even less service, there was bound to be a period of conflict between the P.L.A. and customers and within the organization itself. This has meant that the foremen are placed in the conflict zone and cannot rely on customary relationships to solve the tensions. The situation is also one of ambiguity, however, because managers themselves oscillate between economic and service norms and many middle managers reject senior management's insistence on profitability as the major goal.[33] Foremen frequently find themselves in the middle between the expectations of customers and company, but in an arbitrary and almost random manner.[34]

Unlike their private sector counterparts, public sector foremen found it difficult to claim legitimate authority based on expertise, because the training of middle management and the bureaucratic role system did not admit that foremen had unique skills. In the private companies, the complexity of dock work and the importance of lifelong experience were recognized at all levels of management, but in the public sector it was assumed that all problems could be brought within the scope of formal rules, and that trained managers were the appro-

---

[33] D. Graves, Unpublished L.S.E. Research Paper on P.L.A. managers, 1972.

[34] Public foremen are more likely to report finding themselves 'in the middle' between customers and the company than are the private sector ones. The scores are 67·3 per cent for private sector foremen and 35·4 per cent for the public (these are weighted figures, 100=low frequency and 0=high). Although the difference is not statistically significant at 0·05 level, it would appear to have some substantive significance because it fits the pattern of replies expected on the basis of the preceding discussion.

priate decision-makers when the rules proved inadequate. Thus, one of the mediating variables between pressure and behaviour was formally ignored in the public sector.

The foremen's isolation and their ability to conceal matters from their managers are together partly responsible for providing the necessary area of freedom in which peer-based role definitions can operate. Certainly, the foremen themselves argue that they had mainly learned their jobs from other foremen and not from the organization. Preceding discussions indicate that peer-based roles are likely to reflect occupational norms of conduct. The bureaucratic rule system makes it difficult for managers to wield their authority over foremen except in clearly defined circumstances, which means that foremen are immune from sanctions provided they are, or appear to be, following the rules. As in many other similar settings, the compliance with the rules needs to be only a minimal, lip-service one for the power of managers to be rendered ineffective. Isolation of strata and the bureaucratic rules combine to give foremen some freedom of action. Thus the P.L.A.'s bureaucratic structure is not in practice hostile to the importation of occupational culture and principles of conduct, despite the formal importance of the vertical, organizational structuring of behaviour. But the tension between the formal expectations and actual conduct shows how the authority is less favourable than the private firms to this importation of occupational elements. It is something which in practice does occur but which in theory runs counter to the principles on which the organization is based.

CHAPTER 6

Industrial Relations and the Firms

The Expression of Conflict

Industrial relations in the docks have been of concern to governments, employers and the unions themselves from at least the late 1940s. Public attention has largely focused on the industry's strike record, because work stoppages in the docks have been thought to have particularly serious consequences for the rest of British industry. Over the last twenty-five years there have been two major official inquiries into matters concerning industrial relations in the docks, the Leggett report of 1951 on unofficial stoppages in the London docks and the Devlin committee report of 1965, while another inquiry by Lord Rochdale was concerned *inter alia* with industrial relations.

The official statistics show how the port transport industry has been extremely 'strike-prone' over the years. The first conventional way of analysing strike data is by a simple frequency count, and according to this criterion the docks industry group has appeared within the ranks of the six most 'strike-prone' industries (out of fifteen major industrial groupings) on seven occasions in the last fifteen years.[1] Construction, vehicles, mechanical and instrument engineering, metal manufacturing and mining have all appeared more frequently in this leading group. Strike frequency data, therefore, show the docks to be in the upper ranges but not in the first rank. An alternative index is also often used in analysis of strike data, the number of working days lost per thousand people employed in the industry. This statistic ignores the different sizes of the various industrial groupings, and shows that the docks group has not fallen below fourth place in fifteen years and has occupied first place in six of those years. By any interpretation, the ports must be in the first rank so far as this second measure of strike activity is concerned.[2]

[1] M. Silver summarizes strike data for 1959–71 in 'Recent British Strike Trends: A Factual Analysis', *British Journal of Industrial Relations*, 11, 1973, pp. 66–104. *Department of Employment Gazette*, 1974, gives data since 1971 (and revised figures for 1971).

[2] The measure has shortcomings when used for comparative purposes, which means that comparisons must remain tentative. Because it includes time lost by employees indirectly involved, such as managerial, clerical and technical workers, and the proportions of these vary between industries, it is not an accurate index of

Whereas the view that the docks are inherently 'worse' than other industries has appeared to persist in the public imagination, the strike data show that docking has a place among the leading group of industries rather than being a lone industry which is qualitatively different from others. The national context of strike activity over the period from the last war shows a relatively fixed pattern within which the docks have held a fairly constant place. This is the case despite the evidence of an upward trend of activity from the two measures of strike frequency and the number of days lost per thousand workers, and the fact that the bulk of dock stoppages are unofficial. Silver argues that after setting aside data from coal mining,

> the frequency of strikes fell after the war to a notably low level and remained remarkably stable throughout the 1950s, since which time it has risen almost continuously to the highest levels ever recorded. In the last decade the relative contribution of the various sectors of the economy to the overall rise in strike frequency appears to have undergone very little basic change, although the decline of stoppages in the coal industry has tended to highlight the centrality of certain other industries for Britain's strike statistics. The rate of increase in the number of stoppages has been rising in all the industries examined, and to a significantly similar extent.[3]

The upward trend in the national strike frequency has been matched by increases in the numbers of workers involved and the amounts of working time forgone, but the industrial distribution of strike-proneness has remained almost the same when using the measure of days lost per thousand employees as when using frequencies. The upward trend in stoppages is spread fairly evenly over both the official and unofficial categories, despite annual variations, with unofficial stoppages normally accounting for over 75 per cent of the total number (the Donovan estimate was as high as 95 per cent) and about 75 per cent of all workers involved.

If one takes days lost per thousand employees, the measure which provides the more extreme evidence for the docks, and re-calculates these as multiples of the average days lost nationally per annum, then there were several years in the second half of the 1960s when the docks recorded considerable increases in comparison with the levels which had previously held. See table 6.1. Expressing the data as three-year

---

inter-industry strike-proneness. Nor is it entirely accurate for inter-port comparisons within the port industry after 1967, when the N.D.L.B. ceased collecting the data centrally and relied on employers collecting their own statistics: different employers have different practices, particularly with regard to so-called 'political' strikes.

[3] M. Silver, op. cit., p. 95. Coal mining distorts the picture, because of the strong downwards trend in stoppages in the mines after years as the major single contributor to strike statistics.

running averages irons out some of the yearly fluctuations and clearly shows the 'peaking' in the middle of the second half of the decade which was then followed by a return to lower levels. (The docks occupied first place in the league table of days lost per 1,000 workers for four out of five years between 1966 and 1970.) Apart from this deviation, which coincided with the era of fundamental transformations in the industry from decasualization through Phase 1 to Phase 2, the pattern of stoppages in the docks has followed national trends over the last two decades.

Dock workers are notorious for their militancy in industrial relations, which is a well deserved notoriety if militancy is defined as the willingness to withdraw labour in furtherance of an industrial claim or interest. On the basis of this criterion, strike data indicate militant behaviour in the docks nationally, with London appearing as particularly militant. This is a deliberately restricted definition of militancy, however, limiting the concept to the way in which certain aspects of industrial relations are conducted, and referring to the methods that workers adopt to advance their claims rather than to the attitudes or beliefs they hold. This is *all* that strike data by themselves can reveal. Yet many commentators make statements about militancy in the docks which refer to dock workers' attitudes, and are couched in terms of intense industrial and even class conflict. Kerr and Siegel, for example, infer from dock workers' propensity to strike that they regard the relations between employers and workers in industry and between classes in society as fundamentally hostile.[4] According to this argument, strike propensity can be a good indicator of industrial and social attitudes, and 'mass grievance leads to "class" action'.[5]

While they do not make direct inference from strike data to the attitudes of strikers, two other sociological studies have arrived at similar conclusions about the industrial consciousness of dock workers. The book on the Manchester workers found that all the people interviewed had formed stereotypes of their employers as ruthless, tricky and out only for profit, views which emphasized the dichotomous nature of industry and laid great weight on antagonism and exploitation.[6] Goldthorpe and Lockwood cite this as evidence when they described dock workers' orientations as solidaristic with an alienative involvement in the firm and accompanied by a class-conscious view of society.[7] All these arguments ultimately account for strike-proneness in terms of

[4] C. Kerr and A. Siegel, 'The Inter-Industry Propensity to Strike—An International Comparison', reprinted in A. Flanders (ed.), *Collective Bargaining* (London, 1969), pp. 138–60.

[5] ibid., p. 142.

[6] *The Dock Worker*, p. 90. The study noted, however, that many people thought the firm was as good as any firm could be and felt a sense of loyalty: pp. 91 and 95.

[7] J. H. Goldthorpe, D. Lockwood et al., *The Affluent Worker* (Cambridge, 1968), vol. 1, p. 74. They ignore the ambiguity concerning loyalty to the firm which *The Dock Worker* notes.

cultural isolation. The class-consciousness which leads to strikes occurs because dock workers live in communities outside the mainstream of working-class culture: they become introverted, develop a strong group solidarity and see fundamental lines of cleavage between themselves and their employers.

Although these analyses may accord with views widely held outside academic circles, it needs to be made clear that the evidence of such attitudes is confined to the book on Manchester docks, which is the only work to study attitudes directly. There is no evidence about the consequences of attitudes, because no one has published any research on the actual conduct of industrial relations in dock firms. Indeed, Devlin was notably more cautious than the authors whose views were described above, because he described the poor state of industrial relations and emphasized the strike record but inferred only that dock workers displayed a lack of 'responsibility' in their attitudes. Devlin and Rochdale assumed that the real problem which accounted for strikes and other expressions of conflict was the defective institutional structure of the industry. They thought that the primary defect was the absence of proper employment, which prevented the development of any stable negotiating or other relationships between a worker and a firm, discouraged managers from trying to develop competent personnel policies and eased the way for unofficial labour leaders because the unions were unable to establish a proper shop steward organization. Casual employment bred casual attitudes among men, managers and unions alike. So militancy as a type of behaviour was not seen as a reflection of any deep-seated attitudes about industry or society, but merely as the response to structural inadequacies.

These remarks about the docks indicate a more general problem of understanding the 'causes' of strikes and the meanings which individuals attach to going on strike. This problem applies equally to other forms of industrial action, for example absenteeism, working to rule, non-co-operation, etc. Two basic points can be made immediately. The first is that strikes presuppose a minimum of worker solidarity and organization almost by definition, because the strike is a collective action.[8] The second is that strikes can be, but are not always, the tangible expressions of an awareness of the divergence of interest which is inherent in the employment relationship. The first point is obvious but the second needs elaboration on two counts.

In the first place, many British strikes appear to be 'caused' not by conflict with employers but by conflict between workers themselves, or by other issues. For instance, strikes caused by inter-union demarcation and jurisdictional disputes and strikes which reflect the workers' concern with established patterns of differentials between trades or work groups give some plausibility to the popular argument that much of the dynamic

[8] R. Hyman, *Strikes* (London, 1972), p. 54.

of British industrial relations lies in occupational rivalry and competitive bargaining within the ranks of labour. This situation may well bring workers into conflict with their employers, but those involved may not necessarily see the underlying issues as being part of a simple employer–employee conflict. Other strike issues can also be divorced from the immediate employer–employee conflict. For example, over 80 per cent of all days lost in the docks in 1972 were connected in one way or another with the fears of reduced labour demand and underemployment consequent on the rapid introduction of new technology.[9] But the animus focused mainly on agencies other than the employers of dock labour, who were not thought to be really culpable in the issues causing concern. Hostility was directed against the courts which restricted the definitions of dock work to exclude non-Scheme ports, and against the shipping lines and warehousing firms which were responsible for the speed and manner in which the new methods were introduced.

However, it is probably unwise to carry such arguments to extremes, because the second point of elaboration concerns the way in which people perceive divergences or conflicts of interest. People in industry have always recognized that shopfloor workers are aware of an opposition between their interests and those of their employers, but this knowledge has often been ignored by academic commentators concerned with 'motivation' or 'human relations'. The belated rediscovery of the cash nexus in contemporary industrial sociology points up quite clearly how even those who appear to be the least militant of workers share an oppositional view.[10] Opposition of economic interest between workers and employers is obviously a major source of industrial conflict.

The problem is to go beyond these basic propositions so as to generalize more extensively about the causes and meanings of strikes or other forms of industrial action and the inferences which the sociologist can draw from data on such acts. Although many strikes reflect an awareness of a conflict of interest, bearing in mind the many that do not easily fit this category, the act of striking provides little indication of the intensity or depth of this awareness. There are several reasons why this is so. In many firms and industries the strike is merely the quickest and most efficient means to achieve certain ends, and thus reveals little about the motives of those taking part. This is relevant to the argument often propounded by specialists in the industrial relations area and favoured by the Donovan Commission, that the overt expression of conflict in strikes largely reflects the inadequacy or failure of those institutional arrangements which have been created in order to resolve points of conflict without workers resorting to direct action.

[9] *Department of Employment Gazette*, June 1973, pp. 563–4.
[10] J. H. Westergaard, 'The Rediscovery of the Cash Nexus', in R. Miliband and J. Savile (eds.), *The Socialist Register 1970* (London, 1970), pp. 111–38.

Once the efficacy of the institutions has been improved by raising the quality of collective agreements, strengthening the machinery of dispute resolution and modifying payment systems, then workers will cease to find direct action any more advantageous than negotiation, or so the argument runs. Thus the variable incidence of strike-proneness should partly reflect the failure of the institutional structures rather than the distribution of workers with more antagonistic feelings towards their bosses. Devlin clearly believed this to be the explanation in the docks and assumed that the primitiveness of the institutional arrangements created a situation where those sorts of issues which arise in other industrial settings and are often settled without industrial action could not be settled in this way in this industry. By implication, the incidence of dock strikes described the most efficient means dock workers had for achieving certain commonly held ends.

Many other explanations of industrial conflict and strikes exist, from the argument about agitators to which the Leggett and Devlin reports occasionally resorted when discussing the docks, to more strictly sociological and economic explanations.[11] What is quite clear is the very restricted scope of the generalizations which can be made about the inherent meanings of strike action. Returning to the issue of the hostility workers feel towards their employers and the perceptions they have of the social structure, the willingness of individuals to take strike action is insufficient evidence of such attitudes.

During the casual era industrial conflict clearly existed and was openly expressed. This is suggested by the evidence of the official inquiries, the Manchester study, and the recollections of those involved, taken in conjunction with strike data. Devlin and Rochdale clearly hoped that the decasualization of labour might pave the way to employment relationships which were less full of conflict. By changing the institutional arrangements of the industry the two inquiries anticipated more than the simple regularization and containment of conflict, which is all that most adherents to an institutional view would hope for. It was also expected that dock workers might become involved in their firms in new ways and their attitudes be changed, so that conflict might be overcome by a growing sense of the identity of interests in a unified organization. Devlin phrased this aspiration eloquently:

> But the ultimate objective is to create better personal relationships, a sense of mutual obligations, loyal service in exchange for care and interest.[12]

One of my aims, therefore, was to see how far the traditional notion of dock workers' hostility towards their employers was correct, and to

[11] R. Hyman, op. cit., gives a summary of the various explanations.
[12] *Devlin Report*, para. 257.

what extent that particular unitary vision of the employment situation shared by Devlin and many others had in fact been realized under the conditions of permanent labour. To this end, the people interviewed in the survey were asked a series of questions about the nature of their attachment to their firms and their feelings about management. Some of these questions were taken from other research for comparison purposes.

The answers were evaluated in the light of the three common modes of attachment which are relevant to this issue. These include 'alienative' involvement, intense feelings of antagonism towards managers and the firm and even sentiments of class conflict, which is the mode character-istically assigned to dock workers by popular and academic writers alike. 'Moral' involvement is also defined by intense feelings or 'affect',[13] but it covers a positive rather than a negative commitment, draws on significant non-economic motives such as the need to participate in a supportive social community of workers and managers at the workplace, and is manifest in loyalty and identification. Such attachment has been the goal of the exponents of human relations and official inquiries alike. 'Indifference' means the absence of strong feelings, whether positive or negative, so that the individual appears to have little sense of being personally involved in his firm in any way. This mode of attachment may well reflect the fact that many employees appraise the employment relationship as an economic transaction and bond, in which sentiments of 'affect' have little relevance. The evidence from the survey can be summarized briefly.

The men were asked whether or not they felt that the firms they worked for were good ones. Presented with this straightforward question, 80 per cent replied in the affirmative. This overall approval reflects a variety of responses, as can be seen in table 6.2. Some men felt that their firms were the same as all the others and offered no particular advantages. If this group is combined with those who felt that their firms were definitely not good ones, then 37 per cent of the sample had little to say in favour of the companies which employed them. But only 16 per cent of the men appeared to feel antagonism to their firms. On the other side of the coin, 45 per cent cited good relationships with manage-ment as one reason for regarding a firm as good (though nearly 90 per cent of the men in company No. 1 cited good relationships with management).[14] The tenor of these replies suggested that the fairness and basic human respect which managers displayed towards their employees were the qualities appreciated. With the exception of the first

[13] These terms are taken from A. A. Etzioni, *A Comparative Analysis of Complex Organizations* (Glencoe, 1961), pp. 9–11.

[14] The men in this firm were the only ones to put forward an analysis of relations with management which emphasized expressive and affective elements and to claim that the firm was superior to others in this respect.

company, the emphasis thus lay on the manager's basic politeness in formal relationships rather than on the supportive relationships and informal interaction which advocates of human relations have stressed as sources of moral involvement.[15] The frame of reference was that the relationships between men and managers were good in comparison with what had existed previously, rather than by any absolute standard, and no better than could be found anywhere in the docks at that time.

There was a fairly stable attachment to the various firms, though it must be remembered that there was very little chance to change employers within the industry itself at the time.[16] There were variations by company, however, and in one firm (No. 2) slightly over half reported that they had considered quitting (see table 6.3). In most cases this stability of attachment was not based particularly on feelings of loyalty, identification or involvement. The predominant response was negative, and suggested indifference, because emphasis was placed on the impossibility or pointlessness of changing firms: 48 per cent of the men gave these reasons for staying when they were asked what kept them in their present employment. About one sixth gave reasons connected with management or feelings of positive identification,[17] and company No. 1 was once again non-typical (see table 6.4). Some people emphasized the instrumental attractions of their firms, which in the present context of a hostile or favourable involvement fits the alternative mode of indifference.

These replies suggest neither great hostility nor positive identification, though a number of men could be found with feelings of 'alienative' or 'moral' involvement. The majority was fairly indifferent, though this had some positive elements because the men appreciated the improved quality of the formal interaction between men and management which had developed over the years. The earlier discussion of orientations showed the importance of instrumentality for dock workers and also demonstrated the links which dissatisfaction over pay had with the likelihood of thinking of leaving the firm or giving negative reasons for staying. Instrumentality and the sort of indifference found among these dock workers tend to complement each other: the premium placed on instrumental rewards inevitably emphasizes the nature of employment as an economic exchange, to the relative disadvantage of any other characteristic.

[15] Indeed, if the replies from firm No. 1 are excluded, then in table 6.2 the proportion citing good relationships of any kind drops to 30 per cent.

[16] The proportion considering leaving in *The Affluent Worker* study was 47 per cent: J. H. Goldthorpe, D. Lockwood *et al.*, op. cit., vol. 1, p. 26.

[17] Excluding those who reported that they had thought of leaving, in order to consider those who appeared to be more attached, causes only slight changes in the overall pattern. Negative reasons decline in magnitude while the human relations or identification reasons increase, but the rank order does not alter.

The Manchester study had found considerable aggression towards middle and top management but feelings of loyalty and commitment to the firm itself.[18] This suggested that dock workers might be favourably disposed towards their companies but hostile towards individual managers, even though the questions about the firms had given little indication of this. However, analysis of the replies to my questions specifically about managers shows that most dock workers were as favourably disposed towards their bosses as they were to their firms. 73 per cent thought that there were 'good relations without conflict between the men and management' in their firms, and 71 per cent also felt that their managers were competent at their jobs. When asked what changes they would like to see in the way management ran things, 37 per cent wanted instrumental changes concerned with improved earnings, and 14 per cent wanted improved human relations.[19] Dock workers obviously found their day-to-day dealings with managers perfectly tolerable, which fits the preceding discussion of attachment.

Variations occurred between companies and even between different branches of the same firm. This is apparent in the comparison between companies 1 and 2, which were both branches of the same firm yet produced widely different feelings among their employees. Local differences in the ways companies were managed, particularly the policies and personalities of those concerned, were responsible for variations in people's attachments. Company No. 1 was unusual for several reasons. It handled a lot of modern ships which were easy to work on and the local manager made a policy of giving generous allowances, so the men were extremely well paid. The manager was unusually approachable and well-intentioned in comparison with traditional dock managers and the men responded to his style of management. The second branch worked on small, old-fashioned vessels which did not allow the men to boost earnings and had a local manager who was very concerned to cut labour costs. This manager also saw little point in treating the men in any way differently from the methods which had been used successfully during the casual era. The interview data confirmed what had been obvious during the observation, that most people were only aware of their local branch and appraised this rather than the firm as a whole.

Some writers have recently been concerned with workers' 'images' of employment relations, assuming that these broader pictures of industrial relations influence the workers' own industrial behaviour. In order to investigate these 'images', I employed the question used in other research, which presents two statements based on an analogy between

[18] *The Dock Worker*, p. 95.
[19] 73 per cent thought that there were good relations without conflict between men and managers, and 71 per cent thought managers were good at their jobs.

the firm and a football team and asks people to choose between them.[20] The results presented in table 6.5 show that 56 per cent of the men saw the enterprise in a 'harmonistic' way, 'or perhaps, to be more precise, have a conception of the enterprise in which recognition of the interdependence of management is generally more powerful than awareness of conflicts between them', to quote another study.[21] This proportion is not much lower than the 67 per cent found among the affluent workers of Luton.

However, the question was found to be ambiguous during the pre-testing of the questionnaire. People were unsure whether the question required a descriptive evaluation of industry at that moment or whether it was concerned with the inherent and essential nature of employment over time, a 'normative' evaluation. I overcame this by presenting the statements first as two contrasting descriptions and then asking those who chose a 'conflict' description whether they thought there was a reasonable chance of a change in this state of affairs. 32 per cent of the men thought that teamwork was missing at the moment but that there was a reasonable chance of improvement, and less than 10 per cent thought that teamwork was impossible. Thus most believed that the harmonistic 'image' of industry either existed already or could come some time in the future.

Dock workers are aware of a 'divergence of interests between employers and labour on issues concerning the actual conditions on which employment rests and "teamwork" takes place';[22] despite their harmonious picture of industrial relations, 80 per cent of the men felt that their employers could afford to pay more without harming the firm's long-run financial viability, and the great majority of the reasons given for believing this concerned the size of the profits which the firms were thought to be earning. The men are aware of the latent conflict of interests over the way in which the products of labour are distributed. Reasons such as the wage-effort bargain or pay comparisons with other groups, both of which are commonly used by commentators on industrial relations to explain workers' pay aspirations, were conspicuously unimportant. This view of profits is independent of specific firms and dissatisfaction with relative pay, and is shared by the group as a whole.

The interpretation of the foremen's replies to these questions is less clear-cut. Differences in the degree of attachment between the foremen and men are not great, except that far fewer foremen have considered leaving.[23] There were marked variations between different groups of

[20] Statements taken from J. H. Goldthorpe and D. Lockwood *et al.*, op. cit., vol. 1, p. 89: (a) 'Some people say that a firm is like a football side—because teamwork means success and is to everyone's advantage.' (b) 'Others say that teamwork is impossible—because employers and men are on opposite sides.'

[21] ibid., p. 74.

[22] ibid., p. 89.

[23] Difference significant at 0·01 level.

foremen when they discussed whether their companies were good ones to work for, which makes any generalization about this set of replies inconclusive. There was a fairly even division between the indifferent, positive and other reasons given for remaining in a particular firm, though considerably more foremen than men gave positive involvement reasons concerned with human relations.[24] The substantial number of foremen who cited intrinsic job interest as a source of attachment were also considered as positively attached, because they usually regarded this as an attribute of the firm itself.[25] If the P.L.A. foremen were excluded, then these sources of positive identification were evenly distributed by company, though the other reasons varied. It was shown earlier that, just as with the men, there was a noticeable correlation between certain feelings about pay and foremen's attachment to their firms.[26] Foremen were not as strongly attached as one might have anticipated on the basis of their jobs and length of service in their firms.

Foremen were of course far more constrained and dependent on their firms than dock workers. On the one hand, they were less marketable, since their expertise was to some extent specific to individual firms and not easily transferable, because of their age and because firms preferred to reward their own employees with promotion to supervisory posts. Foremen could only change firms by returning to the labour force where, as dock workers, they had easily transferable skills and the protection of the Scheme. On the other hand, they were more dependent because they were long-term employees who had not changed firms for years and found it difficult even to think of leaving now, whereas most dock workers had become accustomed to moving from firm to firm prior to decasualization (even if they had worked mainly for one firm most of the time) and had only worked permanently for any firm since 1967. P.L.A. foremen were even more dependent than those in the private sector, because they had mainly clerical skills and could not fall back on dock labouring, while their earnings were more than they could expect elsewhere with their qualifications. The stability of the foremen's attachment in both sectors must therefore be seen with these factors in mind.

It seems that the firms they worked for were comparatively unimportant for many of the men. The indifference which most displayed certainly supports the notion that the firms played a small part in their frames of reference. The occupation and industry were of greater significance. But the firms were more important to foremen, which was

[24] Difference significant at 0·05 level.

[25] The men regarded intrinsic interest as the property of dock work, regardless of a particular firm's cargoes or ships.

[26] There were major dissatisfactions with pay. Foremen were as likely as the men to believe that their firms could afford to pay them more without damage, but the *basis* of the belief was the pay of dock workers relative to that of foremen, rather than the wage-effort bargain or the correct distribution of profits.

suggested by the difficulty foremen had in envisaging changing firms. Foremen were dependent and constrained, but their jobs were very secure as long as they remained with their employers.

Relations with managers as distinct from the companies can be mentioned briefly. Given the evidence in other chapters of a fairly high degree of co-operation between managers and foremen in the private sector, one would expect harmonious relationships. This sector was, in fact, generally well disposed towards its management, whereas the P.L.A. foremen's evaluation of management as a whole was consistently negative and their views about their own individual traffic officers scarcely more favourable. Thus, regardless of company, over 80 per cent of private sector foremen rated their immediate boss at the time highly on technical competence, while only 42 per cent of P.L.A. foremen did so. Ninety per cent of all foremen thought that they could easily do the superintendent's job, because there was nothing about the work which would prove inherently difficult for a foreman. This is what one would expect in the light of previous statements that foremen teach their superintendents how to do their own jobs. Some foremen complained that managers failed to uphold their authority and status, which were both devalued by the men. But the private sector foremen had few complaints that their managers failed to recognize the importance of the foremen's job or that they would refuse to stick up for their foremen in the event of trouble with the men or senior management. The P.L.A. foremen were less well disposed and criticized managers for completely devaluing the foremen's importance and position. The public authority foremen displayed a critical and even hostile attitude towards their managers, a characteristic response of bureaucratic employees who feel that their own moral commitments are not rewarded by proper treatment and due regard from their superiors.

Foremen's 'images' of industrial relations were interestingly different from those of dock workers. When presented with the descriptive statements, foremen more frequently chose the conflict view of industry. In normative terms, however, foremen were slightly less likely to regard conflict as inherent in employment. Their descriptive view is in opposition to the images found in two other studies of junior non-manual employees, where an industrial ethos of harmony prevailed.[27] Many foremen obviously felt that the conflict which dock workers saw as latent was in fact manifest, which reflects foremen's views about the situation in the docks.

In sum, dockers found little to complain about concerning the social relations involved in production. They found their employment

---

[27] J. H. Goldthorpe, D. Lockwood et al., op. cit., vol. 1, p. 73, and A. J. M. Sykes, 'Some Differences in the Attitudes of Clerical and Manual Workers', The Sociological Review, 13, 1965, pp. 297–311. These were both groups of clerical workers with less direct experience of the labour force than dock foremen.

tolerable; they reported a low degree of industrial conflict and their attitudes showed the inaccuracy of common views about dockers; while they were more integrated into their firms than earlier reports have suggested, though this integration was largely passive. This harmonious situation reflected the men's power: they were able to control their immediate working environment, including the social relations with foremen and managers. Other participants did not find things so easy-going, in particular foremen who found their traditional dominance overthrown and were now subjected to effective worker control in certain areas; for them, social relations in the industry were indeed conflict-laden.

Payment Systems and Control

It is impossible to assess the impact of decasualization on the character of industrial relations in the docks. First, there were too many other changes occurring in the industry and outside during the late 1960s and early 1970s for the effects of one event to be identified. Secondly, not enough is known about dock workers prior to permanency for anyone to state confidently that the non-antagonistic attitudes found here do in fact indicate a recent change in awareness. These attitudes may demonstrate only how mistaken some people have been in the past. Thirdly, the strike record of the last years of the 1960s contains too many marked fluctuations to make categorical statements about the effects on this index of industrial relations of changes to the institutional structure of employment. In any case, one might reasonably expect that it would take time for a fundamental change of this sort to result in changes of behaviour and that the impact of permanency would be seen in the long term. Indeed, because permanency was such a major disruption of established practices and interests, the effect in the very short term was to cause a major strike in 1967. However, notwithstanding the difficulties of discussing permanency in isolation from other changes, at least two recent books about the industry have tried to interpret the post-decasualization experience so as to show that permanent labour was not the institutional change required to alter the industrial relations record. They suggest, rather, that the abolition of piecework was the most important change to bring about.[28] This step was taken when a flat weekly wage was introduced as part of the Phase 2 arrangements in 1970.

There is a widely shared belief among commentators that payment by results is the cause of many of the 'problems' of contemporary industrial relations.[29] The first objection is that payment-by-results

[28] D. F. Wilson, *Dockers* (London, 1972), pp. 293–6; M. Mellish, *The Docks After Devlin* (London, 1972), p. 137.
[29] e.g. A. Flanders, 'Measured Daywork and Collective Bargaining', *British Journal of Industrial Relations*, 11, 1973, pp. 368–92.

schemes such as piecework tend to 'decay' and fail to meet the managerial objectives which led to their installation; in particular, they fail for various reasons to persuade people to maintain levels of effort and productivity.[30] But at the same time, piecework leads to 'wage drift', because the payment system 'takes on a life of its own as individuals and groups seize on any chance of raising their earnings to a level that they think is "fair" ', so that earnings become less and less related to output.[31]

Thus the second objection is that piecework sours industrial relations at the workplace by making overt the latent conflict between men and management. Workers learn that they can increase their earnings by industrial action rather than increased output, because managers acquiesce in the face of pressure from the workers rather than risk losing production. Piecework also creates numerous occasions for conflict, because all variations on the shop floor have financial implications which lead the men into wage bargaining with management: changes in product or working methods, however minor, delays and stoppages, sub-standard components, all lead to continuing re-negotiation of the employment contract. In addition, piecework leads workers to generate their own 'custom and practice' rules of job regulation. Because all working practices have financial implications under a piecework payment system, workers are obliged to limit management's prerogative to act as it sees fit, and to assert their own rights. Thus the generation of informal rules at work is given sharp impetus by piecework payment schemes. Shop stewards act as 'guardians' of the rules and owe much of their rise in numbers and influence over the last two decades to these rules.[32] Workers tend to function as groups rather than as individuals when they follow the informal rule system at work, so another consequence of piecework and of the need for job regulation via informal rules has been the rising importance of work groups in workplace industrial relations.

Formally, the payment of conventional work in the docks until mid-1970 had two elements. The first was a piecework scheme based on the amount of cargo handled, plus a time-rate when the job was held up. The second was a guaranteed minimum or fall-back wage should piecework earnings be too low for any reason.[33] These arrangements and the precise rates were negotiated between union officials and employers in the National Joint Council for the Port Transport

[30] Though the effectiveness of financial incentives for stimulating greater output has frequently been questioned.

[31] National Board for Prices and Incomes, Report No. 65, *Payment by Results* (London, 1968), Cmnd. 3627, p. 29.

[32] A. Flanders, op. cit. (1973), refers to them as the custodians of the rules.

[33] A major criticism of the casual era was the insecurity and fluctuations of earnings. Even though wages were higher during Phase 1, they still fluctuated considerably because of piecework.

Industry. In fact, a complex informal system of additional allowances had developed over the years to recompense men for exceptional conditions. For example, time spent idle for any reason, be it poor weather or a breakdown in the flow of cargo as the result of the complex division of labour, would always be paid for at a rate above the time rate to be negotiated between men and management. If work slowed down, because of 'long runs' (when cargo has to be moved a greater distance than normal), dirty or dangerous cargoes, or inadequate equipment, then allowances would again be negotiated. Money was paid in addition for work associated with preparing the ship for receiving or discharging cargo: i.e. for uncovering ship's hatches, rigging lifting gear, placing protective wooden dunnage between the layers of cargo and other preparatory tasks. Because 'exceptional' conditions could cover almost anything, allowances were particularly important to both men and managers.

Until decasualization, allowances in the private sector were negotiated between the gangers and the foremen, according to what the foremen were willing to concede. In addition, premiums were often offered for exceptionally fast work, to complete loading or unloading by a certain deadline. Foremen were given complete authority by their managements to negotiate deals for all these exceptional cases and the foreman's decision was rarely challenged. During Phase 1, however, managements themselves were compelled to take a much greater interest in wage matters, for reasons connected with the decasualization of the labour force. The labour costs of permanency were higher when the firm had to maintain a permanent labour force rather than hiring men by the half-day, while the security which dock workers enjoyed during Phase 1 allowed them to be more aggressive in their demands. The firms and their foremen could no longer use the power of hiring and firing to keep the men in line.

Despite losing control over piecework, foremen clung to it as a means of persuading the men to maintain output. They saw it as a substitute for their loss of personal control over the men, and 79 per cent wanted some incentives based on output to remain under Phase 2 conditions. Foremen were convinced that the only way to make the men work hard was to offer them other incentives in addition to the proposed high basic wage. With reference to the then anticipated Phase 2 deal, two foremen expressed the common view most succinctly:

You need either the whip or money. We've lost the whip and now we're going to lose the money.

If the men are going to be paid £39 per week for doing nothing, what are we going to pay the men who do something?

Interestingly, 66 per cent of the men favoured the retention of a financial incentive during Phase 2, for much the same reasons as the foremen. They argued that an incentive element on top of the basic wage kept people on their toes and maintained interest in the work, and that many men were naturally lazy and had to be pushed. But 89 per cent wanted the existing piecework scheme to be abolished in favour of a much higher basic wage, largely because this would make earnings more predictable and secure, but also because it would reduce the strain of work and lead to safer working conditions (men would no longer cut corners).

Despite the evidence from many other studies that piecework normally fails to maintain effort and output levels, it is worth considering the way piecework worked in the docks because both men and foremen considered it to be an effective motivating factor. Statistical information on piecework in the docks does not and cannot provide a meaningful analysis of the motivating effect, for a variety of reasons. No job is the same as another because the types and mixes of cargo, the ships and the equipment used differ every time; wages include complicated but substantial allowances; delays and stoppages are widespread and unpredictable. It can be shown that earnings vary considerably between individuals on a yearly basis, despite the existence of uniform rates, but it is difficult to relate these variations to differences of effort because of the factors just mentioned. (Table 1.3 presents the earnings of those interviewed.) Analysis of piecework must in fact rely on the perceptions of those involved and on observation.

Dock work was suited to piecework payment, because it was labour-intensive in the operations where piecework prevailed. Payment systems which rewarded physical effort could be applied, because the pace of work was operator-controlled and not dependent on machines (though hold-ups could be caused by failures in the division of labour or by the weather). At the same time, restriction of output and stock-piling techniques were not always rational methods of protection for the individual: the volume and earning potential of work were so unpredictable that restriction could be counter-productive and spinning-out work might mean missing a good job the next day, since neither the men nor management knew precisely what work would be available until half an hour before starting. The fluctuations in work flow were too great and unpredictable to be ironed out by stockpiling.

The structure of the payment system, however, contained elements which were potential disincentives. The rates themselves were complicated and often obsolete. There were over 1,000 different rates in existence, each referring to a different type of cargo. The last comprehensive review of rates was in 1929, though there had been across-the-board increases since then and some selective revisions. The obsolete nature of these rates, in terms of proportional differences between types of cargo, created a system in which the easiest cargoes to handle could often pay more than the difficult. Cars were the prime example, since the volumetric measure of these was large but handling was simple (they could be wheeled easily along the quay and in the ship's hold); whereas bag-work, which involved considerable physical effort, rarely earned as much in a given amount of time.

There were in addition critical thresholds below which piecework provided little incentive to maximize output. There was an official minimum earnings guarantee of £3.40 per day in London, which was later raised to £5.50 at Tilbury for loading jobs on board ship as the result of a local agreement.[34] These minimum earnings guarantees acted as disincentives if piecework earnings could not exceed them, and in the case of the special Tilbury rate piecework had to be quite well-paying to lift earnings over this threshold, though the disincentive effects of these negotiated guarantees ought not to be exaggerated in view of the unofficial and higher guarantees given by the companies individually. On top of this formal structure were the many allowances negotiated on a 'one-off' basis between gangers or stewards and individual superintendents. The effect of these allowances was to raise the thresholds at which piecework became a paying proposition to the dock worker; indeed it was sometimes the case with low-paying cargoes that allowances could be won equal to what could have been earned had the men worked flat-out all day on piecework.

Management conceded many legitimate demands for allowances, where work was definitely held up by extraneous causes, but there was an increasing movement towards allowances which were not justifiable on these grounds.[35] Allowances became a way of buying industrial peace, since management had no more control over the men than did the foremen. Foremen dubbed this practice as 'choking the men with fivers' in order to buy off trouble. Bribery was not the refuge of junior management alone, however, but was sanctioned both by the senior managers of the stevedoring firms and by the shipowners themselves, who often demanded that the stevedores pay their men extra: a few hundred pounds on the shipowner's labour bill was a relatively cheap way of avoiding trouble, in comparison with the port charges, the crew's wages, and the loss of earnings and return on capital which extra time in port involved.[36] The men obviously took advantage of this situation, so that slow working was used as a means of raising allowances when conditions were favourable, as, for example, on Friday afternoons

[34] This agreement was made because of the way P.L.A. gangs held up the cargo flow and reduced ship gangs' earnings. The P.L.A. piecework system rewarded weight rather than volume, the *reverse* of the private sector system. Thus P.L.A. gangs saw no reason to work fast on precisely those cargoes which were important to ship gangs.

[35] Wage records do not distinguish between genuine and false allowances, so quantification is not possible.

[36] *Devlin Report*, para. 24.

T.D.—5

when a ship was nearly loaded and would have had to wait until Monday if work slowed down.

The result of this 'decay' in the payment system was wage drift. When I first started this research, managers in one of the largest companies had worked to an unofficial but clearly sanctioned formula of a minimum wage of £6 per day; if piecework earnings fell below this, then allowances would be fixed to make up the difference. After eighteen months this had risen to £7.50 per day. During this period, allowances as a percentage of the total labour costs per ship had risen from the range of 20 to 30 per cent to that of 50 to 70 per cent in the largest of the local branches of this firm. In the company as a whole, the proportion of total gang earnings which resulted from cargo piecework as opposed to non-piecework earnings of all sorts (including overtime) fell from 61·2 per cent in the year ending September 1966 to 55·9 per cent in the year ending September 1969. Some of this increase in non-piecework wage was due to the failure of piecework rates to keep up with inflation, and the need to compensate the men for this. But much of it represented a real increase in the dock workers' level of remuneration: over a four-year period this increase was sufficient to raise them from ninth to second place in the league table of average earnings.[37] From January 1966 to January 1970, average earnings in the docks rose by nearly 57 per cent, despite the absence of any officially negotiated wage increases in the industry (apart from some increase in the minimum earnings guarantee). This compared with an average rise of only 27 per cent for wages elsewhere in British industry.[38]

Despite these features, the payment system did have some incentive effect. Allowances often complemented piecework by raising wages which had fallen below unofficially agreed minima. Moreover, both parties regarded allowances of this sort as a bargain to work well, as a re-negotiation of the reward–effort relationship. In many cases this was done explicitly, by laying down that the work was to be completed in a certain time to qualify for the allowance, but more usually it was an implicit understanding. The allowance system thus had a double-edged effect. It led to a spiralling process in which the piecework and allowance thresholds were continually rising, so increasing the amount of money which had to be offered in order to keep the men working. But in conjunction with the piecework system it appeared to be important for maintaining output and productivity at the high level characteristic of the London docks over many years.

There was one form of incentive which was difficult to debase and which ought to be treated as part of the reward system, even though it was a non-monetary reward. This was leisure. Continuity rules meant

[37] Department of Employment and Productivity, *Report of a Court of Inquiry under the Rt. Hon. The Lord Pearson, C.B.E.* (London, 1970), Cmnd. 4429, para. 35.
[38] ibid., para. 36.

that once a job was finished the gang could not start another job until the next 'turn'; i.e. 8 a.m. or 1 p.m. 'Job and finish' was the normal working arrangement, whereby the men were free to leave on completion of their original work. Even if the job did not actually finish, it was often informally agreed that the men could stop work once they had moved a certain amount of cargo. Payment by the piece rather than by time meant that there was no point in working slowly, unless to win a bonus allowance, because the dock worker was effectively working on his *own* time and not his employer's. Indeed, the largest firm calculated that the average working week of all their dock workers was 30·7 hours during the second quarter of 1970. The firm included in this figure all those hours spent on the job but not actually worked due to delays, but excluded overtime, public and annual holidays and 'proving attendance': i.e. the figures covered the 'normal' working hours.[39] Some of this leisure was undoubtedly the result of lack of work, though average earnings for this period suggest that there was not much of a shortage, but most of the leisure time shown in these figures was attributable to the practice of 'job and finish' on an extensive scale. Leisure had always been an integral part of dock work, but it was something the men had to create for themselves after permanency and full trade gave them regular work for most of the week. The way to create leisure was to finish the job as quickly as possible.

The abolition of all incentives on the introduction of Phase 2 demonstrated that the payment system in its totality had indeed played an important part in maintaining high levels of output up to then, however it may have decayed towards the end. There was a noticeable decline in effort and speed of work when handling cargo, with the result that productivity on general cargo-handling dropped by between 23 and 26 per cent in the first six months of Phase 2. Output levels on conventional work have been low ever since.[40] However, the increased use of unitization kept the overall drop in productivity to around 7 per cent. Just as serious for output as declining effort was the revelation that piecework had been a substitute for efficient administration, which became clear when the men refused either to chase cargo or to assume work-programming responsibilities any longer. The men stated that these were managerial duties which they had only ever assumed in order to maintain their earnings and to finish the job quickly, and that they would no longer perform them when their wages were guaranteed and

---

[39] 'Proving attendance' involved a dock worker signing on in the morning and afternoon when there was no work for him to do; he had to do this to qualify for his guarantee. Between 5 and 10 per cent of the labour force on average was in this situation throughout Phase 1. This was little different from the yearly averages of the casual era.

[40] A bonus scheme was finally introduced at the beginning of 1975 and productivity per man after six months was 27 per cent greater, back to about the levels which had obtained prior to 1970.

their working hours fixed. Phase 2 showed that the men had indeed continued to perform various supervisory and managerial tasks after 1967, despite the foremen's complaints.

Payment by results did not create the weak managerial control characteristic of the docks. Rather, it made managers' relative lack of power *more* tolerable by providing the men with a reason to supervise and discipline themselves. On the other hand, it did give rise to a continual series of minor disputes which, if not settled satisfactorily, threatened to disrupt work. 26 per cent of the foremen said that they would prefer a flat wage in place of the existing piecework because this would reduce the number of disputes and so improve industrial relations. The experience of the docks was similar to that of other industries in this respect: piecework multiplied the occasions when the interests of men and management were in overt opposition and when open conflict was likely to occur. But given the weakness of management in the docks, the capacity of piecework to generate conflict was probably a small price for managers to pay if piecework solved other problems.

In theory, disputes over piecework payment could be settled by appeal to an 'area committee' composed of union and employers' representatives for a whole dock. But these committees took time to convene, which exacerbated disputes, and their settlements often failed to satisfy the men. Managers in fact preferred to bargain directly with the gangs or the newly created stewards. (The Devlin reforms introduced shop stewards as part of decasualization.) The routine negotiation of allowances was conducted with the gang, so that stewards were called in only when disagreements occurred or when the men knew that an allowance was likely to be disputed. Stewards played a key role in the bargaining process between management and men. In many ways, stewards could make life easier for managers by lubricating the machinery of negotiation. In the first place, the men would normally continue working if they knew that steward and manager were tackling their claim, rather than withdrawing their labour until the dispute was settled. In the second, stewards acted as very effective links between men and management, with the result that managers knew more speedily and accurately what was happening around the dock. In the third, managers knew that most stewards could deliver the goods so far as persuading the men to accept the results of negotiation was concerned. In the docks, there were few cases of 'unofficial unofficial' action typical of the motor industry, when workers revolt against their stewards as well as their unions.[41] Stewards kept sufficiently in touch with the men to gauge what was likely to be acceptable. But stewards did not passively reflect the men's dictates: they had enough moral authority within the labour force to resist demands which they regarded as unreasonable, and to

[41] H. A. Turner *et al.*, *Labour Relations in the Motor Industry* (London, 1967), p. 223.

refuse to support the men against management.[42] Dock stewards acted as leaders as often as they followed, which from the management's point of view was part of their value in contrast to union officials who could often do neither.

The notion that demands could be unreasonable highlights the importance of the informal, 'custom and practice' rules which existed in the docks, many but not all of which were concerned in one way or another with piecework. Such rules of course develop in all industrial settings as the result of employees' desires to control the environment in which they work and are not dependent on piecework. It is interesting to see how these rules are created, whether workers actively assert their will to control or whether they passively accept what managers unwittingly give them. A recent discussion of 'custom and practice' rules has argued that managers are a more significant source of these rules than either stewards or the labour force generally. It is claimed that managers make errors of omission and commission which allow workers to control parts of their working environment; once control has been allowed to change hands in this way, then workers defend what has been conceded against future attempts to regain control.[43] Indeed the role of stewards in the creation of rules has been regarded as passive by an influential body of academic opinion since the Donovan Commission's report on the state of British industrial relations described them as the guardians rather than the creators of 'custom and practice'. However, it became obvious that in the docks both the men and stewards were extremely active and aggressive in trying to extend the rules with regard to payment and that the stewards were ahead of the men on many occasions.

So far as the men were concerned, bargaining with management was a matter of both the amount of the allowances and the occasions when allowances were payable. Phase 1 saw an extensive re-definition of what counted as 'exceptional' or 'abnormal' conditions as the result of pressure from the men. This was the case throughout the whole London system, but was most noticeable at Tilbury. Here the influx of men from the various upriver docks and wharves had brought with it a wide variety of new 'custom and practice' rules, which were based on those existing in the docks from which the new men came. The accepted definitions of 'long runs' became shorter and 'dirty' cargoes became cleaner throughout London during Phase 1. At the same time, the placing of

[42] A typical example concerned the practice of 'spelling', whereby a gang would agree to let certain members take time off work and the remaining men would produce the same output as if the gang were fully manned. Management would pay the absent men as if they had worked. However, when the gang failed to maintain output, managers would not give extra allowances to raise earnings, because the gang had chosen to work short-handed. Stewards refused to support the men if they complained.

[43] W. Brown, *Piecework Bargaining* (London, 1973), pp. 98–105.

'dunnage' between layers of cargo, which had traditionally been done free of charge at Tilbury though not in some places upriver, became a payable item in order to compensate the men for time lost performing the task. Another new allowance came from the London Dock, which had only handled small coasters with small tonnages and where it had become customary to pay piecework on a sliding scale giving higher rates for lower tonnages. With the closure of London and the transfer of ex-London workers to Tilbury, this practice was adopted first in the P.L.A. and then in the private sector. Thus dock workers were actively involved in modifying the informal rules in order to increase their earnings, and creating what was often entirely *new* 'custom and practice'.

Stewards could hardly be passive in this creation of new rules. Even if they were to act only as agents, reflecting the men's wishes rather than leading opinion, the stewards had to assume a forceful stance towards management. In fact, the men always had rather vague expectations of their stewards, hoping for no more than that the stewards would try to work the allowance system to their advantage. It was largely up to the stewards which of the existing customary rules they chose as being ripe for re-definition. Stewards and men could not re-define 'custom and practice' unilaterally nor could they do so with any great speed, because managers obviously resisted such attempts to destroy the status quo to their disadvantage. It was necessary that both parties should accept new practices for these to become rules or 'custom and practice'. Certain statements of a general nature can be made about such workplace rules. The rule-like quality of 'custom and practice' lies in the way both parties are bound by it, however temporarily. This binding force can result from a sense of the legitimacy of the rules, or from the superior power of one party which enables it to coerce the other to follow the rules. In the second case, it cannot be assumed that both parties regard the rules as possessing a moral legitimacy. In the docks, the relative strength of the men's situation in the years following decasualization and the unwillingness of shippers to suffer delays placed managers in a position where in fact they had little chance of resisting such demands. They therefore acquiesced in the face of superior power.

There was at least one fundamental change in the rules of the workplace where the stewards clearly led rather than followed the men. This was the trend towards the equalization of earnings in the last eighteen months of Phase 1. This carried the work-sharing ethos to an egalitarian extreme, because it denied the right of some gangs to earn more than others for a higher output. Any gang which had high earnings was to be placed on low-paying cargoes until its earnings came into line with the average, and vice versa. This entirely negated the principle of payment by results. The trend was started in one large firm in the Royal Group, where the stewards were committed to the principle and managed to persuade the men to agree though many had initially opposed the idea. Stewards in other firms and docks took up the idea and some were successful in persuading their men to agree, though in at least one Tilbury firm the men vetoed the change when it was suggested. Managers certainly disliked equalization, because it removed all the incentive effect from the payment system, but they found it difficult to resist when the stewards had the support of the men. Had the Phase 2 deal not been implemented, it appears that payment by results might anyway have been killed off by this development.

The movement towards earnings equalization emphasized two of dock workers' characteristic responses. It demonstrated the traditional concern that the lower-paid members of the occupation, often the older or less fit, should be guaranteed a decent living by the others. It also showed how the large numbers of men who were less than happy with such a radical change in the relationship between effort and reward would nevertheless acquiesce to the majority or most vocal opinion. Both responses illustrate the immense solidarity which is traditional in the industry, and which in most major conflicts with employers overcame the sectionalism inherent in casual labour.

Sectionalism was also a likely consequence of piecework payment and the gang method of organizing work, both of which were continued into permanency, but now the solidarity was easier to maintain even on a day-to-day basis. Elsewhere in British industry, systems of work group organization and payment by results have tended to create fragmented labour forces which are internally divided by their competitive sectionalism. Shifts in the conduct of collective bargaining in Britain over the last two decades, as documented by the Donovan Commission, have led to the decline of the old, formal and industry-wide bargaining in the face of 'informal' workplace bargaining. The interests of different workers within an industry or firm are not homogeneous, and different groups pursue their individual interests independently: they act as autonomous bargaining units, particularly under piecework conditions.[44] It might reasonably have been assumed that the docks, with both gangs and piecework, would have fitted this pattern. This was not often so, however, because occupational solidarity was strong enough to overcome fragmentation. Thus shop stewards in the docks were elected by all the workers in one firm, rather than by more limited groups as is common in other industries, with the consequence that stewards represented the interests of all. Part of the stewards' role in piecework bargaining was to ensure that new gains made by one gang were extended to all and that the creation of new 'custom and practice' rules

[44] For a critical review of recent literature on the 'informal' system and a development of the present discussion, see S. R. Hill, 'Norms, Groups and Power: The Sociology of Workplace Industrial Relations', *British Journal of Industrial Relations*, 12, 1974, pp. 213–35.

was uniformly distributed throughout the firm. The stewards were helped in this by the fact that most dock workers did not value the gangs very highly. Gangs remained work units and displayed no tendency to become anything more.

Industrial relations in the firms were therefore different from what might have been anticipated. Dock workers displayed strong feelings of solidarity with each other but were not antagonistic towards their employers. Their sense of occupational membership was perfectly compatible with harmonious industrial relations and did not create any great sense of hostility: solidarity with 'us' did not presuppose conflict with 'them'. This solidarity was concerned with feelings of belonging to a community, which remains an issue completely separate from that of industrial conflict. Of course, dock workers had already won control over much of their employment situation and they were often able to define industrial relationships on their own terms. This apparent reversal of the normal shop-floor power relationships may partly have explained the feelings of harmony which prevailed among the men, because managers so often deferred to the men's wishes. But even so, dock workers were still aware of the potential conflict of interest which lay beneath the employment contract.

Piecework meant that the employment contract was continually re-negotiated, because the terms of employment were discussed every day. Piecework meant also that the informal rules governing the workplace became particularly important to all parties, because these rules reflected the relationships between men and management and the terms of employment which were to prevail. Piecework and the concomitant rule system thus became the disputed ground which revealed the relative power of the parties.

In the long run, of course, the shop-floor strength which dock workers possessed during the late 1960s and early 1970s may be weakened by structural changes *outside* the workplace. In particular, decisions taken by shipowners, manufacturers shipping goods and judges may affect the power of the men at their workplaces. The decline of the Scheme ports as against those outside and the introduction of labour-saving techniques lead to under-employment, a declining dock system and the threat of redundancy in the long term. Strictly, this situation does not affect the controlling power of those men who are still employed, though it may lead to a decline in their numbers over the years. But the men themselves may lose their will to control for fear of speeding the decline of their ports: they may realize that one of the *reasons* for the growth of non-Scheme ports and the spread of new techniques is the concern felt by those who make the important decisions in the transport field about the extent of dock workers' present power and the manner of its use.

CHAPTER 7

Trade Unionism

The long-standing paradox of dock trade unionism is that a union movement which has contributed so much to the development of organized labour in this country should have been riven by internal fragmentation and disorder for most of its existence. For about forty years, between the 1880s and the mid-1920s, the ports played a dynamic role in the British labour movement in two important ways.

In the first place, dock-based unions showed that it was possible to organize unskilled workers, who were moreover casually employed, to win major concessions from their employers and to hold together a vast organization of dockers and ancillary occupations at least during the struggle itself. Membership of the waterside unions fluctuated greatly; but the main union (the Dockers' Union) solved the problems of earlier, short-lived labourer unions—which could not achieve continuity of organization—by maintaining stable nuclei in selected industries and localities, rather than by spreading the organizational base too thinly and relying on spontaneous action: this helped make the effective unionization of unskilled workers possible.[1] The London dock strike of 1889 and the national strikes of 1911 acted as an example and inspiration to other groups of workers who had been left unorganized by the old-established craft unions. Indeed, the 'dockers' tanner' strike of 1889, during which the Dockers' Union was born, can claim to be 'the most famous strike of the nineteenth century';[2] it was the culmination of the great outburst of trade-union militancy of the late 1880s.

The docks contributed to the theory and practice of unskilled unionism and showed by their example what collective strength could achieve. But their contribution to the labour movement at this time went beyond example, to the point of involving active collaboration with the miners and railwaymen in an alliance of over a million unskilled workers. Although the Triple Industrial Alliance had a chequered

---

[1] The Dockers Union was a general union rather than one restricting itself to a single trade as did craft unions, and picked up members from all the waterside trades and even from beyond the docks completely (e.g. it had strong organization among the tinplaters in south Wales). See E. J. Hobsbawm, 'General Labour Unions in Britain, 1889–1914', *Economic History Review*, 1, 1949, pp. 123–42.

[2] A. Bullock, *The Life and Times of Ernest Bevin* (London, 1960), vol. 1, p. 27.

history, and won its main victories by the threat of joint action rather than by carrying out its threats, it was a significant experiment in trade union solidarity, to which the dock workers contributed loyally, particularly in 1926.

The second achievement of dock trade unionism was to lay the foundations of the Transport and General Workers' Union. Numerous unions organized different ports, and different groups of workers in and around the docks, at the turn of the century; but in 1911 twenty-six of these were organized into the National Transport Workers' Federation, largely at the instigation of Ben Tillett—the creator and leader of the largest of these unions, the Dockers. The Dockers' Union played a leading part in the great strike wave of 1911/12—a period of labour unrest and militancy unparalleled since the early decades of the previous century. The Federation, which was born out of this crisis, mainly covered dock-based groups—though it extended into those other sectors of transport which impinged on the docks, and created the first effective co-ordination of the ports and waterside occupations. Dock workers clearly saw the benefits of solidarity. Ernest Bevin of the Dockers' Union, together with other union leaders, built on this foundation to create in January 1922 the new Transport and General Workers' Union, the majority of whose members at this time worked in the docks, on trams or buses or driving lorries.

Despite these major achievements and the solidarity which they demonstrated, the subsequent history of dock unionism has been one of fragmentation of effort and internal disorder within the movement, particularly within the T.G.W.U. Fragmentation resulted when most of the stevedores and some of the lightermen who had been in the 1911 Federation refused to join the new general union. They set up a rival body (National Amalgamated Stevedores, Lightermen, Watermen and Dockers Union) which was confined to port workers alone and had a less authoritarian structure than the T.G.W.U. In 1927 the watermen and lightermen split from the N.A.S.L.W.D.U. to create their own union. The two small unions were known as the National Amalgamated Stevedores and Dockers', and the Watermen, Lightermen, Tugmen and Bargemen's Union. Competition for members followed, and the inter-union rivalry between the N.A.S.D. and the T.G.W.U. has been a constant feature of the industry until the present day, particularly in London. Some of the implications of this are discussed later in the chapter.

Internal disorder within the T.G.W.U. itself broke out within eighteen months of the new union's creation: in 1923 the London docks went on unofficial strike in opposition to an officially negotiated wage settlement, and after the collapse of the strike many thousands of lightermen and dockers left the T.G.W.U. to join the newly formed N.A.S.L.W.D.U. Throughout the twenties, dock workers connived with their employers to ignore the registration schemes which the union had negotiated in many ports,[3] and in 1926 the unofficial leaders of the London dockers tried to form a rival union (without success). Finally, in 1932, the Glasgow dock workers did leave and set up their own union. Although dock workers saw the benefits of size and solidarity, many found the T.G.W.U. the wrong instrument for their struggle, feeling that it covered too many different trades to promote the interests of the ports, and resenting its bureaucracy and the frequently authoritarian stance of its general secretary, Ernest Bevin.

These early examples of fragmentation and disorder reveal a significant parallel between the early history of dock unionism, and the well-documented inter-union rivalries and unofficial movements of the postwar period—movements which have continued into the 1970s and given dock trade unionism much of its distinctive character. At this stage, it must be emphasized, however, that the terms 'fragmentation' and 'disorder' refer to the institutions which organize labour, and not to the dock workers' own solidarity, which is unaffected by the difficulties facing the unions. It has been the failure of the unions, in particular the T.G.W.U., to win the trust and leadership of their members, which has been the main characteristic of dock unionism in London over the last thirty years. In 1951, the Leggett Committee reported on unofficial stoppages in the London docks and showed how the unofficial leaders claimed that 'they are at heart good trade unionists, who have been compelled reluctantly to resort to unofficial action because of the inability or refusal of their respective Unions to pursue wholeheartedly the true interests of port workers' (though the committee thought the leaders were politically inspired wreckers).[4] In the same year, *The Dock Worker* found in Manchester, which was a T.G.W.U. port, a striking gulf 'between formal trade union organisation and everyday life in the docks',[5] between full-time officials and the men.

In similar vein, fifteen years later, Devlin noted the rise of the Unofficial Liaison Committee in London to a position in which 'the unofficial leadership is strong enough to amount to a rival power' (to the unions).[6] Devlin criticized both the N.A.S.D. and the T.G.W.U., but felt that the failings of the latter were the more significant, given that it was a much larger and more important union. One of Devlin's main recommendations was that the unions should try to establish themselves as the men's representatives. It was argued that a revitalized union movement would help to remove the causes of 'dissension and inefficiency' in the industry, by giving the employers well-organized and disciplined bodies to deal with and so frustrating the aims of the

[3] ibid., pp. 372–3.
[4] *Report into Unofficial Stoppages in London* (London, 1951), Cmnd. 8236, para. 32.
[5] *The Dock Worker*, p. 135.
[6] *Devlin Report*, para. 116.

'wreckers'.[7] In view of the history of unionism in the industry and the strictures of the official inquiries, it is obviously highly relevant to find out what meaning unionism had for the people whom I interviewed and what were their attitudes to the two union organizations.[8]

Attitudes to Unionism

Certain observations can immediately be made. Little was to be gained by asking people why they had joined unions, because all manual, clerical and supervisory or managerial employees are required to be union members: the men refuse to allow non-union labour to work in the docks. So membership tells us little about the nature and extent of people's involvement in their unions. The reports of the frequency with which people attend branch meetings and vote in branch elections are more informative and demonstrate some discrepancies between the two unions: by and large, blue union members attend slightly more frequently than the whites and they definitely vote more often.[9]

Differences between the two unions are indeed to be expected because, for a variety of reasons, the N.A.S.D. has always been the better supported. One reason which used to count in the past was the old stevedoring basis of the union: it developed out of the original Stevedores' League, which organized those who worked on board ship, and the stevedoring element has remained influential until recent times. Historically, stevedores were an élite sub-group who practised a skilled and dangerous trade and typically worked in very small firms; the combination of these factors created a strong sense of solidarity which was manifest in the old League and almost certainly carried over into the new union.[10]

The sectional solidarity of this group should not be exaggerated, however, because the membership division between blues and whites is by no means clear-cut. Those working aboard ships in Tilbury have always rejected the blues and preferred to join the T.G.W.U., while even upriver, where N.A.S.D. traditionally has a large membership, workers

[7] ibid., paras 114–16.

[8] Because of the different colours of their membership cards in the past, the T.G.W.U. is known as the 'white' union and the N.A.S.D. as the 'blue' in the docks. This terminology is often used in what follows.

[9] 83 per cent of the men and 74 per cent of the foremen were T.G.W.U. members, and the rest were all N.A.S.D. 15 per cent of the dock workers and 45 per cent of the foremen in the T.G.W.U. attended 'regularly', while the respective voting figures were 46 and 51 per cent. 26 per cent of N.A.S.D. men and 13 per cent of foremen attended 'regularly', while the voting figures increased to 96 and 92 per cent. *The Dock Worker*, p. 122, found that only 18 per cent went to at least 1 in 4 branch meetings. B. C. Roberts, *Trade Union Government and Administration in Great Britain* (London, 1956), pp. 95–7, estimates attendance in most unions at between 3 and 15 per cent, the bulk in the range 4 to 7 per cent.

[10] J. C. Lovell, *Stevedores and Dockers* (London, 1969), pp. 76–82.

performing stevedoring functions often join the rival union. N.A.S.D. has in fact acted for many years as a minority union working in the same field as a larger rival, and there is no natural line of demarcation between the two. This has led the blues to recruit dockers since the foundation of the N.A.S.D. Dockers have always been in the minority in this union, but this does not mean that they have occupied a subordinate position. The union is organized into two sections for stevedores and dockers, both of which are equally represented on the executive council. The chairman is drawn from each section in alternate years and has a casting vote. Thus while the bias of membership has been towards stevedores, the blue union has always managed to present itself as the union of dock workers as a whole.

A second aspect of the blue union, which is often believed to account for the greater loyalty of its members, is the democratic nature of its internal structure, which attempts to maximize popular control. Therefore the union has regular elections for all posts, the occupancy of these being for a limited period of time rather than for life. The most senior positions in the union hierarchy are included in this arrangement. Attendance at elections and certain meetings is supposed to be mandatory for all members, in order to enforce participation. Decisions of any importance are decided by all members, either in the branches or in special mass meetings. Such a democratic structure may well reflect or foster a sense of possession, so that the union is not regarded as an alien body in the way that white unionists seem to regard their organization. This structure assumes that the union belongs to its members, so that union officers do no more than administer routine affairs. A sense of possession means that the notion of official leadership is an alien one to union members, since officials can be no more than custodians: Devlin described the general secretary's position as being that of 'the voice of the Union rather than its leader'.[11] It should be noted, however, that Devlin and many in the industry believe that such extreme democracy leads the N.A.S.D. into a state of semi-paralysis where few decisions are taken and new initiatives are left to the more forceful T.G.W.U. whose officers are more independent of the membership.

Other indicators of the extent and nature of involvement reinforce this pattern of strong loyalty on the part of the blues and a less enthusiastic response on that of the whites. Indeed, the whites' criticisms of their union are quite strong, as one would have predicted from the events of the last twenty years and the references already quoted. In view of Devlin's particular criticism of the white union's failure to lead its members and to enlist their loyalty and support, everyone interviewed

---

[11] *Devlin Report*, para. 105. This was more in condemnation than in praise of the blues, because such a system of accountability to the rank-and-file meant that the union was hamstrung in negotiations. Devlin wanted the union negotiators to have more power.

by me was asked how they thought their union rated on this issue: 'In your opinion, has your union the respect and leadership of its members in the sector in which you are employed?' Table 7.1 shows the division between the two unions: a majority of the white unionists replied negatively while the blues were affirmative. Interestingly, the foremen were more extreme in both cases, since white foremen were more critical than the men and blue foremen were more in favour. This supports the view that the blue union was trusted more completely by its members than the white union at the time.

The desire which most people had for changes in their unions provides further evidence of this. 87 per cent of white union dock workers and 78 per cent of foremen reported that they would like to see changes, making 84 per cent of the two groups combined. Among blue union members, 52 per cent of the men and 92 per cent of foremen, making 72 per cent in all, wanted some changes. This compares with the results from the study of Manchester Docks (all T.G.W.U. members), where nearly three-quarters of the whites were dissatisfied with some aspect of their union.[12]

If one looks at the types of change desired in table 7.2, then the nature and extent of the dissatisfaction with the T.G.W.U. become more apparent. The theme which runs through the criticisms expressed by men and foremen is that the union is insufficiently representative of, and responsive to, the members. The majority of changes suggested by both groups is concerned with reducing the gulf between the union and its members and with making the union more representative of their wishes. It should be noted, however, that a larger proportion of men than of foremen were concerned with the union's lack of representativeness. Differing classifications of replies make direct comparison difficult, but the overall results are fairly similar to those of the Manchester study, in that issues relating to union democracy and the power of members are the crucial ones.[13] However, the actual replies within this overall category differ slightly from those of the previous study. There is no direct mention of national union policy and little of the officials above the local level, while issues such as the size and heterogeneity of the union, the nature of the negotiating machinery and information about union affairs are never mentioned at all. Yet these issues were all significant ones in Manchester. The largest single set of complaints in London was in fact about local officials and their terms of appointment: the union's remoteness and lack of representativeness were seen primarily in *local* terms, and not in terms of the union structure as a whole. (Of course, the local level may well be the more important to members.) The inference is that T.G.W.U. members were fairly satisfied with their union apart from the problems encountered at local

[12] *The Dock Worker*, p. 128.
[13] ibid., pp. 127-9.

level. They were not critical of national policy nor of the actions of the docks' trade group within the national structure.

The T.G.W.U. has been faced with two particular problems which have marked it off from the N.A.S.D. and made its relations with its members difficult. The first is that as a general union, albeit with a separate trade group for the docks within the overall structure, it has not perhaps been as concerned with dock problems as a purely dock-based union might have been. Secondly, the way in which the Scheme's provisions for employee participation work means that the T.G.W.U. is in an ambiguous position, because it shares responsibility as the men's ultimate employer and the enforcer of discipline. Moreover, by sharing control with management, the T.G.W.U. is accused of being too close to the operating employers.

In the blue unionists' case, the suggested changes were less critical of the union than the whites'. The men were fairly evenly divided, with most of those who desired change stressing the need for union members (not officials) to adopt a more modern outlook. By this was meant a greater receptivity to new mechanical handling devices and a greater willingness to allow flexible manning. The second desired change was for one port union to represent the interests of all who worked in the docks. During the time I was in the docks this was a frequent topic of conversation, since the blue union had long suffered a declining membership and those who remained appeared to be increasingly elderly.[14] Thus blue union members were concerned about the future of their small union and usually favoured some alliance with other dock groups to form a new organization. But the traditional hostilities were too great for them to consider merging with the T.G.W.U.

The Devlin Report suggested that the union movement, and in particular the T.G.W.U., should launch a great campaign in order to establish its authority and leadership, both of which had been usurped by the unofficial committees. Part of this massive drive was to be a long-term reorganization of the white union's structure, so as to institute a shop steward system in the industry. Shop stewards were recommended for two main purposes: relieving the local full-time officials of the minutiae of industrial relations, such as dealing with foremen about the men's grievances, and improving communications between the union's officers and committees and the men.

> For if it is admitted, . . . that the branch no longer provides a satis-
> factory means of communication between the dockers and their
> union, then the shop steward must serve in its place, not only in
> relation to day-to-day issues on the job but also in relation to major
> general issues.[15]

[14] From a maximum of 14,383 in 1955, the blue union's membership nationally had declined to 6,381 in 1969.   [15] *Devlin Report*, para. 288

The white union did make some effort to improve relations between dock workers and the hierarchy in the early 1970s. There was a considerably more 'open' atmosphere, with officials calling mass meetings in order to explain the union's position during negotiations and to gauge the opinions of the members. There were also some structural reforms, as opposed to the less tangible ones of 'atmosphere' or public relations, which attempted to revitalize the branch system. One reason for the branches' loss of vitality had been the oversupply of branches, too few of which, in addition, were in the right places: population movements resulting from East End slum clearance and the drift of trade downriver made the numbers and distribution of branches obsolete. During Phase 1 and the early months of Phase 2, many moribund branches were merged with others, so that numbers dropped from 80 in 1967 to 52 in 1971.[16] However, the data on attendance presented earlier shows that branch life at this time was still not very thriving.

This was really the limit of the 'great campaign' so far as the reform of institutions was concerned, since Devlin's most important suggestion was only half implemented. This was the proposal that a new shop steward system should be established, and be linked in some way with the union hierarchy. The stewards were indeed created, but their links with the unions were not well established.[17] Devlin appeared to envisage that officials and stewards would bypass the branches, liaising directly, whereas at least one T.G.W.U. proposal was to link stewards to the branches themselves. Neither scheme was implemented in the event. The blue union objected to the stewards, who often represented both white and blue members in the same firm, being linked in this way to the T.G.W.U. structure. At the same time the individuals elected to stewards' jobs frequently refused to see themselves as dependent on either union because they regarded themselves solely as the men's representatives.

Indeed, the new steward system contained the seeds of another unofficial movement similar to that which organized dock labour at various times in the 1950s and 1960s. This movement came forward most dramatically during 1972, when local steward committees led the campaign against the way in which containerization was being introduced into the industry and bypassed the unions entirely. The old Unofficial National Shop Stewards Committee was resurrected in order to co-ordinate the activities of the local unofficial movements run by the stewards. The national committee persuaded dock workers to ignore the official T.G.W.U. appeal to postpone the national dock

---

[16] Details given in D. F. Wilson, *Dockers* (London, 1972), p. 197.

[17] Though following the legal judgements in *Heatons v T.G.W.U.* under the 1971 Industrial Relations Act, the white union clarified the role of its stewards in all industries, including the docks. T.G.W.U. stewards are now more clearly part of the union hierarchy so far as union officials are concerned.

strike and also organized the extended campaign of blacking and picketing the inland container bases. But this new unofficial movement never received the same support as the old, as was shown clearly when most docks refused to heed the national committee's call for another national strike in late 1973, this time in support of a pay claim. In London, there was a small and temporary stoppage in part of the Royal Group but the rest of the port worked normally.

The relative lack of support for the unofficial movement may allow the unions to re-establish their moral authority in the long run, and recently the T.G.W.U. has been more concerned to improve its standing at the local level by becoming more responsive to rank-and-file pressures. The national policy of the union throughout the 1970s has been to consult stewards more fully during negotiations and generally to introduce a more democratic element into the traditionally rather autocratic practices of the union. This policy has been forcefully argued for by Jack Jones, the present general secretary. The effects of this in the docks were felt after I completed my research, so the attitudes of members towards their union may be more favourable now and the criticism of officials may have abated.

As was shown earlier, dock stewards do not represent sectional interests because they represent all the men in a firm and not just specific work groups. The people whom I interviewed were extremely well disposed to the new steward system and gave it considerable support, as can be judged from the replies to a question asking whether or not they thought that stewards were a good idea. (It was not possible to check support by the frequency of voting in steward elections, because many firms had only had one election since decasualization.) 90 per cent of the men approved the system, though some had reservations, and 62 per cent of foremen approved as well, though more of them with reservations. People who agreed in principle with the system but had reservations normally had doubts about particular individuals. The reasons given for approving the shop steward system all centred on the shop steward's role in improving industrial relations in the companies. 58 per cent of men and 45 per cent of foremen thought that the speed and efficiency of grievance settlement was the major source of improvement, because this prevented disputes festering and developing into serious trouble. Another 21 and 19 per cent respectively thought that managers were more likely to listen to stewards than to the men themselves, while 11 per cent of the men felt that stewards were more in touch with the men than anyone else.

The point about the steward system is that it tends to lead to settlements which are acceptable to the men, as was noted in an earlier chapter. This explains the equal weight men gave to efficiency and to speed. Stewards were seen to act as a linking agency with management, representing the men's interests and persuading management to consider their views. This was valued as proof of their efficiency. Running through most of the replies were overt or implied criticisms of the unions, since the functions performed so well by stewards were the ones in which the unions had failed in the past. Interestingly, half of those who objected to stewards did so on the grounds that they were doing the union's job.

Foremen tended to agree with the view that the steward system had improved industrial relations in the firms, although they displayed nowhere near the same unanimity as the men. Over a third gave the alternative view, that stewards either caused trouble and the loss of supervisory control, or at least were easily swayed by the men. It is in fact surprising that so many foremen did see the positive advantages of shop stewards, given that the rise of agencies to represent and protect the men's interests at the workplace has led to a curtailment of the foreman's traditional autonomy and to the bypassing of foremen by stewards and managers.

Significantly, neither the men nor the foremen mentioned the role of shop stewards as part of the union structure, nor as a source of information about union affairs. It is possible that stewards closed the gulf between the members and the official structure by representing the men's views to union officials, but the men never made any reference to this nor to the dissemination of union views to the members. Given the criticisms of the T.G.W.U. at the time, one can probably assume that stewards had little impact in either area of communication so far as the men were concerned.

Foremen were very much in favour of having a section of the union just for themselves, 81 and 83 per cent respectively of foremen in the two unions arguing in favour of this. P.L.A. foremen were not in fact in the same section of the union as their manual workers, since all P.L.A. staff were regarded as clerical workers and thus found themselves in the clerical and supervisory part of the T.G.W.U. Private sector foremen, however, normally continued in the same section and branch to which they had belonged as dock workers, although some chose to join the non-manual section and thus to separate themselves from the men.

All the blue union foremen were part of the same structure as the men, and members of the same branches. This system appeared to have worked in the foreman's interests at one time, because in the past he was able to use the union machinery to discipline poor workmanship or conduct unbecoming to the union, when the union acted to maintain craft standards. Now, however, blue union foremen found this situation increasingly intolerable, since they felt that the men objected to foremen's membership of the same branch. Table 7.3 shows that the major reason for wanting a separate union section in both unions was the belief that the foremen's problems and interests differed from those of other groups and required special attention. Blue foremen went further than this, to stress that the existing system led the union to neglect their interests because the men actively opposed the branch action on behalf of foremen. By a separate section, most foremen meant one separate from all other groups, not merely from the men: for the P.L.A. foremen this included separation from both the writers and assistant foremen.[18] Just as most foremen saw themselves as separate groups in their firms, so they wanted to be treated as separate entities by their unions.

In summing up the findings so far, one can draw a number of conclusions. The two unions stimulated very different responses from their members, the blues generally reacting favourably to the actions of their union, while the whites were fairly critical of certain areas of their union's performance. The whites' criticisms were mainly concerned with what was seen as the union's lack of sensitivity to its members' interests and wishes, which was expressed as the union's failure in one way or another to represent the members. Consequently, members did not respect the union or acknowledge its leadership. Interestingly, very few criticisms were directed above the local level: it was at this level that the union was regarded as inadequate, often because of specific individuals.

Shop stewards were welcomed because they provided a more efficient and rapid means of dispute resolution at the local, workplace level, and because they improved industrial relations in the process. Members of both unions shared this view of the role of shop stewards. However, they were not seen as part of the union structure to any great extent, but probably represented an alternative channel for conducting industrial relations.[19]

Foremen differed from the men on some issues, but the overall impression is that there were few consistent or substantively significant differences in their attitudes towards the unions. There is certainly no evidence that foremen as a group were more hostile to the unions than the men, though there was a sizeable minority which was hostile to shop stewards. Indeed, the high value which foremen placed on unionism can be seen in their desire to form their own section, in order to protect their interests more effectively.

The meaning which trade unionism has for union members is not necessarily clear-cut. It has been argued that unionism in the past was

[18] A P.L.A. 'writer' was a senior clerical worker of the same status as a foreman, who worked in the same office and dealt with the paperwork.

[19] There was a separate system for the resolution of disagreements, based on area committees, where union officials but not stewards acted as representatives of the men. These committees became moribund during Phase 1, because both men and management preferred to use stewards. These committees were abolished after Phase 2 and the stewards were given more recognition.

a form of collective action with social and political aims wider than the workplace itself, which represented more to the worker than simply a means of economic betterment. Workers with 'traditional' outlooks still share this view of unionism, whereas certain groups of 'modern' workers regard trade unionism as having relevance only for issues which are economic in nature and local in scope, being confined to meeting instrumental objectives in the workplace.[20] At the same time, membership of unions has been seen as a feature traditionally distinguishing manual from non-manual employees. This is no longer so true as it used to be, though one should avoid over-estimating the degree to which non-manual unionism has grown in the manufacturing sector,[21] but it is not entirely clear what meaning union membership has for non-manual occupations.[22] The people whom I interviewed here included both supposedly traditional manual workers and foremen whose manual status is ambiguous. The meanings they give to unionism are therefore well worth examination.

It is often held that collective bargaining for narrowly economic ends is but one method of achieving unionism's more basic aim, which is to give workers more control over their working lives.[23] This fundamental trade union objective requires job regulation and control in the industrial setting and political power in the wider society. In the workplace this is thought to involve encroachment on, and participation in, the exercise of managerial authority. In society, this involves power as an interest group in the political system in its broadest sense, and in the Labour Party specifically. One way towards the study of the meanings of trade unionism is to ascertain people's views on these aspects of union objectives. Thus foremen and men were presented with a series of statements on these aspects and asked to say how far they agreed with them (see section H, question 11 of the interview schedule).

Most people thought that unions should have greater influence in management. Over three-quarters of both men and foremen agreed that, 'unions ought to get their members a say in management', and there were no real differences between the two groups. See table 7.4. This contrasts with the Luton engineering workers, only 40 per cent of whom thought that unions ought to gain more influence for their

[20] J. H. Goldthorpe, D. Lockwood et al., The Affluent Worker (Cambridge, 1968), vol. 1, p. 113.

[21] G. S. Bain, Trade Union Growth and Recognition (London, 1967), para. 40. Unfortunately, more recent statistics of white-collar unionism collected by the government do not allow the sectors in which people are employed to be differentiated. Bain notes the very different proportions of different non-manual groups joining unions: 9 per cent of manufacturing foremen in 1964 against 49 per cent of draughtsmen and 30 per cent of all technicians.

[22] G. S. Bain, D. Coates and Valerie Ellis, Social Stratification and Trade Unionism (London, 1973), review the evidence concerning the meaning of unionism for white-collar workers.

[23] e.g. A. Flanders, Management and Unions (London, 1970), pp. 130-47.

members.[24] The reasons these people gave for their views are particularly interesting, because they suggested that union members could restrain managerial incompetence and thus run the docks more efficiently than they were run at that time. That is to say, dock workers and foremen felt that they knew more about the running of dock work than their managers, and could ensure the economic viability of the port better. This in turn would be in the workers' interests, since job security and pay would be improved in a more efficient industry. There were scarcely any comments about the possibility of greater autonomy of job regulation as the result of greater influence. (The men of course already had a significant amount of control over their work.) Two quotations give the flavour of the typical sort of reply:

> Supers are important for some things, like keeping the shippers happy, because they speak the language and we don't. But they know nothing about stowages compared with us—how can they, when we've spent 20 years down the hold on piece rates, learning how to shave a few seconds off every job. Give dockies control of loading and London'll be the best port in Europe again.

> It makes you sick, seeing these employers ruining our industry. Any dock worker could take on their job and do it a hundred times better. And our living would be saved, too.

Two aspects of trade unionism's role in society were treated. These concerned the power of trade unions in the country and the alliance with the Labour Party in politics. The replies are interesting. On the subject of trade union power the men were nearly evenly divided, with as many as 40 per cent agreeing with the statement that 'the trade unions have too much power in this country', while 49 per cent disagreed; while two-thirds of the foremen felt that the power was excessive. On the subject of the union–Labour alliance, even more people in each group were opposed to the union position than on the question of the power of the unions. In both instances, dock workers took a line which was at least as critical as that of other groups of workers elsewhere.[25]

These findings are *not* surprising, despite the weight which many sociologists have previously given to these aspects of trade unionism. In the first place, the extra-industrial aspects of union power represent

---

[24] J. H. Goldthorpe *et al.*, op. cit., vol. 1, p. 109.

[25] M. Moran, *The Union of Post Office Workers* (London, 1974), p. 54, found that 79 per cent of postal workers disapproved of their union's affiliation to the Labour Party. J. H. Goldthorpe, D. Lockwood *et al.*, op. cit., vol. 1, pp. 112–13, found that 53 per cent opposed the Labour alliance and 41 per cent thought that unions had too much power in society. In the survey reported in R. McKenzie and A. Silver, *Angels in Marble* (London, 1968), p. 127, 56 per cent thought that unions had too much power. *The Dock Worker*, p. 132, found only 17 per cent hostile to the alliance with Labour.

the 'needs' of unions as institutions and such 'needs' are not necessarily sanctioned by the rank-and-file membership.[26] The 'needs' themselves may be more historical than current: a recent study of the linkage between the engineering union and the Labour Party in the 1950s and 1960s shows just how little influence union leaders sought to use, despite their potential power in the party at national and local levels.[27] Nor do all manual worker unions feel the 'need' to form extra-industrial alliances which increase their social and political power, such as the link with the Labour Party. That union of supposedly traditional proletarians, the N.A.S.D., has steadfastly refused to affiliate to the Labour Party for many years, preferring both to remain independent of party politics and to act primarily on the industrial front.[28] The dock workers I interviewed were certainly hostile to the traditional alliance between unionism and Labour, refusing to accept the view that these formed the industrial and political wings of an integrated labour movement.

Secondly, it has been suggested that the view that union power is too great is fairly widely shared in the working class.[29] The proportions of dock workers giving the various responses to union power closely matched those reported in *The Affluent Worker* and *Angels in Marble*, so dock workers were quite typical when large numbers agreed that the organizations which represented their interests as wage earners were too powerful in the country.

Thirdly, and in a slightly different vein, it may be that one should expect such replies, in answer to questions which deal with fairly abstract ideas which are also part of a socially dominant ideology. Thus people may *genuinely* agree with the socially dominant view of unions at the abstract level; but they may take a different attitude when they are themselves directly involved. For instance, dock workers in the 1960s were content for the unions to put pressure on the Labour Party concerning decasualization, whatever ideological objections they otherwise had to the union–Labour link. Nor did they disapprove of the Scheme, which was clearly the result of union influence on the Labour Party and the brainchild of Ernest Bevin, ex-union leader turned Labour cabinet minister. The consequences of the alliance rarely meet with disapproval.

The discrepancy between people's replies to general questions which

---

[26] A. Flanders, op. cit., p. 29. M. Moran, op. cit., passim, shows how the union leaders and a minority group of lay activists in the postal union are responsible for maintaining affiliation to the Labour Party.

[27] I. Richter, *Political Purpose in Trade Unions* (London, 1973), passim.

[28] M. Harrison, *Trade Unions and the Labour Party Since 1945* (London, 1960), pp. 325–34, points out that many minor manual unions do not affiliate to the Labour Party.

[29] R. McKenzie and A. Silver, op. cit., pp. 126–33, whose question wording was used here.

do not specify particular situations and what one knows to be their opinions about actual cases, may reflect the fact that they have two frames of reference. The first is the acceptance of dominant values, which general questions about unions and other issues normally reveal. The second is the subordinate value system which arises out of people's own experience and that of others in the same situation, and regards as legitimate those acts of which the dominant values would disapprove.[30] Both frames of reference are equally valid and 'real', but are adopted in different situations.

Foremen and men obviously differed on the subject of the unions' power in society. In view of the evidence of other research, that political party allegiance differentiates between various degrees of hostility to union power,[31] the results were analysed while controlling for party allegiance. There was a chance that the difference between foremen and men was due to the fact that there were more Conservative foremen than men. However, table 7.4 shows that foremen who regularly voted Labour were more likely to disapprove of union power than Labour-voting dock workers (though the extent of the difference between Labour foremen and men is less than that between all foremen and men). That is to say, the difference between foremen and men is mainly associated with status rather than political persuasion.[32] Within the ranks of foremen, however, Conservative voters were generally more hostile than Labour ones. Taking the two groups together, Labour 'constants' were considerably more likely to disagree with the statement that unions have too much power in this country than were the Conservative 'constants'.[33] While considering the impact of party allegiance on views about unionism, it is worth noting how more than half of Labour-voting dock workers and foremen disapprove of the alliance between their party and the union movement.[34]

This evidence, that many London dock workers share a fairly com-

[30] F. Parkin, *Class Inequality and Political Order* (London, 1971), pp. 79–102.

[31] R. McKenzie and A. Silver, op. cit.

[32] There were no significant differences between Conservative and Labour dock workers. The difference between Conservative and Labour foremen was significant at 0·05 level: $X^2 = 4·62$ with 1 degree of freedom. The difference between Labour dock workers and Labour foremen was significant at 0·06 level: $X^2 = 3·74$ with 1 degree of freedom. (These values of X^2 are expressed with 1 degree of freedom because the neutral response was dropped from the calculations, which were based on a simple dichotomy of 'Agree' or 'Disagree'.) There was no significant difference between Conservative dock workers and foremen, but the small numbers and highly skewed distribution of voting behaviour may well explain this.

[33] Labour foremen differ significantly from Conservative foremen at the 0·01 level on the statements about support for the Labour Party and the necessity of unions: $X^2 = 9·55$ and 20·4 respectively with 1 degree of freedom.

[34] The four statements about unions were tabulated against other variables in addition to political allegiance. Age, which was differentially distributed between the two groups, did not account for any of the differences in attitudes towards unionism. Among the foremen, views about 'teamwork' in industry did not correspond with

mon antipathy to unions' extra-industrial activities and power, does by no means imply any weakening of attachment to the idea of unionism or the value placed on collective bargaining. Both groups were asked how far they agreed that, 'trade union action to improve wages and living standards is no longer so necessary as it used to be, since everyone today can raise their own standards of living by hard work and ability'. This statement was chosen because collective bargaining over financial benefits has always been central to unionism, and because the belief in individual bargaining has in the past separated non-manual from manual workers, being part of the individualistic non-manual ethic which is hostile to unionism.[35] Table 7.4 shows that very few dock workers and comparatively few foremen were willing to agree that trade unions had lost their importance for protecting and improving their members' economic interests. In other words, the value of collectivism and unionism as the means of protecting the individual is still central to the beliefs which these groups hold about the nature of industry.

Some strands can now be drawn together. Dock workers are divided on the question of social power and support for the Labour Party; that is, on the extension of union power beyond the limits of industry. But within the industrial setting they are happy to see some limitation of managerial power in favour of employees having a greater say. This fits the picture which began to emerge earlier. The information about dock workers' views of the steward system and the nature of their criticisms of the white union indicated that much of their attention was focused on labour organization so far as it concerned local matters at the workplace. Discontent was rarely voiced against the T.G.W.U. as an organization, above the local level, nor did this discontent influence the men's evaluation of collective action and unionism as such. Unions are still valued for the economic benefits they confer, for their role in bargaining, and this favourable evaluation remains despite other criticisms. McKenzie and Silver found that unionism had a similar meaning for their sample of working-class voters, and their conclusions appear appropriate for many of the dock workers:

Thus, unions are widely seen as necessary agencies of defence, rather infrequently praised with basic enthusiasm, and often criticized for a variety of alleged faults and failings. Agreement with the unions'

any of the views on unionism; among the men there was a significant but slight correlation (·21) between 'teamwork' and the trade union power statement. Table 10.10 shows that the inter-correlations between most of the four statements are definite and moderately sized, which suggests a reasonable consistency of response.

[35] e.g. A. J. M. Sykes, 'Some differences in the Attitudes of Clerical and Manual Workers', *The Sociological Review*, 13, 1965, pp. 297–311,

goal of improving the lot of ordinary people very often does not involve a thoroughgoing approval of unions as institutions or political organizations.[36]

Two conclusions can be made about the meaning of unionism for foremen. Foremen were slightly less well disposed to certain aspects of unionism than dock workers, but in absolute terms were not hostile to the idea of unionism or collective action. Compared with the men, foremen were more likely to agree that unions had too much power in the country, that they ought not to support the Labour Party, and that collective action was less necessary than before.[37] There was little difference, however, on the subject of greater participation in management. Taking foremen on their own, unionism is meaningful to them. The meaning is one of union action at the workplace level combined with hostility to extra-industrial activity. Thus two-thirds feel that unions are too powerful and three-quarters oppose the political alliance, but the great majority want more say in management while nearly two-thirds disagree that unions are no longer needed for instrumental ends. Foremen agree with the limited aims of the union movement, but not with its overall power and position in society. Moreover, when political allegiance is controlled for, then those foremen who constantly vote Labour are more favourably disposed towards the wider aspects of unionism than the others. However, differences between foremen and men remain.

A real problem when assessing foremen's attitudes is the lack of comparable data from other studies. Information on non-manual unionism shows the wide variation between different occupations within this general category, so that it becomes difficult to generalize about all non-manual workers.[38] Data on the extent of unionization among foremen are not entirely accurate, because it is not possible to ascertain exactly how many are union members (some unions do not keep figures for foremen separate from those for manual workers). Since most foremen are promoted from the manual side, one might expect their attitudes to differ from those of clerical and other non-manual workers. (Though in this study the P.L.A. foremen, who were all ex-clerks, were little different from the private sector foremen.) However, the fact that they have been promoted obviously means that foremen may differ from the rest of the men, because selection must

[36] R. McKenzie and A. Silver, op. cit., p. 133.

[37] The differences on the subjects of power and necessity are significant at 0·01: $X^2 = 15·01$ and 10·96 respectively with 1 degree of freedom; the difference on the subject of the relationship with the Labour Party is significant at 0·05: $X^2 = 5·73$ with 1 degree freedom.

[38] G. Bain et al., op. cit., passim. B. C. Roberts, R. Loveridge and J. Gennard, The Reluctant Militants (London, 1972), pp. 231–88, show how meanings can vary even among very similar non-manual occupations.

indicate that managers prefer an individual to his mates for some reason. The indices of participation, attendance and voting, did not greatly differ between men and foremen, but there was a wider divergence on the general issues of unionism. There was no rejection of the idea of unionism, but the desire to form a foremen's section showed that these foremen were not happy with the men as their allies in collective action and preferred a form of separatism which would better protect their different interests.

Occupational Solidarity

Some consideration of the nature of occupational solidarity is appropriate at this point. In the first place, trade unionism has often been co-extensive with occupational solidarity or awareness as can be seen in the growth of craft unions based on specific occupational groups. To some extent, this had been the case historically with the N.A.S.D. Secondly, occupationally based unionism of this sort can lead to sectionalism within the working class, which is manifested in demarcation disputes between unions, and rank-and-file concern with differentials. Such sectionalism can prevent solidarity between groups which might otherwise be united. This is particularly so when the original bases of the distinction between groups have disappeared, as in the docks, so that multi-unionism divides what is in other respects a single occupation.

One strand in the history of dock unionism has been the well-known rivalry between blues and whites. The stevedores' union emerged and consolidated very much earlier than the white one, establishing its position by the end of the nineteenth century.[39] This was the progenitor of the N.A.S.D., which claimed to represent the interests of all dock workers and tally clerks and set itself up as a direct competitor to the T.G.W.U. Stevedoring was traditionally regarded as the most highly skilled work in the port, and stevedores were clearly at the summit of the hierarchy of occupational groups with dockers at the bottom.[40] This distinction was based partly on the technical knowledge and skill required to work on ship and partly on the greater physical danger of the job. However, the differences which underpinned the distinction between the groups have declined in importance throughout this century, though the speed of this decline should not be exaggerated. These differences were partly bound up with the technology of sail and early generations of motor ships: the cramped holds, the need continually to consider the ship's trim and the reliance on the ship's gear (derricks and winches), which have progressively disappeared from ship work. In the techno-

[39] See J. C. Lovell, op. cit., passim.
[40] ibid., pp. 35–43, where the many specialisms of nineteenth-century dock work are described.

logically most advanced operations, such as packaged timber and containers, these aspects of ship work have entirely disappeared. It is still true, however, that certain residual differences in skill requirements remain today on conventional operations, since the space constraints of the hold, the need to pack the maximum amount of cargo, the need to avoid damaging it, and the physical dangers of downhold work demand a greater precision and a greater knowledge of techniques than on the quay. Ship work is also physically more demanding.

But the differences are now much smaller than before, and provide a poor basis on which to divide dock workers. Other ports have always made less of a distinction between the work of the two groups and historically, P.L.A. dockers have always performed the ship work when unloading in the London Dock or St. Katherine's. More recently, the common register of 1967 broke down the barriers between the two unions in London, unifying working practices and facilitating the further integration of the two groups of workers at the workplace. This ensured that only one category of dock worker existed and that docking was an undivided occupation. A few blue stevedores at first resisted the final abolition of what they saw as their élite status, but they rapidly accepted the common register once Phase 1 got under way. In so doing, they removed the last risk that the old status distinctions might re-emerge in London as a threat to the solidarity of dock workers as a whole. Phase 2 recognized the residual task differences by giving ship work a cash value, but only of a few pence per day.

Significantly, the blue union gave up this last vestige of stevedoring's separate identity because its insistence on demarcation rules threatened its stevedoring members' livelihoods in the face of the changes introduced into the industry. Modern unitized cargo-handling techniques and purpose-built facilities made the old ship–quay distinction completely meaningless, and it was obvious that integrated operations would be forced through. Moreover, since these new methods were based on Tilbury, where the N.A.S.D. had never been accepted, the blues could not even try to enforce demarcation. At the same time, Tilbury was taking conventional work as well out of the upriver docks and away from the blues. Finally, the P.L.A. began to emerge as an employer worth working for, with modern work and equipment and high earnings potential, instead of being the employer of last resort. The P.L.A. had never recognized the blue union, partly because it refused to accept the union's demarcation rules with regard to unloading a hold.

The relations between the N.A.S.D. and the T.G.W.U. have frequently threatened to split dock workers into sectional groups. The earliest occasion of inter-union dissension was the refusal of the old Stevedores' League to join the new transport union in 1922, which led to the subsequent battles for membership in the 1920s which seriously divided the occupation at the time. There has been recurrent strife between the two unions ever since, becoming worse over the years, until open warfare broke out between 1945 and 1954 with the large-scale poaching of white members by the blues. This infringement of the Bridlington agreement led ultimately to the T.U.C. disaffiliating the N.A.S.D. in 1959. The Devlin committee noted that this dispute 'greatly weakened the trade union side with grave consequences'.[41] It also noted that the prospects of reconciliation were slight in the mid-1960s. Since Devlin, overt conflict has declined, the relative peace largely resulting from the blue union accepting a minority status.[42]

The most significant aspect of this inter-union rivalry, however, is how little it has damaged the occupational solidarity of dock workers themselves. The rivalry had the potential of dividing the labour force into sectionalist camps, as in other instances of union rivalry, but this has rarely occurred in docking. So far as can be seen, rivalries between individuals may have occurred, but usually when neither party was in dispute with an outsider. In most disputes with employers, for instance, workers of one union have supported those of the other. Devlin described the inter-union dispute in these terms:

> It has remained a dispute between leaders. But the rivalry between the leaders does not appear to excite any great animosity in the rank and file. In London . . ., Blues and T. and G. members work together in complete amity and gangs are often mixed. If the Blues in a gang decide to stop work . . . the T. and G. members of the gang will most likely stop work out of a sense of solidarity.[43]

Support for the view that occupational solidarity transcends union rivalry can be found in the nature of the old unofficial liaison committees and the modern steward system. On the one hand, the committees were an expression of the discontent at that time with the remoteness and lack of responsiveness of the major union, so that individual union members were unlikely to identify with their leaders' battles. On the other, the old committees always contained a cross-section of members from the two unions and avoided all taint of sectionalism. Given the support which dock workers showed for the unofficials, this success shows how different groups were united on a wide occupational basis. The steward system has worked in the same way. Union membership is not relevant: it has been shown how blues represented whites and vice versa, while voting in steward elections was organized on a company basis without reference to union division. In Tilbury, one senior steward during the research period was a blue, even though his company employed only ten other blues and over five

[41] *Devlin Report*, para. 103.
[42] D. F. Wilson, op. cit., p. 209.
[43] *Devlin Report*, para. 103.

hundred whites. Now, as in the past, being a dock worker is more important than the union one belongs to.

Another impetus towards greater solidarity was the mixing of previously discrete groups of workers during Phase 1. The casual system had ensured that dock workers interacted with a fairly wide range of their colleagues, since workers were not divided up into separate companies. But even under the casual system, interaction had been restricted by specialism and by the separation of docks. Although decasualization permanently split people into different companies, which may in the long run weaken occupational solidarity, one short-term consequence of Phase 1 was to mix people more thoroughly than before. The closure of various docks, wharves, and warehouses meant that many people who had spent most of their working lives in one dock, or who had specialized in one aspect of dock work, such as short sea trade vessels or warehousing, were uprooted and put alongside others with different experience. 23 per cent of the men and 7 per cent of the foremen I interviewed had moved docks after decasualization.

Individual docks during the casual days had attracted their own regular workers, regular in the sense that they would seek employment from any of the companies in that dock before moving to another. Movement between docks was probably never very high. The consequence was that all docks developed their own 'characters', which were widely recognized by those involved in the industry in London and appeared to be stable over time. That is, dock sub-cultures developed which were highly localized. The characteristic most frequently mentioned and the one most noticeable in practice was the willingness to take industrial action. Thus the Royal Group and the old London and the St. Katherine's Docks (when the latter were still open) were the most militant, Tilbury and the West India/Millwall were somewhat less so, while the Surrey Commercials were the most passive. When unofficial strikes were called, the various docks would normally halt work in this order.

So far as can be told from the impressions of those in the industry, the mixing which occurred after permanency went some way to breaking down these localized sub-cultures. Managers in Tilbury, for instance, complained that dock workers from the old London dock had introduced new working practices (restrictive ones from the managerial view-point) and new norms of piecework bargaining, as discussed earlier. Both of these had become established among those who had always worked in Tilbury. In interactional terms, a more generalized interaction between occupational members must have occurred as the result of labour transfers. This interaction contributed to the further generalization of occupational culture, so that any localized and sectional elements became submerged.

The dock workers and foremen whom I interviewed had a sense of solidarity with others in the occupation. They were asked whether they thought it right to take industrial action in support of other dock workers, whether in London or other docks, if they themselves were not directly involved. 86 per cent of the men and 71 per cent of foremen were in favour of action to support others. A further ten and eight per cent of the two groups said support would depend on the issue. The nature of the replies to this question centred on the need to protect the occupation: solidarity was seen as being in the long-term interests of all who worked in the docks.

In order to make the discussion more concrete, people were also asked about their views on the container ban, which was in force throughout the period of my interviewing and prevented the opening of any more unitized berths (though it did not interfere with existing operations). The unions justified the ban on the grounds that it was a bargaining device in the struggle to improve pay and conditions throughout the industry: no more groups of workers would be allowed to receive the special deals involved in container work unless everyone benefited. 83 per cent of the men and 69 per cent of foremen accepted this principle, even though it meant a personal sacrifice for many of those in Tilbury. The 1970 national dock strike also demonstrated the strength of dock workers' solidarity: London dock workers supported the national dock strike, which was intended to bring the other ports up to the standards of London, even though they themselves did not initially expect to benefit from this action.

Questionnaire replies and these examples of recent industrial action indicate that occupational solidarity has a real meaning for dock workers. They have shown themselves willing to support people they have never met for no immediate gain of their own, but because they share feelings of occupational loyalty. However, the strength of this solidarity nowadays is probably not always as great as many in the industry would like to claim. Industrial action since about 1972 has rarely been concerted and the sectionalism between ports has been a constant disappointment to the National Shop Stewards' Committee. The situation is that a few ports have expanded at the cost of others, mainly at the cost of London and Liverpool, within the context of an overall decline in the demand for dock labour. In this situation, solidarity has been strained and inter-port rivalry has been strong.

What solidarity there is might of course prove segmental within the context of the labour movement as a whole, because strong occupational loyalties often prevent feelings of solidarity with those outside the occupation. These loyalties can easily breed an inward-looking attitude which hinders a more universal world view. Those theorists of working class consciousness who locate its origins in geographically and socially isolated occupational communities have rightly been taken to task recently, on the grounds that parochialism is the most probable result of strong occupational solidarity.[44] But in this case, dock workers appear to have overcome any sectional tendencies and have developed fairly all-embracing world views. This universalism can be shown in both attitudes and deeds.

Dock workers have always been willing to help other groups of workers involved in disputes by blacking cargo, so that goods cannot be loaded or unloaded. Weakly organized occupations like the seamen have particularly benefited from this, because they have been able to use the threat of dock delays to strengthen their hand in negotiations with employers. (Dock workers have always had close links with seamen: 13 per cent of the foremen, for instance, had worked as seamen prior to entering the docks.) The dock workers' absolute insistence that only union members enter the docks to work has also helped spread unionism among lorry drivers, a notoriously difficult occupation to organize, and much of what solidarity exists among drivers can be attributed to this.[45] The people whom I interviewed were in some agreement that dock workers ought to help others involved in industrial action on occasion, though most added that they would need to be clear about the dispute involved and in agreement with its aims. 51 per cent of the men thought it right to help out in certain cases, 32 per cent thought it wrong, and 17 per cent did not know. Foremen were somewhat less likely to support the idea of sympathetic action for workers outside the industry, 43 per cent stating that it might be right in certain cases and 52 per cent opposing the idea. It can be seen, therefore, that dock workers do indeed have some sense of affinity or identity with other groups of workers outside their own occupation. In this, they are similar to printers, whose work experience and values create a sense of identity which transcends occupational self-interest and particularism.[46]

Whether this universalism is class-conscious is not clear from the evidence presented here. Later discussion of political attitudes shows that the social consciousness of these dock workers contains few elements of traditional class perspectives, though the evidence presented there may not necessarily be conclusive. The impression which is given by these data on unionism and occupational solidarity is that the universalism is a trade unionist one: a belief in the industrial ideals of the union movement, so that all unionists help each other should the need arise or help weaker brethren who are not yet organized. This complements the previously noted hostility to the extra-industrial aspects of union behaviour and the rejection of the notion of a united politico-industrial labour movement.

[44] See J. Westergaard, 'Sociology: The Myth of Classlessness', in R. Blackburn (ed.), *Ideology in Social Science* (London, 1972), pp. 119–64.

[45] P. G. Hollowell, *The Lorry Driver* (London, 1968), p. 49.

[46] I. C. Cannon,'Ideology and Occupational Community: A Study of Compositors', *Sociology*, 1, 1967, pp. 165–87.

CHAPTER 8

Foremen and Men

Different aspects of the relationship between foremen and men have been described at various points so far. It was suggested that a fundamental transformation of the relationship has occurred over the last fifteen years or so as the result of a more general modification of dock institutions. A series of changes has resulted in the destruction of the personalistic tie in its various forms, notably the dyad, which used to be the basic institution of employment; in the truncation of the foreman's old role with regard to personnel and industrial relations and in the parallel development of new links between the men and their firms and the growth of stewards as the men's agents. Thus the erosion of the traditional position of the foreman is more than just a change in the patterns of supervision: it represents a massive transformation in the institutional fabric of the docks and the rise of what are normal aspects of employment elsewhere in industry. Two issues remain to be discussed: what the labour force thinks of foremen and what further consequences the events of the last few years have produced.

By and large, the men whom I interviewed were reasonably well disposed towards foremen. 90 per cent claimed to get on well at a personal level and said that their relationships with foremen were good, without much conflict. These findings are similar to those reported in *The Dock Worker*.[1] Moreover, 73 per cent recognized the necessity and importance of the foremen's job for the running of the work and acknowledged that everyday routine could not be carried out without them. However, only 53 per cent thought that the majority of the foremen with whom they worked were good at their jobs. And whereas the foremen had claimed that their job could not be done well by someone whose only training was experience of docking in the labour force, the men denied that the job required any special skills which they as dock workers did not already possess. 83 per cent felt that they could easily do the job if it were offered them.[2] In other words, dock

---

[1] *The Dock Worker*, p. 94.

[2] Though only 35 per cent would in fact accept the job if it were offered, which puts dock workers in the middle of the range of workers wanting promotion, according to other studies: see H. Beynon and R. M. Blackburn, *Perceptions of Work* (Cambridge, 1972), pp. 88–9. There was no clear pattern of replies rejecting promotion, but there was no suggestion of hostility to management.

workers did not agree with the foremen's inflated view of the difficulty of the job and also doubted the competence of many individual foremen.

It is noteworthy that dock workers in fact expected very little of their foremen. When they were asked what they thought were the most important qualities of a good foreman, large proportions of the men were concerned primarily that he should know his own job and be technically competent, such competence of course influencing the men's chances of earning well under piecework conditions. See table 8.1. Another sizeable group was concerned with autonomy and being left alone by foremen, because they wanted to get on with the work without frequent contact with supervision. Less than twenty per cent thought that those attributes of good human relations which can be categorized as 'consideration' were important. These attributes include politeness, treating the men as individuals and knowledge of people's capabilities. Indeed, the overall tenor of the replies suggests that most dock workers are fairly unconcerned to develop close social bonds with foremen and that the quality of personal relationships is not especially important. This impression is reinforced by the reactions to the Phase 1 practice of rotating men from one foreman to another with each separate job: less than forty per cent wanted to stick permanently with one foreman, and they were mainly concerned to develop teamwork between men and foremen purely for the instrumental reasons of increased earnings and greater safety.[3] Most either preferred rotation or had no preference one way or the other, or even thought that the question was irrelevant. See table 8.2.

Scarcely any dock workers mentioned the role of foremen as 'leaders' of the workforce. Yet much of the writing about supervision has concentrated on just this aspect, with the very practical aim of finding some way in which to gain the commitment of the labour force to the firm's goals. Because foremen are thought to be integrated into their firms and are also in direct contact with the men, they are regarded as the agents most likely to succeed in bringing about this commitment. Such 'leadership' theories fall into two categories, those which treat leadership as a process of influence and those which treat it as the provision of supportive relationships.[4] The first refers to the foreman's ability to influence his superiors in favour of his subordinates; i.e. from the subordinates' viewpoint, it usually concerns their foreman's ability to provide instrumental benefits. The second refers to types of

[3] There was no association between those who gave a 'Way he treats men' reply to the last question and those who wanted a regular foreman.

[4] R. Likert, *New Patterns of Management* (New York, 1961), chapter 8, is concerned with 'supportive' relationships which contribute to a person's sense of personal worth and importance. D. Pelz, 'Influence: A Key to Effective Leadership in the First-Line Supervisor', *Personnel*, 3, 1952, pp. 209–17, remains the classic statement on influence.

inter-personal relationship, ranging from considerate to autocratic behaviour.[5] These two are not necessarily related: one can conceive of situations in which foremen are 'good' on the influence dimension but 'bad' on the inter-personal style, or they can be 'good' on style but 'bad' on influence.

With regard to leadership as a process of influence, dock workers were sceptical of either the foremen's ability or their desire to act as workforce leaders in dealings with managers. Less than half (42 per cent) thought that their foremen would try to stand up for them with management in the event of any dispute between an individual and the managers, though these replies varied slightly between companies. When given the hypothetical case of the foremen actually deciding to stick up for their men, even fewer (30 per cent) thought that the superintendents would listen to the foremen's views on this subject. Significantly, 94 per cent stated that they would choose *other* agencies to represent their case to management, because these could do it better than foremen and would be more successful in influencing management. The usual pattern was to approach the ganger first and then the shop steward, the steward generally being reckoned the more useful. As the foremen themselves had insufficient autonomy to decide issues of payment and discipline, the two areas of major concern to the men, the men's response was a realistic one in this situation.

With regard to supportive relationships, it has already been demonstrated how little the men valued this aspect of supervision. Nor did the foremen themselves see the provision of these supports as part of their job: even more than the men, foremen thought that technical competence and certain personal attributes unrelated to dealings with the men were the basic qualities required in the job. They rarely selected the ability to get on with the dock workers as an important quality. See table 8.1. Foremen were hardly concerned that their jobs could require them to act in ways which they knew the men would dislike, though 51 per cent reported conflict between their own feelings towards the men and the duties of their position. But only 12 per cent of foremen reported that this conflict would cause them any anxiety. The fact that most foremen had risen from the hold did not mean that they still identified with the men: most were adjusted to being foremen and realistic about what this involved in dealings with the labour force. As a matter of expediency, if it helped to complete a task, 85 per cent of foremen were willing to consider the men's views when taking decisions but did not feel that the men had any legitimate claim on

---

[5] Another style of leadership has been identified by R. W. White and R. Lippitt, 'Leader Behaviour and Member Reactions in Three "Social Climates"', in D. Cartwright and A. Zander (eds.), *Group Dynamics*, 3rd ed. (London, 1968), pp. 318–55. This is the 'laissez faire' style, in which the leader leaves his followers to their own devices.

them. These findings suggest that the foremen themselves are not oriented towards the men to any great extent and scarcely regard themselves as workforce leaders.

If dock foremen preferred any particular 'leadership style', it would almost certainly be what is labelled 'laissez faire', which is really non-leadership because the leader leaves his men to their own devices. This is of course highly congruent with what many dock workers prefer. Foremen showed no interest in the 'considerate' or 'democratic' modes, nor really much interest in the 'autocratic', because all they wanted to do was to give the men orders for the day and then to get on with their own work. Any style of supervision which increased contact with the men at the cost of the foremen's real work would have been resisted. Historically, of course, dock foremen have never been group leaders: the analysis of the casual system showed that foremen did not need to intervene in the men's work, because the combination of hiring practices and craft-like orientations made this unnecessary. Indeed, this could probably have been said at some time or other about all occupations which have regulated themselves at the workplace and have relied on internally created and enforced standards of work behaviour.

Men in the middle?

The earlier discussion of role revealed that foremen did not regard dock workers as significant role definers. Yet changes exactly like those which have occurred in the docks over the last ten years or so have caused foremen considerable role confusion elsewhere. This confusion is often discussed in terms of the 'man in the middle' syndrome, which has the following elements: the foreman is caught in a position of role conflict, in which often incompatible pressures are received from both managers and workers, who together form his role set; this results from his occupancy of a position between the two parties, where he is an agent of management but also in some sense a member of the shopfloor workforce; at the same time, according to this approach, the authority and status of the foreman's position have been eroded by structural changes in industry, so that he has become powerless to control or influence his situation; the result of this conflict is acute psychical strain, which can only be resolved by identification with one or other of the sources of pressure.[6] Those changes which occurred in most other industries over a period of several decades prior to the 1950s have been completed in the docks much more rapidly. Thus dock

[6] The clearest exposition can be found in E. V. Sneider, *Industrial Sociology*, 2nd ed. (New York, 1969), pp. 167–75. Parts of this section have appeared in similar form in S. R. Hill, 'Supervisory Roles and the Man in The Middle: Dock Foremen', *British Journal of Sociology*, 24, 1973, pp. 205–21.

foremen have personal experience within their own careers of the conditions which elsewhere transformed supervisory roles during an earlier era and over a longer time span. Their reactions to this experience throw light on their own position in the industry and their position vis-à-vis the men.

An outsider might easily assume that supervision in the docks was of a variety which enabled foremen to minimize the man-in-the-middle conflict. The descriptions of what foremen did showed that they were relatively unconcerned with labour control (the traditional mode of supervision) and with the personnel functions of hiring, firing, discipline and remuneration. Therefore foremen were not directly concerned with two areas of considerable potential conflict. Managers appeared to want foremen to spend more time in supervision, but the foremen were not aware of this. Work co-ordination did not involve much contact with the men, being more concerned with co-ordinating outsiders, nor was it a function which was likely to lead to role conflict of the man-in-the-middle variety. Work direction did involve a greater contact with the labour force and this could on occasion cause some conflict, insofar as it affected the men's piecework earnings or work autonomy. However the situation might have appeared to be to the outsider, the foremen themselves did think that they were men in the middle and they were nearly unanimous in saying so: 67 per cent said they were in the middle 'nearly all the time', 10 per cent said 'quite often', 15 per cent said 'sometimes', and only 8 per cent said 'rarely or never'. Table 8.3 gives the distribution of replies by company and sector.

However, the information contained in these results ought to be clarified, in order to ascertain just what foremen meant when they said that they were in the middle. Despite the way the question was phrased, asking about conflicts when men and managers wanted foremen to do different things, many foremen (43 per cent) did not have role performance in their minds nor could they quote any specific instances. Instead, they complained of general abuse from both sides. They interpreted this as a way in which the men and management vented their grievances or feelings of frustration with the other party, which they could not do directly for fear of hazarding their delicate and ongoing relationship, or their frustration with the situation in the docks generally. The point about this abuse was that it involved no role pressures, and no behavioural responses were possible: the foremen saw themselves as scapegoats for displaced hostility. In their vernacular, they were the 'pissing posts of the industry'. Their great merit as 'pissing posts' was that they were powerless and so could not retaliate. Any action on their part would, in fact, have jeopardized industrial relations.

The rest of the foremen took the question in the way intended and were able to quote specific instances or general cases. These produced some interesting replies. 32 per cent said that the different expectations of the two parties were not really role pressures in the accepted sense, because both sides regarded the foremen as 'messenger boys' on these occasions: foremen were not expected actually to do anything in response to the pressures except to pass them on to the other side. The outcome of such situations was that managers and the men got together to bargain or compromise, leaving the foremen aside. Even though many of these situations concerned working methods, they always involved piecework earnings as well and thus were outside the foremen's competence.

The smallest group (17 per cent) gave instances which could reasonably be classed as examples of what is conventionally regarded as role conflict, when the foreman was faced with two sets of opposed expectations which both related to the same subject. These invariably concerned alterations in working methods which would affect piecework earnings: the usual case being one in which the men took short cuts to maximize earnings while the superintendent insisted on the job being done properly.

The sanctions which either group could bring to bear on foremen should be considered, because the nature of sanctions and the likelihood that they will be used are probably related to the strain which supposedly characterizes people in this conflict position. If pressures can be ignored with impunity then one would imagine that the foremen's feelings of stress would be reduced. The foremen were asked to describe what the two groups would do if their expectations were not met. They reported that their superintendents rarely took any action in these cases and that verbal reprimands were the limit on these rare occasions, because most superintendents knew that the foremen were powerless in face of the men, and dealt with anything connected with pay themselves. The men could take action by slowing down the work, but they usually preferred to negotiate directly with management or to call in the stewards to negotiate on their behalf if the problem were a serious one.

The obvious conclusion to be drawn from these examples is that the man-in-the-middle epithet is a misnomer in this case: the 'man outside' is a more apt description. This conclusion has been anticipated to some extent by references to the 'marginal men of industry',[7] in which some stress is laid on the isolation of foremen from other groups. But this view is neither systematically developed nor seen as an alternative to the man in the middle. The essence of the man-in-the-middle view is that, however isolated foremen may be in terms of their social relationships with other groups, they nevertheless form part of the firm's chain of command or vertical system of communication. In such a situation, they really are in the middle because they have to act on decisions over

[7] D. E. Wray, 'Marginal Men of Industry: The Foreman', *American Journal of Sociology*, 54, 1949, pp. 298–301.

which they have no control and which are resisted by the other party. The usual movement of communication is thought to be from the top downwards, though presumably it could be vice versa. The communication content is never discussed in expositions of the man-in-the-middle idea, but it is assumed to be relevant to work in one form or another, and not purely expressive.

The alternative description, however, has a different set of implications: the foreman is seen to be outside the main lines of communication and command, either because his role is that of a scapegoat or because he acts merely as the relayer of messages. In the first case, the content of communication is purely expressive, which is possible precisely *because* the foreman is irrelevant to the chain of command. In the second, communication is work-centred in a general sense and the foreman is in the vertical line of communication. But he is expected neither to act as an occupant of a vertical-line position in the way predicted by the man-in-the-middle argument or by the tenets of classical organization theory, nor to exercise authority, nor to act to reconcile conflicting pressures when expectations prove contradictory. What is required is direct contact between men and managers, which occurs as the result of the foreman passing messages, and the line of command passes the foreman by.

Foremen were shown in a previous chapter to be able to define their roles and to persuade management to accept these definitions, in the private sector at least. This was bound up with the structure and functioning of the variety of organization typically found in the docks and the nature of dock work, both of which allowed the foreman to claim the status of expert and to be accepted as such by managers. Such freedom from organizationally derived role pressures helped to minimize role conflicts of all varieties, including that of the man in the middle.

Freedom had more far-reaching effects than this, however, because it allowed the foremen themselves to define the foreman's role as that of the man outside. This definition was in one sense a continuation of the pre-permanency supervisory role, because the old behaviour patterns were retained in dealings with the men. But the effects of such behaviour and the consequences of such a role definition could not be the same in the new situation. The foremen themselves were aware that this was the case: the maintenance of the overt behaviour associated with the traditional role in fact became the means of defining the foreman's position as removed from the arena of industrial conflict. Indeed, under the changed conditions of permanency, such a continuation of old behaviour patterns was to assert a new definition of the foreman's role, whose novelty was disguised by its apparent continuity with previous definitions and by the sanction of traditional occupational norms.

It has been demonstrated that foremen had no need to enforce labour control by means of overt supervision during the casual era because the employment situation of the men made such activity unnecessary. In this situation, the foremen could emphasize other aspects of their job. The labour control function was thus built into the foreman's role, but in such a way as to involve him in no action beyond the act of hiring the individual or gang. Those customary norms of supervisory behaviour which regulated the relationship between foremen and men were in fact predicated on this situation, and both groups expected that the foreman would leave the men alone while he got on with sorting out the work flow. Thus a foreman's role did involve personnel functions such as hiring, firing, discipline and payment, but the power of his position meant that there were no problems associated with the performance of these functions and gave him time to devote himself to the technical areas of the job. The labour control and personnel aspects of supervision required little action on the foreman's part, but they were still significant elements of his old role.

Under the new conditions following decasualization, foremen would have needed to alter their behaviour considerably in order to retain the control which they had exercised over the men before. The problem, of course, was that no one in supervision or management could control the men once permanency was established and the foremen rightly saw no point in attempting to regain ground that was lost for ever, or at least for as long as dock workers had security of earnings and employment. Indeed, managers had unwittingly made the foremen's loss of control even more absolute by removing remuneration from their hands in order to try and centralize wage policy: the unintended consequence of this decision was to deprive foremen of the only real sanction or bargaining counter left.

Faced with this emasculation of their power, foremen probably exaggerated the definition of their role as technical experts. This definition corresponded to the way in which they had traditionally acted and was sanctioned by the occupational norms which men and foremen shared. Moreover, managers had always accepted this definition and appeared likely to continue to do so in the future. The freedom from managerial pressure meant that other foremen's conceptions of the job and the prescriptions of the occupational culture continued to be the most significant influences affecting role creation. Foremen reacted in similar ways to the structural conditions facing them, creating and reinforcing a definition of the supervisory role which was a mutation of the old one. Not only did this definition emphasize technical expertise, but it attempted to pre-empt any demand that foremen reassert their authority over the men. It was noticeable that one of the definitions which foremen had created, and which management had accepted, was precisely that of the man outside: because they had persuaded management that they were powerless to control or command the men, foremen were in fact rarely called upon to enforce managerial directives. In this way, private sector foremen neatly avoided the strains and tensions of the classic man in the middle.[8]

Foremen felt little need to identify either with management or men as the consequence of conflicting pressures; identification with one or other source of pressure is what the man-in-the-middle argument predicts. The low level of involvement with the men has already been noted, while evidence will shortly be presented to show that identification with management was none too high either. But the 'man outside' syndrome did produce some emotional response of a different kind: anger and frustration. 88 per cent thought that they had insufficient authority over the men and that it had declined over recent years, while another 84 per cent thought that the foreman's prestige had declined with it. The result was the isolation of the foreman from his previously central role in docking, the response to which can be summed up in the two phrases previously mentioned: 'We're the pissing posts of the industry' and 'We're just glorified messenger boys now.'

This description of the 'man outside' raises the question of where foremen are to be placed in the hierarchy of their firms. They are obviously not members of the labour force, but their place in the ranks of management is ambiguous if they are so often outside the normal lines of command and communication. 'The first line of management' phrase rings hollowly in this industry as it does in many others. The foremen certainly do not regard themselves as being part of management but locate their position as 'staff'. By saying this they do not identify at all with the white-collar, clerical workers who man the offices, but see themselves as a group which is closer to management and entirely separate from these other employees. They are an élite of non-managerial employees, close to but not a part of management. Public sector foremen see themselves slightly differently, in that they also regard foremen as a separate group, but one which is at the top of a very finely differentiated staff hierarchy and which is in no way close to management. They in fact adopt and identify with the official bureaucratic pecking-order of occupations; so much so, that they accept into their group the status-equivalent, non-operational clerical rank (the 'writers') but exclude assistant foremen with whom they work and whose jobs are similar to their own. They accept the organization's definition of their position. Interestingly, both public and private foremen feel that the foremen in their firms tend to stick together as groups on their own. This provides additional evidence in support of the view that foremen form a separate stratum in most firms, identifying with neither the men nor management but with their colleagues. See tables 8.4, 5.

[8] Definitions in the public sector were more bureaucratic, but foremen were protected against conflicting pressures by poor communications.

The foremen's own self-assessment of their position and their identification with a non-managerial grouping of other foremen can be supplemented by a brief consideration of their structural and normative integration in management. Structural integration was probably not high, to judge from the data on interaction obtained during the activity analysis, which demonstrated that many foremen had little contact with managers and what little contact they did have was with immediate superiors rather than anyone more senior. (Management above superintendent level appeared to be a different world from the foremen's.) The evidence of the 'man outside' syndrome certainly suggests that integration is not complete in some areas of the foreman's role.

The extent to which managerial norms were accepted is less clear-cut.[9] P.L.A. foremen clearly did not accept many of the rules which were supposed to govern their actions and used communication blockages in order to conceal their evasion of these rules. Private sector foremen were far more integrated in this context and rarely disagreed with the rules of behaviour, partly of course because they in fact defined many of the managerial norms themselves. Though even among the private sector foremen there was apparently disagreement with some of the rules of behaviour, which is most noticeable in the pejorative references they made to 'the man outside'; these indicated that they were not entirely happy to be by-passed on certain matters. Overall, private sector foremen conveyed the impression that they were integrated into the management hierarchy neither in terms of inter-action nor in terms of their self-perception (nor in terms of promotion and career prospects), but that they formed a separate group. However, they were more firmly integrated normatively and agreed with management on most of the rules of action, whereas the public authority foremen appeared to be alienated from management in every respect.

When social scientists have been concerned with the relationship between foremen and men, their interest has mainly centred on the leadership potential and the role conflicts of first-line supervisors. The two go together: because his position allows him to act as a work group leader, the foreman is also potentially in the middle between his group and his managers. Such arguments assume both that foremen have their proper place in the firm's hierarchy of communication and authority and that their roles are organizationally determined. Integration of foremen in their firms in any sense of the phrase, is not thought

---

[9] Norms were chosen rather than goals, because organizational goals assume that there is a consensus between managers, at least, about what these goals are, and that they are sufficiently explicit to be described, neither of which assumptions necessarily applied to the docks. The P.L.A. had conflicting goals, and different levels of management had different views about the purposes of the organization. There were fewer conflicts in private sector firms but their goals were rarely made explicit.

to be a problem. It can be argued that such assumptions are plausible in the U.S., where most has been written about supervision, and reflect the structural features of industrial organization in that society. But it would seem that they become less plausible in the different structure of the London docks and in many other British firms.

The system of supervision found in the docks and some other industries depends on occupational rather than organizational roles. Sub-contracting of the hiring and management of labour to foremen was firmly rooted in British industry until the early years of this century, particularly among craft occupations.[10] Sub-contracting has died out, but the withdrawal of managers from certain areas of labour administration often survives to the present day. The system has always been most effective, indeed it has only really been possible, when strong occupational cultures and sanctions have provided internalized controls and standards of workmanship.

Two factors made possible the use of occupational roles. In the first place, early nineteenth-century principles of laissez faire provided factory owners with an inadequate and even perverse basis for the large-scale social organization of production. Thus pre-industrial models had to be adapted, one of which was the craft-occupational.[11] In the second, mechanization spread so slowly in many British industries that a number of crafts had industrial roles of central importance and élite status until at least the early twentieth century. It can be argued that in this situation other occupations and employers continued to follow and emulate the craft model which remained highly visible, for various reasons. Not the least of these reasons has been the great importance of occupational consciousness at all levels of British industry and the high social status accorded crafts and professions, which have typically regulated work on non-organizational principles.[12]

This model of industrial experience was probably fairly common in Europe, but experience in the U.S. appears to have been different. Organizations appear to have been designed more self-consciously and

---

[10] K. E. Thurley and H. Wirdenius, *Supervision: A Reappraisal* (London, 1973), p. 5. Many supervisory roles have, of course, been consciously created by managers when there have been no relevant occupational roles: the chemical and electronics industries are good illustrations.

[11] The enlarged personal household was another: see J. Foster, *Class Struggle and the Industrial Revolution* (London, 1974), pp. 174–82, and C. Hill, *Society and Puritanism in Pre-Revolutionary England* (London, 1964), Chapter 13. S. Pollard, *The Genesis of Modern Management* (London, 1965), Chapter 7, discusses the problems facing early industrialists. (Whereas, imperial Germany, another example of early industrialization, did have an effective model of social organization appropriate for factory production; I am indebted to Donald G. MacRae for this information.)

[12] For a fuller discussion of the effect of this, see S. R. Hill and K. E. Thurley, 'Sociology and Industrial Relations', *British Journal of Industrial Relations*, 12, 1974, pp. 147–70.

organizational roles given precedence, at least from the early twentieth century.[13] Moreover, in the U.S. a foreman is often correctly described as the first level of management and is integrated into the vertical line, because he has a real prospect of promotion through the hierarchy. The usual British tradition, on the contrary, has been that most foremen are not promoted further, with the result that the job of supervisor is the last in the manual hierarchy rather than the first in the managerial. Therefore, many traditional social science propositions about foremen appear to be culturally specific and do not apply in at least certain areas of British industry.

Therefore it is scarcely surprising that dock foremen should see themselves neither as leaders nor really as men in the middle. The history of supervision in the docks and the model of supervision which still exists in many other industries have created a different tradition of foremanship. What is noticeable in the docks is how both the men and managers share with foremen similar conceptions of the supervisory role. Foremen and men share a common occupational culture which contains expectations of certain types of supervisory behaviour in many areas of the role, while managers accept the definitions of these two groups as legitimate and inevitable. Significantly, the previous work experience of many managers has probably provided them with little knowledge of other modes of industrial organization.

Dock supervision is now changing, however. The growth of a new type of employment relationship for the men and the greater sensitivity of firms to labour costs effectively destroyed the sub-contracting element of supervision. Much of the old dependence and personal loyalty which bound men and foremen disappeared as a result. This left only the shared occupational model of the foremen's rights and duties as the underpinning of the traditional form of supervision. But without any sanctions of their own, without any network of personal bonds and without the exercise of managerial authority on their behalf, foremen then found that they could not enforce the traditional rules. Over a period of years much of the old custom and practice was destroyed, often deliberately, because dock workers discovered that they had no reason to comply with traditional modes of behaviour and could improve their lot by new types of action. In other words, the men realized that those occupational norms which had once constrained their interests could easily be redefined once the power of foremen and managers was shown to be ineffective: without sanctions, the occupational model was found to be hollow inside.

Foremen reacted to the men's initiative by modifying the content of

[13] The great emphasis on the self-conscious and deliberate designing of organizations can be inferred from the creation and dissemination of organization theory and management science in the U.S. from Taylor onwards. This contrasts with the reluctance of the British to have much to do with such notions, at least until recently.

the old role while preserving the outward forms. They exaggerated the technical aspects and made no effort to regain the old personnel functions. But how long this mutated role can last is another question. Two further types of pressure on foremen might be anticipated. Managers may become disenchanted with an occupational role which fails to deliver the goods and try to develop some organizational definition which will bring foremen back into the vertical line and make them men in the middle. This bureaucratization of the foreman's role is unlikely to occur without the prior bureaucratization of the organization as a whole, however. Nor will it have much success until managers themselves regain their lost authority, which implies major alterations in the balance of power in the industry and the modification of the Scheme. Alternatively, supervision could be further devalued so that it 'withers away'. Given the amount of autonomy the men already have, they could easily be allocated some of the foremen's technical functions. On mechanized berths, where the technical component has been simplified, such a redistribution of functions would probably be viable. Self-regulating, autonomous work groups would recognize and try to build on the reality of shopfloor control, though the men would have to be persuaded that the conflicts of interest between themselves and management could be reconciled sufficiently for them to act on behalf of their employers. But in either of these hypothetical developments foremen would no longer act as the messenger boys and 'pissing posts' of men and management, and it may well be that both sides would prefer foremen to continue to act as the shock absorbers of industrial relations rather than alter the situation.

CHAPTER 9

Community, Friends and Family

Occupational Community

There is a popular belief that dock workers, like members of some other occupations, form distinct and closed social communities:

> The miners, the sailors, the longshoremen . . . form isolated masses, almost a 'race apart'. They live in their own separate communities: the coal patch, the ship, the water-front district . . .[1]

The structural position of docking, which is carried out only in the one industry, in a small number of locations and frequently in geographical isolation has indeed fostered the growth of docking neighbourhoods around the dock gates of many ports. It is obviously important to establish to what extent such occupational communities occurred in London during the late 1960s and early 1970s.

In its simplest form, the notion of occupational community holds that workers in some occupations mix socially outside the workplace more often with people in their own line of work than they do with people in other jobs.[2] The social community of occupational members need not form a physical neighbourhood; all that is necessary is that people should seek out the company of other occupational members more often than not. Occupational membership is held to be so significant for the individual that he allows his work to spill over into his leisure: work is thus a central life interest which dictates life outside work. More recently, some people have linked occupational community with working-class traditionalism: occupational communities which are co-extensive with geographical localities and form physically distinct neighbourhoods, and in which there are 'closely knit cliques' of friends, workmates, neighbours and relatives who share the same work, tend to be more traditionally proletarian than other sorts of community.[3]

---

[1] C. Kerr and A. Siegel, 'The Inter-Industry Propensity to Strike—An International Comparison', reprinted in A. Flanders (ed.), *Collective Bargaining* (London, 1969), pp. 138–60.

[2] R. Blauner, 'Work Satisfaction and Industrial Trends in Modern Society', in W. Galenson and S. M. Lipset (eds.), *Labor and Trade Unionism* (New York, 1960), p. 350.

[3] D. Lockwood, 'Sources of Variation in Working Class Images of Society', *Sociological Review*, 14, 1966, pp. 249–67, and J. H. Goldthorpe, D. Lockwood *et al.*, *The Affluent Worker* (Cambridge, 1968), vol. 2, pp. 74–5.

The structural position of such communities, which are typically inward-looking and isolated, means that they are insulated from the dominant social ideology and often generate their own sub-cultural values in opposition. The solidarity of these communities is linked to the sociability of individual members at work and outside.

There are two ways in which membership of an occupation may be related to patterns of sociability. The first is the direct extension of social ties from the workplace into leisure: the continuation of associations made at work into leisure-time friendships. The second is more indirect, because it is not work but the local community which is important: for example, friendships made with neighbours, ex-schoolmates or friends of friends and kin. If the community contains a large proportion of people from one occupation the friendship patterns are likely to reflect this distribution but the links with the workplace will be incidental. In the first case it is the workplace and occupation which matters, while in the second it is the outside community which is important. These two ways may be distinct practically as well as analytically. For example, members of an occupation may share an orientation to work which devalues the place of workmates as non-work friends. But at the same time, they may also share what is thought of as the usual working-class characteristic of making friends from the 'givens' of social life, many of which involve the local community.[4] The occupational structure of the local area may thus create patterns of friendship which appear to be the carry-overs of work relationships.

Some separation can be seen between work and community in the London docks. It was shown earlier that sociability between members of work groups or more widely based work associations was not particularly important: people did not lay great emphasis on the quality of the personal bonds and human relations at the workplace. A corollary of this is that work-based associations outside the dock gates are relatively unimportant: there is very little direct extension of work friendship into leisure. 47 per cent of men and 36 per cent of foremen stated that they saw a lot of other people from the industry outside work, but the more significant figures are those which show that only 23 and 19 per cent respectively reported that they saw much of the people with whom they actually worked. Discussion of the quality rather than frequency of friendships indicates that only 32 and 18 per cent respectively of the two groups included 'close friends' among these docking friends. Analysis of the nature of social contacts shows that most were casual or semi-casual, even for the sub-groups with work-based friends, over 90 per cent occurring in pubs.[5] These patterns of

[4] The terminology of the 'givens' of social life is coined by J. H. Goldthorpe, D. Lockwood et al., op. cit., vol. 3 (1969), p. 91.

[5] Other information indicates that the entertaining of friends at home was fairly common, but few of these docking friends were in the home-visiting category.

association show just how little spill-over there is of work into leisure.[6]

Data on friendship patterns more generally provide further information about the role of the occupation. I asked people to think of their three best friends, the people closest to them who were not their relatives, and to say what jobs they did. Dock workers gave 337 friends, of whom 43 per cent were employed as dock labourers, tally clerks or foremen in the docks. Foremen gave 194, of whom 23 per cent were employed in the industry. (A recent study of shipbuilding, an occupation similar to docking, found that 33 per cent of the shipbuilders' friends were employed in the same industry.[7]) If the data are expressed as the proportion of people who had at least *one* close friend working in the industry, then 56 per cent of men and 31 per cent of foremen had one or more friends in the docks.[8]

Such friendships do depend partly on contacts originally made in the docks, though not always as the result of working together. Most friendships were more indirect, however, and depended on dock workers getting to know each other through institutions not related to work.[9] Table 9.1 shows how important the local area of residence was for making friends, via agencies such as pubs and clubs, schools and neighbourhood. Kin was also significant, but to a lesser extent. The impact of the local community can also be gauged by comparing the proportions of docking friends in the different areas in which people lived. London's East End, the urban district of Thurrock and Gravesend are all areas which have traditionally contained large numbers of dock workers.[10] People who live in these areas are more likely to have dock friends than those elsewhere. See table 9.2. In addition, more than 80 per cent of the men in the East End and Thurrock reported that their

---

[6] It suggests, moreover, that the aspect of work as a central life interest which is concerned with the overlap of work and leisure companionship does not apply here.

[7] R. K. Brown *et al.*, 'The Contours of Solidarity: Social Stratification and Industrial Relations in Shipbuilding', *British Journal of Industrial Relations*, 10, 1972, pp. 12–41.

[8] Both sets of differences between men and foremen are significant at 0·01 level: $z=4·55$ and 3·38 respectively.

[9] The reliability of this approach, which is used frequently in other research, is debatable, because the information on the origin of friendships relies entirely on the respondents' recollections of where they first met their friends. In many cases, friendships had lasted well over twenty years and the origins were somewhat obscure in the minds of respondents. At the same time, when people both work in the same place and live in the same area, difficulty in distinguishing the two may be expected.

[10] Gravesend is not usually referred to as a separate area in analysis because of the very small numbers living there. It is, however, included with the East End and Thurrock as part of the docking area. Thurrock includes Tilbury and Grays. The East End areas in which people lived included: Bethnal Green, Stepney, Poplar, Cubitt Town, Mile End, East and West Ham, Plaistow, Canning Town, Silvertown, Southwark, Bermondsey, Deptford and Lewisham. 45 per cent of the men and 38 per cent of foremen lived in Thurrock; 21 and 22 per cent in the East End; 2 and 5 per cent in Gravesend, and 32 and 35 in other areas.

areas contained a lot of dock workers, against 45 per cent of those who lived elsewhere. People who lived outside the traditional communities had dock friends, and had come to know many of those friends they mentioned during earlier periods of residence in the East End or Thurrock.[11] The distinction between traditional and other areas should not be overdrawn, however, because the coefficients of association between area and dock friends are not high and fair numbers of people in other areas also described their areas as having a lot of dock workers.[12]

Several conclusions can be made about foremen. The most significant is that they have fewer docking friends than the men, which holds good even when area of residence is considered. Foremen rely much less on social bonds formed with others in the industry than do dock workers. Their dock worker friendships mainly originated outside the docks and were not work-based, although all their dock foremen friends stemmed from within the industry. Differences in the extent of docking friendships are related to the area of residence, as was the case with the men. It is clear that foremen are more inclined to hold themselves separate from other people in the industry outside work, and occupational membership is less salient for them than it is for the men.

The areas in which dock workers lived were rarely 'self-contained', because the occupational composition of neighbourhoods included a wide mix of mainly manual occupations. Everyone was asked what jobs their immediate neighbours had, to which only 12 per cent of men and 3 per cent of foremen replied that they had neighbours who worked in the docks. Patterns of friendship reveal the same situation, given that most contacts originated in the local communities. Between half and two-thirds of those who lived in the East End and Thurrock areas had at least one friend working in the docks, but it is equally true that 61 and 60 per cent respectively of the men in the two areas either had no friends at all in the industry or had one at the most. Taking all the men and foremen regardless of area of residence, 69 per cent of men and 87 per cent of foremen had at the *most* one friend in the industry.[13]

Data from the 1961 and 1966 Census can be used to describe the areas under consideration, though the sizes of the Census districts are too large to be really useful (they may conceal smaller areas where docking is more heavily represented). Table 9.3 shows that, in 1961, Bermondsey had the highest concentration of dock workers and docking formed the largest single occupation in the borough. Poplar, Stepney

[11] It is interesting that many people moved from the old docking areas in order to buy houses, property being more easily available outside the old areas.

[12] $\Phi = \cdot 34$ and $\cdot 24$ respectively for the men's and foremen's data in table 9.2, significant at the 0·06 and 0·05 levels respectively. The coefficients of association between area and having at least *one* dock friend are ·31 and ·24 at the 0·01 and 0·05 levels respectively.

[13] These figures are percentages of those who reported having friends and not of the whole sample, some of whom had no friends.

and Thurrock had large proportions of dockers. Comparison of 1961
and 1966 shows that the proportion declined in Thurrock in those five
years, but the changeover to the new and much larger Greater London
boroughs makes comparison impossible in the East End. However, the
halving of the number of London dock workers since 1961 must have
had an impact on the traditional East End docking communities, while
the massive rebuilding of the area and relocation of the population
over the last twenty-five years has made the preservation of old communities even less likely. The single-industry area with one dominant
occupation could not be found in the places where these workers
lived.

The people whom I interviewed lived in widely dispersed areas,
often many miles from work. Table 9.4 shows no significant clustering
of homes around the gates of the Tilbury and the West India/Millwall
docks. In the Manchester area, 40 per cent of the dock workers used to
live within one mile of the dock gates and formed a docking community.[14] 21 per cent lived more than four miles away. Among these
London workers, less than 20 per cent lived within one mile of their
workplace at either dock. 43 per cent of those at the West India/
Millwall and 27 per cent of those at Tilbury lived within two miles,
while well over half of both groups lived more than two miles away;
there were about equal numbers of people living over four miles away
as lived less than two miles from work.

The men who lived closest to the docks did not participate more
noticeably in occupational communities outside work than those who
lived further away. Cross-tabulation of the friendship data with the
distances from workplaces gave no indication of strong docking communities in the immediate vicinity of the docks. Men living within half a
mile of the workplace were no more likely to have one friend or more
of dock worker status than those living even four or more miles away,
and the distribution of all friends of dock worker status was evenly
spread up to a four-and-a-half-mile radius.[15]

What is more important than geographical separateness or isolation
is how far people choose members of the same occupation from the
fairly wide range of potential friends which the geographical neighbourhood provides, and how far they regard themselves as forming a
community. People in Thurrock and the East End are obviously more
involved in occupational communities than those who live elsewhere,
though the coherence and exclusiveness of such communities must not
be exaggerated. Local neighbourhoods are important for the initial
contacts between dock workers, but the further development of friendships may have as much to do with the shared values and experiences of
docking as with those of the neighbourhood. In other words, the job is

[14] *The Dock Worker*, pp. 43–7.
[15] Beyond 4½ miles there was a decline.

probably influential in determining which acquaintances become close friends.

These relatively open patterns of sociability have little impact on the strength of occupational solidarity and identification, because sociability is not necessarily related to a sense of identification in the ways suggested by theories about traditional workers. It was shown earlier that gangs at the workplace can be manifestations of occupational solidarity but not involve sociability, while dock workers can identify with men in other ports whom they have never met. There are no grounds for believing that further sociability outside work is a necessary underpinning either of this sort of solidarity or of a more extensive working-class consciousness.

Friends

Friendship patterns provide information relevant to the discussion of social class as well as the nature of docking, because they constitute the relational element of class analysis. The men interviewed in this survey are set firmly in the contemporary working-class tradition so far as the status and origins of their friendships are concerned: less than a sixth of all their close friends had white-collar jobs and all the rest were manual workers. See table 9.5. 74 per cent of the men had only manual workers as friends, leaving 16 per cent with one or more white-collar friends.[16] These friends were made the same way as their dock worker ones, via the local area and the family. See table 9.6. Area and family overlapped of course, because friends made via relatives were often resident in the neighbourhood. The description of how other manual working-class individuals make friends fits these dock workers:

> ... they would appear to build up their friendship relations largely on the basis of social contacts that are in the first instance 'given'. Actually *making* friends—through personal choice and initiative— from among persons with whom no structured relationships already exist could not be regarded as at all a typical feature of their way of life.[17]

Foremen had far more friends of non-manual status than the men. 44 per cent of all the friends they mentioned were in white-collar occupations, while 58 per cent of all foremen had at least one close friend who was a white-collar worker, which indicates a considerable amount of interaction between foremen and middle-class individuals outside work. It is not clear how far this pattern is the result of foremen

---

[16] This compares with the similar figure of 76 per cent which was found in the Luton study: J. H. Goldthorpe, D. Lockwood *et al.*, op. cit., vol 3 (1969), p. 109.
[17] ibid., p. 91.

consciously choosing their friends in the manner commonly expected of members of the middle class.[18] Foremen claim to have met many of their friends, manual and non-manual, in the same ways as dock workers met theirs: via the 'givens' of social life rather than via unstructured relationships. But it is noticeable that foremen's white-collar friends tended to originate in certain of the 'givens' rather than in others: the pub or club and school are slightly less important, and neighbours slightly more important than with their manual friends.[19]

Area has an obvious effect, but it is not possible to tell whether foremen live in separate areas which are more middle-class than the men's, or whether they live in the same areas but choose to associate more with the white-collar residents than the manual workers. Both alternatives assume that areas have mixed populations of manual and non-manual workers, though the former presupposes a greater proportion of non-manual workers than the latter. The first alternative is compatible with the idea that people do not really 'choose' their friends, because foremen's friendships merely reflect the social composition of their neighbourhoods (though the decision to live in a particular area may be a deliberate choice which is influenced by the possibilities of meeting certain types of people). The second suggests that foremen do actively select their friends in the supposedly middle-class manner.

The census is not sufficiently discriminating to identify the characters of separate localities within broader areas, but the two main docking areas, Thurrock and the East End, have fairly similar social mixes. The data in table 9.3 show that one of the London boroughs has a very small proportion of white-collar employees but the other main docking boroughs and Thurrock are similar, while the boroughs on the periphery of the docks are more white-collar. The overall similarity of the two main docking areas may be surprising at first glance, because of the different patterns of development over the last two decades. The urban district of Thurrock is part of the corridor alongside the Thames in South East Essex which has expanded rapidly since the early 1950s with the advent of new industries, many of which are technologically modern and employ a variety of occupational groups, and with the increase in numbers of office workers commuting to London. The Thurrock population increased by half between 1951 and 1971. This buoyant growth compares with the static or declining populations of the various London boroughs and the steady movement of manufacturing industry out of the area. Yet both are predominantly proletarian localities which contain large minorities of white-collar inhabitants. Within the areas

[18] How far choice and non-structured friendships characterize all the middle class is not clear, of course, given the paucity of information.
[19] Kin may be more important for the white-collar friends of foremen than of dock workers because of the differences in the numbers of non-manual relatives.

used as census boundaries there were obviously communities with significant numbers of middle-class, non-manual residents, but the extent to which these formed segregated communities is not apparent from the available data.

The interviews show that area of residence and home ownership are associated with friendship patterns. For example, table 9.7 shows that in Thurrock the proportion of dock workers with only manual-worker friends was higher than in the areas classified as 'other',[20] while the East End workers came between these two extremes. The spread between localities was not so great among foremen but the 'other' areas still produced fewer people with only manual-worker friends than Thurrock or the East End. This suggests that the social compositions of the other areas probably differ from Thurrock and the East End.

Patterns of home ownership also varied between areas, so that people living in the East End and Thurrock were considerably less likely to own their homes than those elsewhere.[21] See table 9.8. Home ownership and friendship bear a definite relationship to each other: dividing people into those who only have manual-worker friends and those with at least one non-manual shows small but positive associations between home ownership and white-collar friends.[22] Taking the figures for foremen and breaking them down according to the various areas, these associations can be found in Thurrock and the East End, though only to a small extent.[23] But home ownership and choice of friends are not related in the other areas where white-collar friends are more common for owners and non-owners alike. Thus there are links between home ownership and area of residence on the one hand and, on the other, the friends foremen have. Among the men, there is no significant relationship between home ownership and friendship when the overall association is broken down into the three major categories of locality. However, the small numbers of non-manual friends make such statistical manipulation of the data unrewarding where dock workers are concerned.

Foremen are considerably more likely than the men to be home owners, 63 per cent of the former owning their own homes against 35 per cent of the latter.[24] House purchase has frequently involved changing areas: 39 per cent of foremen and 23 per cent of dock workers

[20] Significant at 0·001 level: $X^2 = 12·5$ with 1 degree of freedom.

[21] Significant at 0·05 level: $X^2 = 6·4$ with 1 degree of freedom.

[22] $\Phi = ·21$ for the men and ·29 for foremen; both are significant at 0·05 level. If the division is made on the basis of manual only vs. non-manual only, then the association among foremen becomes much more powerful: ·52 at same level. The small number of men with only non-manual friends makes it impracticable to use this division for dock workers, however.

[23] $\Phi = ·34$ and ·29 respectively, both significant at 0·05 level.

[24] Difference is significant at 0·001 level: $X^2 = 16·32$ with 1 degree of freedom.

(61 per cent and 67 per cent of the home owners in the two groups) reported that they had moved from one area to another, because there were more houses available for purchase outside the traditional docking areas.[25] Movement of this sort shows the relative instability of local communities which has been characteristic of the docking areas for many years and has influenced patterns of sociability. Among the people interviewed here, 76 per cent of foremen and 69 per cent of men had moved house at least once during their adult lives: 65 per cent of foremen and 46 per cent of men had moved out of one area into another, while the rest had moved within the same area. The information about how close people live to their parents also reflects the relative instability of local communities. Less than half the men in any area live near their parents, while those in the East End and other areas are less likely than the Thurrock ones to live near.[26] Population movements, for the purposes of home ownership or otherwise, suggest that stable working-class communities, let alone stable occupational communities, are not as common as might have been anticipated in dockland.

Foremen are more likely to own their homes and to have moved from one area to another for whatever reason. This suggests an element of deliberate choice in deciding where to live, which may be connected with the greater proportion of white-collar friends they have. Certainly, when foremen were asked about the sort of people they would like to have as friends, they gave replies which seemed to indicate some preference for friends of non-manual status. See table 9.9. People with good education, with similar backgrounds to their own or with interesting and responsible jobs were the main categories chosen out of a list of possible types of friend.[27] This contrasts with the men's replies where similarity of background was the main response. The replies reinforce the picture created by the various other pieces of information, that many foremen do differ from the men in their lives outside work and display traits which indicate their partial assimilation into the middle class, or at least their desire to be assimilated. It was noted earlier how foremen distanced themselves from the occupational communities outside work, and now it appears that they have succeeded even in distancing themselves from the working class, though this latter process is not as marked as the former.

[25] Home ownership could mean moving some distance. 18 per cent of those men living within 4 miles of the dock gates were owners, against 60 per cent of those over 4 miles. The foremen's figures are 51 and 78 per cent respectively.

[26] The dock worker figures for those living 'near' their parents (i.e. within 5 minutes' car drive) are 28 per cent of East End residents, 31 per cent of 'other' residents and 46 per cent of those in Thurrock. The proportions with respect to parents-in-law are 23, 35 and 52 per cent.

[27] The question and structured replies were taken from J. H. Goldthorpe, D. Lockwood et al., op. cit., vol. 3 (1969). The 'similar background' reply refers to non-manual workers in the foremen's case and manual workers in the men's.

The Family

Traditional working-class family life is often characterized by its lack of home-centredness, particularly as far as the husband is concerned, which is manifest in the segregated leisure activities of husband and wife and the communal kin-based sociability of the family unit as a whole. How far this characterization is now mainly of historical interest is not clear in view of the relative paucity of recent empirical information, but it clearly does not fit the patterns of family life to be found among the dock workers involved in my research.

With regard to the segregation of the husband from his wife and children, two criteria show how little separation there was. On the friendship criterion, most of the people mentioned by husbands were also family friends shared by husbands and wives together; 64 per cent of the men's close friends and 86 per cent of the foremen's were in fact joint friends.[28] So far as leisure activities were concerned, wives were with their husbands nearly all the time except for visits to the pub or club. Table 9.10 shows the proportions of joint activities on different occasions, from which it can be seen that levels of 89 per cent joint activity and over were common in both groups.

The period used for the analysis of leisure activities was the week prior to the interview. During this time about a third and a half of men and foremen respectively never went to a pub or club, while the majority of the remainder visited only once or twice in the seven days. Dock workers' wives accompanied their husbands on two-fifths of these occasions and foremen's wives on nearly half, while only a fifth of all the men and one-tenth of all foremen failed ever to take their wives when they went to the pub or club. Thus visiting pubs and clubs were exceptional activities, which refutes the popular view of dockers as traditional workers who spend most of their free time drinking in all-male company with their mates.

Leisure was largely home- and family-centred as well. 70 per cent of the men and about the same proportion of foremen spent four or more nights at home in the week prior to being interviewed, without going out for any length of time.[29] The great majority spent more than half their free time in the home itself. Those activities outside the home

---

[28] Significant at 0·001 level: $X^2 = 28·7$ with 1 degree of freedom. No data was collected on the extent to which wives had their own circle of friends independently of their husbands, which is one aspect of the segregation of the traditional family.

[29] Number of nights at home includes 'out of home activities' of 60 minutes or less. But *all* visits to pubs, relatives, friends are included even when less than 60 minutes. When these specific activities exceed 60 minutes, they are classified as a whole category: i.e. are not recorded as time at home even when part of the evening is spent at home, say before or after visiting the pub. This in fact *deflates* the amount of time which was actually spent at home.

which were joint were also usually family-centred, suggesting that the total proportion of activities which were not in some way family-centred was small.

The importance of the communal sociability of kin and friends seems to have declined in comparison with earlier times. Most of the people reported that they saw their own parents and their parents-in-law fairly frequently: 73 per cent of the men saw their own parents at least once a week and 69 per cent saw their parents-in-law as often; the foremen's figures were 67 and 50 per cent.[30] The details of activity in the week prior to interviewing indicate that about four-fifths of the men saw some relatives in that time, either at home or in their relatives' homes. About half had more than one contact in the week. Most of the visiting was with parents, parents-in-law and children (if these were independent of their parents): 70 per cent of the relatives the men saw were immediate kin and 75 per cent of the foremen's contacts were in this category. There was relatively little contact with relatives outside the immediate family circle. Wives may possibly have had more contact with a wider circle of kin, though there is no information available on this subject from the interviews. But it is significant that the joint activities of husband and wife involved frequent contact with close relatives and little with wider kin. Familial values are obviously important, but they do not necessarily extend to the wider form of communal sociability.

Nor was the traditional gregariousness of the working-class community particularly noticeable. Visits to the pub or club involved contact with friends and acquaintances, but these visits occurred less often than might have been anticipated. One alternative form of social contact is home visiting, but visiting friends or entertaining them in one's own home accounted for a fairly small proportion of either group's activities in the week prior to the interview. There was some home entertaining, however, which should help to dispel the notion that home visiting is alien to traditional workers, and about three-quarters of both groups said that they and their wives had friends around to the house at least once a month. About a third reported home entertaining once a week.

[30] These figures are proportions of people whose parents or in-laws were still alive, not of the whole sample. Not surprisingly, there was an obvious association between the frequency of contact and the closeness of residence. Among the men, 55 per cent of those who lived within five minutes' car journey from their relatives claimed to see them once or more per week, against 18 per cent of those who lived further away. The figures for foremen were 55 and 13 per cent respectively. People who lived more than 3½ miles from the dock gates were less likely to live near their parents than those who lived nearer the docks. 77 per cent of the men who lived less than 3½ miles from the docks and had parents alive lived near their parents, against 36 per cent of those who lived further away. At 82 and 71 per cent, the foremen's data were not so greatly affected. (Only 43 per cent of foremen had parents still alive.)

In sum, family life revealed a low segregation of leisure time between husband and wife and a large number of joint activities, a considerable degree of home-centredness, social intercourse with very close family members but not with more distant kin, and some contact with friends but not a great deal. In short, both men and foremen had 'privatized' life-styles.

Another aspect of family life is also of interest. This concerns the jobs that relatives do and their place in the occupational hierarchy. I collected data on the jobs of the fathers and fathers-in-law, brothers and brothers-in-law of all the respondents. The information is presented in table 9.11. People's origins, measured by the jobs of their fathers and fathers-in-law, were almost entirely manual working class. Both dock workers and foremen were similar in this respect. But the information on siblings shows a slightly different pattern, because a minority of brothers and sisters (classified according to their husbands' jobs) have in fact moved upwards in the occupational system. Foremen are somewhat more likely than the men to have white-collar brothers and brothers-in-law. The data therefore suggest that dock workers are members of families which are fairly stable working class, so far as their own generation and the preceding generation of close relatives are concerned, while foremen share the same sort of social origins as the men but have brothers and sisters who are slightly less stable members of the working class. Some foremen tend to be members of upwardly mobile generations, though this remains only a tendency because many foremen are indistinguishable from the men in this respect.[31]

The similarity of social background is reinforced when finer categories of occupation than the crude manual/non-manual division are used. The data on relatives show how docking has retained one of its traditional characteristics through to the present day: the kinship system of labour recruitment. The study of the Manchester docks found that 75 per cent of the labour force were the sons of dock workers in 1951.[32] Among the people I interviewed, direct father–son inheritance accounted for 67 per cent of the men and 75 per cent of the foremen (consolidating the categories of dock worker and foremen in table 9.11 into one for the

[31] The differences between the proportions of the two groups with brothers and brothers-in-law of non-manual status are statistically significant ($z=3\cdot55$ and $4\cdot22$ respectively at the $0\cdot01$ level), but the substantive importance should not be exaggerated in view of the comparatively small differences. The positive association which existed previously between area of residence and friends of non-manual status is not repeated between area and the occupations of brothers and brothers-in-law. The second correlate, home ownership, is positively but only slightly associated with the occupations of the men's brothers-in-law ($\Phi=\cdot27$ at the $0\cdot05$ level), but it is not significantly related to the jobs of the men's brothers. There is a positive and reasonably sized association between ownership and the occupational level of brothers in the foremen's data ($\Phi=\cdot37$ at the $0\cdot01$ level), but no significant association between ownership and jobs of brothers-in-law.

[32] *The Dock Worker*, p. 50.

purpose of father–son inheritance). Other categories of relatives, such as brothers, fathers and brothers-in-law, also included large numbers of dock workers. More distant kin were frequently employed in the docks, though here there is no information on precise proportions. Only 10 per cent of men and 8 per cent of foremen could not name one relative who worked in the docks.

Just as docking as an occupation passes down through families, so does the specific job of foreman. 52 per cent of the private sector foremen had one relative who was or had been a foreman in the industry. This was in contrast to the men, only 29 per cent of whom were related to foremen. Both inheritances are illustrative of the ascriptive and personalistic ethos prevailing in the industry. Both are important for the occupation and employers alike.

The presence of older relatives in the industry should facilitate the transmission of occupational culture via anticipatory socialization (i.e. socialization prior to entering the occupation), particularly when these relatives are members of the immediate family.[33] It also strengthens the historical memory of the labour force, so that past events are indirectly experienced even by very young workers in the industry,[34] while the inheritance of the foreman's job shows how employers follow the traditional ascriptive practices when filling positions of responsibility. In the smaller firms which existed prior to the amalgamations, close personal bonds grew up between employers and foremen, with the result that many employers felt that they could trust their foremen's relatives more than they could strangers when appointing to supervisory posts.[35] It was shown earlier how firms had followings of families who were thought to be more loyal and trustworthy workers; the same was true with foremen's families. There would therefore appear to be some anticipatory socialization for foremen as well as workers.

The large proportion of docking kin is relevant to the discussion of the occupational community outside work, mentioned earlier in the context of friendship patterns. A second aspect of occupational community, in some definitions at least, is the overlapping of kinship ties at work and outside. Such overlapping was apparent among the people interviewed here, because so many had relatives in the docks, particularly fathers. This situation must have helped the transmission of occupational

---

[33] Most workers said that contact with extended kin when learning the job was less common than it had been in the past.

[34] The impact of historical memory on the industrial relations of the industry is of course legendary. The high average age and great length of service of most dock workers means that the *direct* experience of many reaches back two, three and even four decades.

[35] It was also true that new foremen were often promoted from the ranks of the gangers, who in turn were often relatives of existing foremen. The blue-eyed system tended to favour the emergence of foremen's relatives as gangers because these men had the most useful ties.

values and norms, particularly in the past when docking communities appear to have been more closely knit. But it has not necessarily led to the sorts of sociability which constitute a community among kin. Earlier evidence suggested that frequent contact with parents was normal for most of the sample but that interaction with other relatives was less common. Indeed, there was evidence of a 'privatized' family life among dock workers and foremen. At the same time, few relatives appeared to be workmates inside the docks, despite being members of the same occupation. One can conclude that, in this respect as others, dock workers and foremen are members of an occupational community to a greater extent than are many other workers in different occupations, but not to the extent that might have been anticipated.

Certain commonly held views about dock workers can now be questioned in the light of the empirical evidence concerning patterns of sociability. The first view is that there are distinct and separate docking communities in the immediate vicinities of the various docks. Data on friendship, kinship, and family life give no support to this view when analysed in terms of proximity to the docks, although slight differences appear among those living more than about four miles away. The evidence suggests that patterns of sociability and labour recruitment do reflect the existence of a kind of occupational community, though this is neither very concentrated geographically nor are people's lives greatly influenced by it, in contrast to what older descriptions of dockland have maintained.

Secondly, the community and family lives of men and foremen suggest that the adjective 'traditional' is an inappropriate description of the working-class communities from which these people come. The docking populations of the various areas covered here are unstable and residentially mobile within and between areas. This mobility frequently involves the separation of adult sons and daughters from their parents and the consequent attenuation of the ties of even the immediate family. When people stay in one area, extensive sociability on a scale which is wider than the immediate family is still rare and extended kin play a small part in people's lives outside work. The characteristic home life is family-centred and private. Some gregariousness is evident, but it falls far short of what is regarded as traditional working-class behaviour.

Foremen were often fairly similar to the men, but there were a few differences which indicated the partial assimilation of middle-class *mores*. These were most notably found in friendship patterns and the extent of home ownership. It was suggested that many foremen consciously chose friends of white-collar status. In the two areas known to be heavily manual working class, home-owning foremen were somewhat more likely to choose white-collar friends than those who rented accommodation. The evidence that home-owning dock workers were more likely to have friends and relatives within the middle class was not conclusive, particularly when area of residence was controlled for. The small numbers in the categories of analysis made statistical manipulation unrewarding, but there was little to suggest that many dock workers were assimilated into the middle class in any way.

CHAPTER 10

Cultural Perspectives

Aspirations

Analysis of the aspirations which people hold for their own and their families' future lives is a useful methodological research device. In the first place, the analysis helps to place groups relative to each other and thus to distinguish between them. Aspirations reflect the cultures to which people belong, so that sub-cultural variations between groups are often manifest as differences between individuals. At least some part of a group's culture is grounded in the structural position of the group, whether its present or historical situation. Thus differences between working-class and middle-class aspirations are frequently demonstrated, and are shown to correspond partly to the 'objective' positions of these groups. Equally, within the working class, variations are found between different groups, these differences corresponding to different structural positions. In the second place, aspirations provide clues as to the nature of people's more general social perspectives or world views and thus facilitate the analysis of individual and group consciousness. The coherence of social perspectives and the differences between groups which emerge from the analysis are both subjects of considerable interest.

Starting with the world of work, attitudes towards promotion form one critical area of aspirations. The idea of a career at work has traditionally been regarded as central to middle-class expectations of work and absent from working-class expectations. In the past at least, this expectation of a career was grounded in the realities of the middle-class employment situation. Whether this situation still holds good in the present day is not entirely clear, but there is ample evidence that the career opportunities and promotion prospects of many junior non-manual employees have dried up.[1] Short-range mobility appears to be unaffected, but mobility from clerical and supervisory positions into middle and senior management is probably increasingly rare. Thus the objective position of many lower middle-class employees no longer permits realistic expectations of promotion and career, and in this aspect of the employment situation working class and lower middle class converge. There is insufficient evidence on the repercussions such

[1] e.g. the study of the career opportunities of a national sample of certain technical, junior non-manual occupations in B. C. Roberts *et al.*, *The Reluctant Militants* (London, 1972), pp. 299–302.

changes have had on middle-class expectations, but presumably career aspirations may become more limited with time.

The facts of the situation in the docks were not entirely clear, because records did not show how prevalent promotion into management had been in the past while policy changes in several firms indicated that career prospects might alter in the future. Historically, a foreman's chances of becoming a manager appear to have been remote. The predilection of private companies for ex-merchant navy officers suggested that few foremen were promoted. The P.L.A. enforced a distinction between 'upper' and 'lower' staff, as they were entitled until recently, which prevented foremen and clerical workers from rising into management.

The situation became fluid towards the end of the sixties and real opportunities for promotion began to be opened, though on a limited scale. The two largest private companies investigated in my research introduced the new policy after 1967 of filling 10 to 20 per cent of superintendent vacancies from the foreman grade. It was anticipated that the advent of shiftwork in Phase 2 might require a further increase in the number of superintendents and foremen. In 1970, the P.L.A. abolished the distinction between upper and lower staff, removing the major barrier to promotion. This was one of the terms which the staff's representatives negotiated in return for agreement to participate in the new working arrangements of Phase 2.

Promotion prospects for manual workers were in the past extremely remote. In the P.L.A. they were literally non-existent, since foremen were recruited from clerical staff, another of the absolute barriers which the rigid bureaucratic hierarchy created. In the private sector, promotion to foreman did occur, but vacancies came up comparatively rarely. Taking the whole sample of foremen, approximately 52 per cent had been foremen for more than eleven years, and only about 8 per cent for less than three. However, the changes of Phases 1 and 2 promised to affect the promotion prospects of the men as well, because the vacancies created by the promotion of foremen to superintendent positions and the increased demand of shift-working should have meant more opportunities for the men to become foremen. (Though in the event, the decline of the upriver docks and the increased unitization of cargo have prevented the dramatic expansion of promotion prospects which seemed likely in 1970.) In the P.L.A., the introduction of Phase 2 was accompanied by reorganization of the foreman's job so that he had more sheds to look after, which in turn meant he needed a greater number of subordinates to help him. A new grade of assistant was created, this being filled from the manual labour force. In theory, an assistant in this post could become a foreman and then rise to middle management as the result of the integration of the two staff categories.

The objective situation was thus changing, though only senior management was really aware of this at the time. There was a feeling among the people whom I interviewed that promotion opportunities were increasing or were about to increase, but tangible evidence was scarcely visible then. The survey evidence on the subjective aspects of career, that is aspirations for and belief in the possibilities of promotion, show certain patterns. The replies in table 10.1 suggest that many foremen fit the middle-class stereotype and value career prospects highly as an attribute of the perfect job; while dock workers place less value on promotion.[2] In other words, the anticipated difference between manual and supervisory workers was found here: many foremen did have characteristically 'middle-class' aspirations (though they rank promotion prospects less often in the three *most* important attributes). But the results also show that dock workers do not all devalue promotion prospects, that 'getting on' in a career is not always irrelevant to them, and that many do not share the limited aspirations and opposition to self-advancement of the traditional working class.[3]

The differences between foremen and men are maintained when the existing job is appraised. Both groups were asked to state how far they were satisfied with promotion prospects in their present jobs. Nearly half the men said that promotion prospects, or the lack of them, were irrelevant to their feelings of satisfaction with their present job, while nearly a third expressed dissatisfaction. Considerably fewer foremen stated that promotion prospects were irrelevant, which is what one would have expected from their previously expressed views on the perfect job.[4] See table 10.2. Nevertheless, it is significant that nearly a quarter of foremen did feel that promotion was irrelevant, because this serves as a caution against assigning a middle-class pattern of aspirations to all foremen. Slightly less than half were positively satisfied with the prospects, while a third were definitely dissatisfied.

The aspirations which people have for their private lives, and in particular those aspirations related to their children's futures, are commonly thought to illuminate social attitudes and so to distinguish between groups and classes. Men with children who were not yet in work were asked what jobs they hoped their children would end up in eventually. In addition, all respondents, with or without children, were asked what advice they would give to a hypothetical son, who was fairly bright intellectually but was aged fifteen and eligible to leave school.[5] The results of the two questions can be seen in table 10.3.

[2] These data are taken from the questions on the attributes of the perfect job, which were discussed in Chapter 4. The differences are significant at $0.01 : X^2 = 15.68$ with 4 degrees of freedom.

[3] See R. McKenzie and A. Silver, *Angels in Marble* (London, 1968), pp. 190-3, for a discussion of the limited aspirations which manual workers display when they *do* desire to 'get on'.

[4] Difference between men and foremen significant at 0.01 level: $z = 3.47$.

[5] This question was taken from R. McKenzie and A. Silver, op. cit.

These findings are significant for a number of reasons. They show the clearly greater ambitions which foremen have for their children, in the context of the occupational hierarchy, than are manifested by manual workers.[6] That is to say, more foremen than dock workers want their children or a hypothetical son to become white-collar, while the type of white-collar job envisaged is also of a higher socio-economic status. These foremen, in fact, have considerably higher occupational aspirations for their own children than have been found in at least one study of clerical workers.[7]

The findings also show that foremen do not share the relatively bounded horizons and aspirations which other studies have noted. These bounded horizons include the sorts of non-manual jobs which can be easily comprehended because they represent a projection of manual work and of a worker's own experience: jobs such as engineering, for instance. But they do not include jobs with a content based on abstract thought or those of which the worker has no direct knowledge: for example, certain types of profession (but probably excluding medicine and teaching) and higher management. The occupations mentioned by dock workers, however, fell largely into this bounded category, unlike those of foremen. In particular, dock workers favoured electronics and computer engineering, two glamorous non-manual occupational areas which carry the legitimacy of technological progress but which can be seen as the projections of more mundane manual jobs. These two areas are also commonly regarded as affording good security and high financial returns. They are regarded as some kind of present-day equivalent to the old-fashioned craft jobs of the skilled trades.

However, if the dock workers are taken alone rather than in comparison with the foremen, who after all display unusually ambitious aspirations, then the nature of their aspirations is also rather surprising. The proportion of those who wanted white-collar occupations for their children is higher than has been found in several other studies and is fairly similar both to Runciman's national sample and the Luton engineering workers.[8] If we take the advice to a hypothetical son, then the findings are even more surprising because two-thirds of all dock workers aspire to white-collar jobs, albeit within the rather limited

[6] Differences between men and foremen in categories 1 and 2 combined are significant at 0·01: z=4·94 and 3·41 respectively for the results of the two questions. Many dock workers had no occupational aspirations but wanted their children to be *happy*.

[7] J. H. Goldthorpe, D. Lockwood et al., *The Affluent Worker* (Cambridge, 1969), vol. 3, p. 131.

[8] The figures are as follows: F. M. Martin, 'Some Subjective Aspects of Social Stratification', in D. V. Glass (ed.), *Social Mobility in Britain* (London, 1954), p. 69, gives 31 per cent; W. G. Runciman, *Relative Deprivation and Social Justice* (London, 1966), pp. 233–5 gives 47 per cent; J. H. Goldthorpe, D. Lockwood, et al., op. cit., vol. 3 (1969), p. 131, give 54 per cent.

range which they usually consider. One obvious reason for the discrepancy is that aspirations for one's own children are inevitably constrained by knowledge of their actual abilities and interests, whereas the hypothetical son question removes such limitations on aspiration.

These high-flying aspirations are significant evidence of social attitudes. They question the assumption that dock workers share those working-class cultural norms which emphasize the importance of group solidarity and supposedly censure attempts to improve one's own position in society or to wish one's children to move up the social scale. They throw doubt on the related idea that aspirations do not extend to those jobs which break up the family, as distinct from the community, by taking children away in either a geographical or a social sense.[9] They demonstrate that these working-class individuals would be happy to see their children 'get on'. Nor are age differences important: older dock workers (and foremen) are no more likely to have traditional, bounded horizons than are the younger ones when presented with the hypothetical son question.

It should be noted that the difference between foremen and dock workers is not the result of greater occupational achievement by foremen's sons than by those of the manual workers. Table 10.4 shows, indeed, how the occupations of children in employment are similar for each group. One expectation might have been that foremen, as men who have to some extent moved upward, would put pressure on their children to be high achievers. This is certainly the impression one gains from the nature of foremen's occupational aspirations. A study of education and the working class has shown how foremen's children tend to have a higher educational, and thus occupational, attainment than the children of other working-class parents, which results from the greater pressure and encouragement the parents bring to bear.[10]

The data on the occupations of children at work (including those of the husbands of married daughters) show that this pressure, if it existed, has not led to differential performance. Children of both groups have been successful in crossing the divide between manual and non-manual work, and approximately half the working children in both cases are in white-collar work or are married to white-collar husbands. As the proportion of the working population engaged in manual occupations in Britain drops towards half, the manual/non-manual division may become less significant as a fundamental class divide and the mobility of dock workers' children across this divide less sociologically meaningful. But the salient fact for our purposes is the similarity of achievement among children, whatever the meaning given to mobility.

[9] F. M. Martin, op. cit., pp. 68–70.
[10] B. Jackson and D. Marsden, *Education and the Working Class* (London, 1962), pp. 73 and 96.

It is noticeable that few sons actually work in the docks, and that parents' aspirations rarely include dock work. The reduced rate of recruitment probably explains why so few sons actually work in the docks, but the absence of docking from parental aspirations cannot be explained in these terms. Rather, there are many other occupations which fathers would prefer rather than to see their sons follow their own footsteps.

Despite the different levels of occupational aspirations, both groups agreed on the way for their children to achieve the desired occupational level: through the educational system. As part of the hypothetical son question, all respondents were asked whether they would recommend his leaving school to get a job, leaving school to become an apprentice, or staying on at school if he could. An enormous majority of both groups recommended staying on at school, 87 and 94 per cent of men and foremen respectively, scarcely any recommending the taking of a job and very few recommending an apprenticeship. The proportions recommending staying on at school were considerably greater even than those found in McKenzie and Silver's research, from which the question was taken, where two-thirds chose the 'stay on at school' reply.[11] When questioned as to why they favoured more education, 77 per cent of foremen and 71 per cent of dock workers stated that the type of job one could get was linked to educational attainment. Unlike McKenzie and Silver's sample, where education was not seen to be clearly related to future occupational position, both dock groups had a clear perception of the relationship. Moreover, it was a strategy of action which they would recommend: there were none of those reservations about educational achievement alienating the child from his parents which have been noted elsewhere.[12]

It is often argued that individuals in traditional cultures have limited wants and expectations of life, particularly with regard to consumption patterns. Although normally used to describe pre-industrial societies, this notion is sometimes thought to apply to 'traditional' sectors in advanced industrial societies. In order to see how far dock workers and foremen had aspirations which included material advancement and a change of consumption patterns, I asked people the deliberately general question, taken from other research in order to ensure comparability, which goes thus: 'Looking ten years ahead, what improvement in your way of life would you most hope for?'[13] The answers given in table 10.5

[11] R. McKenzie and A. Silver, op. cit., p. 140.
[12] ibid., pp. 143–5; F. M. Martin, op. cit., pp. 68–70; J. H. Goldthorpe, D. Lockwood et al., op. cit., vol. 3 (1969), p. 119. The educational attainments of foremen's children still in the educational system were little different from those of dock workers': the use of the educational system as a source of upward mobility for the children of foremen was not conspicuous despite the parents' occupational aspirations.
[13] J. H. Goldthorpe, D. Lockwood et al., op. cit., vol. 1, p. 136.

show different patterns for the two groups. Dock workers had relatively high aspirations for an improvement in their material well-being. Foremen were much less concerned with this, while a substantial proportion was concerned with provision for old age. Both groups were concerned to have more leisure time.

Dock workers' most widespread aspirations were thus concerned with increasing their consumer capacity and the level of their consumption. They did not appear to be inhibited very much by culturally prescribed limits or traditional consumption norms. It should be noted that the proportion of individuals giving these aspirations is not as high as that found among the Luton engineering workers, though the proportion of all aspirations mentioned is similar in both studies.[14] Dock workers were not so overwhelmingly obsessed with constantly rising living standards as the 'affluent workers', but there is ample evidence to support the view that they had instrumental orientations and were concerned with consumption standards to a considerable degree. If anything, foremen were the ones with limited consumption norms and did not aspire to a continually rising living standard.

The difference between foremen and men may partly have been a reflection of the differing situations of the two groups. Taking the situation of foremen over the last twenty years, they have normally been in a better financial position than the men because their earnings have not only been fairly high but have also been regular, which is just as important. In addition, the age of many foremen means that they tend to have fewer dependent children than dock workers. Evidence of better living standards lies mainly in the much greater proportion of home ownership among foremen than among the men. Car ownership is similar in both groups. The fluctuations in dock workers' earnings in the past as the result of casual labour and piecework made it extremely difficult for them to arrange credit, because most companies would only take the fall-back wage as the basis of calculations. Earnings, too, were comparatively low until recently: in 1967, docking came ninth in the list of manual earnings, whereas it came second in 1970. Not surprisingly, 60 per cent of the men thought that their standard of living had risen 'a great deal' or 'quite a lot' over the last ten years, while exactly two-thirds thought that they were better off as the result of decasualization. 48 per cent of foremen thought their living standards had improved over the decade. Dock workers have become affluent, but this is a recent phenomenon for most of them.

Aspirations relating to work were few, apart from a desire to spend less time working which reflects on the physically arduous nature of the tasks and the hours worked. Leisure was valued because it allowed more time to be spent in home-centred activities and with the family. There is strong evidence, indeed, that work was unimportant as a

[14] ibid., p. 137.

central life interest for these home-centred workers. In addition to the negative evidence that work scarcely featured in aspirations, there are the answers to a question asking people whether they talked about their work or the docks generally after they had finished work, or whether they left all that behind them at the dock gates.[15] The great majority of foremen and men, 82 and 83 per cent respectively, reported that they left work behind them at the dock gates and avoided talking about such subjects outside work. Talking shop was confined to the workplace and played little part in after-work life. The only occasions when work was discussed outside was when workers from the docks met each other alone, without wives or outside friends, mainly at pubs or sports events. 44 per cent of the men and 26 per cent of foremen said they might talk shop in addition to other subjects on such occasions. Further positive evidence can be found in the replies to the question about what they would do if they had their time again, when about half of each group had aspirations for jobs of higher socio-economic status, though many wanted these higher status jobs to be within the port industry rather than outside. Table 10.6 gives the results.[16] Information such as provided by these two questions, when taken in conjunction with what is known about the nature and origins of friendships, suggests that work was low in the scale of life interests and rarely the source of aspirations.

In conclusion, foremen displayed more middle-class aspirations than the men. In particular, the high aspirations for children indicated knowledge of the middle-class occupational structure and the desire that their children should participate in it, though the actual occupational and educational achievements of foremen's children differed little from those of dock workers. The men had fairly high aspirations, but these were both more limited and more bounded by working-class horizons than those of foremen. Given these limitations, dock workers displayed little of the traditional working class's supposed conservatism, fear of group disloyalty or concern with family and kin solidarity. Rather, their aspirations for their children and often for themselves implied the willingness to dislocate traditional ties: they desired to see their children socially mobile, even though they did not conceive of this extending to higher managerial and professional occupations, while many desired some mobility for themselves. So far as their children were concerned, they were well aware that occupational placement depended largely on educational achievement. Aspirations also in-

---

[15] This aspect of work as a central life interest is derived from R. Dubin, 'Industrial Workers' Worlds: A Study of the "Central Life Interests" of Industrial Workers', *Social Problems*, 3, 1956, pp. 131–42.

[16] 'Time again' replies were tabulated against area of residence and distance from the docks, in case there were traditional proletarian docking communities in which work was a central life interest: there were no significant variations.

cluded a concern to improve living standards and there was little sign of limited consumption norms in this respect. There were no significant differences between different age groups on any of these items, and there was no evidence that older people were more traditional in their outlook than the younger ones.

Socio-political Views

Dock workers are solidly committed to the Labour Party. In the three elections prior to the period of my research over 80 per cent of this sample voted Labour and on one occasion the figure rose to 86 per cent. See table 10.7. The proportion of those with a completely solid attachment, defined as those who always voted Labour or abstained only once, was, however, lower at just below 70 per cent. This was mainly due to the number of respondents who reported that they would switch parties or abstain from voting at the next election. Without this last set of figures, the stable Labour commitment would have been greater. (I conducted the interviewing immediately before and after the 1970 election, and the traditional Labour voters' declining support for the Labour Party matched the national trend at that election.) These pro-Labour and anti-Conservative votes are somewhat extreme in comparison with the national averages for manual workers of two-thirds and one-third respectively. But the figures show some similarity to those of the Luton engineering research, where the pro-Labour vote was about the same and the pro-Conservative vote did not exceed 15 per cent.

Dock foremen are less homogeneous in their political views and about one-third voted Conservative against a maximum Labour vote of 60 per cent. Stable commitment to the two main parties was just under a half of the sample for Labour and a third for Conservative. Foremen also showed the same swing away from Labour as the men when asked how they would vote in the next election. Pro-Labour and anti-Conservative voting patterns were much less marked than among dock workers, but fell into the pattern of the manual working class nationally: the proportion of Conservative foremen was only slightly over the one-third average for the manual working class as a whole, with the exception of the sharp rise in the intention to vote Conservative at the next election. Compared with one study of white-collar workers, dock foremen are considerably less likely to vote Conservative and much more likely to support Labour.[17]

The dock workers and foremen who were solidly attached to the Labour Party gave similar reasons for this attachment, as can be seen from table 10.8. A general identification with Labour as the party of the working class was the largest single reason given by either group,

[17] J. H. Goldthorpe, D. Lockwood et al., op. cit., vol. 2, p. 12.

demonstrating the importance of class loyalty to Labour in both cases. A second category, 'family tradition', could also be part of this class-based and affective involvement with Labour according to a recent study of political ideology.[18] Dock workers in fact display the same 'diffuse class loyalty' to Labour which was noted among the Luton workers. Many foremen share this loyalty as well, but the tendency is less marked.

Voting patterns therefore show that dock workers and foremen behave in ways which correspond to what is known about the working class generally. In fact, dock workers display these working-class characteristics to a greater extent than is regarded as normal in literature on this subject, which may indicate some elements of proletarian traditionalism. The problem, however, is to know the meaning of voting behaviour. Voting figures can be compared with those revealed in other research, in order to show how far dock workers and foremen fit typical working- or middle-class patterns and thus to place people in terms of these objective indicators. But it is interesting to go beyond this form of analysis, in order to find out how people see society and to place them somewhere in the left–right spectrum.

The data presented so far do not allow inferences of this sort, since commitment to the Labour Party gives only the most general guide to social perceptions. Those who gave class interest as their reason for supporting Labour may be giving clues about their perceptions of society. But the other reasons scarcely lend themselves to this sort of interpretation. The category of 'family tradition', for instance, could well reflect inertia and indifference as well as class loyalty. Indeed, many people themselves suggested that support for a political party would be a poor guide when over 40 per cent of both groups stated that it would make no difference which party won the next election, because the two major parties were either the same or made no difference to the individual. (44 per cent of foremen and 40 per cent of the men said this.) Some further information about perceptions is required.

In order to illuminate people's views more fully, I borrowed various ideological statements about the distribution and use of power in the British social structure from other research.[19] The data in table 10.9 show that dock workers tend to agree with what may be termed the 'Left' responses to the statements. Moreover, the correlation matrix

[18] ibid., p. 18.
[19] 1. 'There's one law for the rich and another for the poor.' 2. 'The men who own the big businesses have too much power in this country.' 3. 'The upper classes in Britain have always tried to keep the working man from getting his fair share.' 4. 'There are no social classes today as everyone is more or less equal.'
No. 1 was taken from J. H. Goldthorpe, D. Lockwood *et al.*, op. cit. Nos. 2 and 3 were from R. McKenzie and A. Silver, op. cit. No. 4 was not borrowed from other research.

presented in table 10.10 shows that there are positive associations of moderate size between the statements, which indicates some degree of consistency among the respondents' perceptions.[20] This suggests that many people react in a coherent manner to various separate aspects of social power and inequality. Dock workers, indeed, are more likely to agree that there are social inequalities than are other groups of workers.

Foremen's replies differ. Foremen display a fairly high agreement with the first statement, that there is one law for the rich and another for the poor, but give lower scores on the subjects of business power and fair shares. They are less likely than dock workers to have a 'Left' view of social inequality and power in response to the statements, and are also less to the 'Left' than other groups of workers on some items. Even when those foremen who regularly vote Labour are considered alone, they still have less 'Left' opinions about these aspects of the social structure than do the men. Political affiliations, however, do differentiate between different foremen with regard to these statements.[21]

The correlates of these ideological statements are interesting. The first thing to notice is the positive but small associations between political party attachment and the majority of the statements.[22] Some association would be expected if voting does in fact reflect some wider social perspective. Secondly, age is unrelated to ideological position in either group, and people do not move to the 'Right' with advancing years, which fits the relative unimportance of age for most attitudes in this research.[23] Thirdly, the perceptions which people have of industry and associated institutions are definitely not related to ideological position as revealed by these statements. There are no associations with replies to the earlier questions about teamwork and the nature of employment and only a few extremely small associations with the statements about unions.[24] It is clear that the 'Left' position with

[20] The correlation matrix includes foremen's data. The internal consistency of the political ideology section of the matrix is greater than another similar study would suggest: M. Mann, 'The Ideologies of Non-Skilled Industrial Workers', in M. Bulmer (ed.) *Proceedings of a SSRC Conference: The Occupational Community of the Traditional Worker* (Durham, 1973), pp. 246–84.

[21] Holding Labour Party attachment constant, foremen and men still differ significantly on statements 1 to 3: Chi Squares = 4·59 at 0·05, 9·01 at 0·01 and 4·06 at 0·05 respectively, all with 1 degree of freedom. Labour and Conservative foremen differ significantly on statements 1 to 3: Chi Squares = 7·57 at 0·01, 6·59 at 0·05 and 6·50 at 0·05, all with 1 degree of freedom.

[22] Associations among the men are $\Phi = ·32$ and $·41$ between party and statements 1 and 2, both significant at 0·05 level. Statement 3 just misses statistical significance. Among foremen, associations for statements 2 and 3 are $\Phi = ·44$ and $·27$ at the 0·05 level. No. 4 just misses significance.

[23] There is a ·25 correlation between age (plus or minus 45 years) and ideological position on statement 1 among foremen, and younger foremen are more 'Left'. There are no other age-related differences among foremen or men.

[24] Neither are teamwork and unionism, nor teamwork and party related.

regards to social inequality and power does *not* imply a particular conception of employment relations nor support for the role of trade unionism. The coherence of the various different strands which are thought to make up a radical proletarian image of society is missing among these dock workers and foremen. The people interviewed in this research appeared to have their views fairly well compartmentalized, so that a particular view about one aspect of society did not predict views about others.

The inferences which can be drawn from these ideological statements are not completely clear. Such statements have previously been taken to indicate the intensity of workers' class-consciousness. If this is true, then dock workers show an intensity of class-consciousness which approaches that of traditional proletarian workers. An alternative interpretation, however, is that the statements are taken at their face value by respondents and are seen merely as statements about social inequality. An awareness of inequality may be a necessary pre-condition of class-consciousness but it would hardly appear to be the same thing. The absence of any strong association between views about industry and unionism and those about inequalities and power certainly suggests that a developed and coherent class-consciousness of the variety sometimes encountered in sociological literature about traditional workers cannot be inferred from this evidence. The disjunction between views about industrial and social life appears to represent a more inchoate form of social awareness.

Differences between the men and foremen suggested that the latter held less obviously proletarian attitudes than the former. Reinforcement of this interpretation is found in the nature of people's self-assessed class position. 83 per cent of the men regarded themselves as working-class whereas foremen were much more divided. Just over half (55 per cent) saw themselves as working class and just under a half as middle class. The number of 'middle-class' dock workers is too small for analysis, but 'middle-class' foremen are sufficiently numerous to show that there is some association between self-assigned middle-class status and a stable attachment to the Conservative Party.[25] There may be reservations about using a forced-choice question referring to the working class and middle class when such concepts may not be meaningfully related to respondents' perceptions of stratification, but the systematic differences which the question reveals between foremen and men tally with other evidence and suggest that it has some rough and ready utility.

It is appropriate at this point to consider the social images or models of the class system which the two groups possessed. The findings on ideology, voting and class assessment showed dock workers as slightly more proletarian than many other groups of workers. But such results

[25] $X^2 = 5·82$ with 1 degree at the 0·05 level.

do not necessarily indicate that dock workers are equally proletarian in other senses of the term, for instance, in the sense that they have a dichotomous model which splits society into two confronting classes on the basis of the possession of power by one and the subjugation of the other. Recent interest in models of class has modified and supplemented the traditional distinction between two-class, 'power' models and three (or more) class, hierarchical 'prestige' ones. A third type which is based on money and which appears to be independent of the others has been identified.[26] Additional complexity can result when individuals possess models which combine elements of more than one pure type, as for instance in the mixed 'power-prestige' model which has occasionally been noted.[27]

Before discussing people's social imagery, I must express certain reservations concerning the assumptions and methodology which are used in 'image' analysis. In the first place, there is often a tendency to assume that manual workers do possess clearly articulated and internally consistent images, when they may in fact be incoherent.[28] Secondly, the ways of classifying statements about society into images appear to rely heavily on the interpretation of the coder, neither the criteria nor the replicability of classification being very clear in existing studies. Thirdly, the relatively wide categories used may lead to distortion of the 'true' image, particularly if there is a wide range of possible images or if these are not as coherent as has been claimed. In more general terms, the complexity of social imagery may be too great to be very useful for the simple classification of populations at present demanded of it. Fourthly, even when images do exist, are coherent and can readily be categorized, their salience to the individuals holding them cannot merely be assumed. For these reasons, the imagery presented here should be regarded as being useful for categorizing foremen and men in a crude fashion, but it should not be given the weight which other users of the approach have claimed for it.

The imagery which is classified and presented in table 10.11 is based on what people saw as the nature of social inequality and contains no reference to the number of social classes described. Counting the precise number of classes creates more complexity and is less important than the bases of social divisions for classifying perceptions. The table shows that a simple power model of 'us' and 'them' is held by small proportions of men and foremen, less than 15 per cent of either group.

[26] J. H. Goldthorpe, D. Lockwood et al., op. cit., vol. 3 (1969), pp. 147–50.
[27] e.g. Elizabeth Bott, Family and Social Network (London, 1957), pp. 174 and 178.
[28] This is argued by M. Mann, 'The Social Cohesion of Liberal Democracy', American Sociological Review, 35, 1970, pp. 423–39. 33 per cent of The Affluent Worker sample either had no social images or such diverse ones that they could not be classified: J. H. Goldthorpe, D. Lockwood et al., op. cit., vol. 3 (1969), p. 149.

When this is supplemented by a mixed money and power model, then the broader power category accounts for about a quarter of the sample. This mixed model conceived of one class containing all employees, manual and non-manual alike, and a second, smaller class of people who lived off the efforts of the bulk of the population.[29] This is why this type of image is classified along with the simple power one. It should be noted, however, that the large central class was in turn internally divided into a multiplicity of grades based on money and consumption patterns. But these internal divisions could be surmounted, whereas the other barrier was more absolute.

The central tendency among dock workers, however, was towards a money model of social divisions, in which the amount of cash one earned and the nature of one's consumption patterns were the major determinants of social position. The 'pure' money model accounted for nearly half the sample of dock workers, nearly the same proportion that was found in the Luton study.[30] This indicates just how prevalent the concept of a stratification system based on money is among all manual workers.

The problem with a money model, however, is how to distinguish it from power or prestige ones in every case. It is possible that differences in income and consumption may represent merely the tangible manifestations of other principles of stratification, or that respondents talk about these differences because they lack the analytical vocabulary to express more abstract concepts. Thus the concept of an élite may be expressed in the language of money or be tangible because of the spending power of élite members, but may in fact be part of a power rather than a money model as noted earlier. On the other hand, the mixture of money and prestige bases can be equally difficult to disentangle, since many dock workers think that the two go together. A proportion see high social status employment and high income as inextricably linked. A variation on this is represented by the foreman who said that he was middle class because of his income, but that his school teacher nephew was upper middle class because he had roughly the same income but a higher-status job: money and status were here seen as overlapping systems of stratification, whereby money would get one so far up the class ladder but status was needed as well in order to reach the upper rungs.

Among foremen, the central tendency was as much towards prestige and status hierarchy as towards money principles of stratification. Fewer foremen than dock workers gave a 'pure' money classification,

---

[29] This élite group was seen as parasitic or referred to in terms of the ownership of the means of production. The élite in the money model of *The Affluent Worker* study is described as being qualitatively different from other strata, which appears to be close to what I have here called a *power* model: ibid., p. 149.

[30] ibid., p. 150.

while more gave a prestige one. The proportions of the two groups giving mixed money and prestige were similar.

Certain conclusions can be drawn from these models, bearing in mind the limitations of this form of analysis in general. In the first place, dock workers as a whole do not claim to see society in terms of a power-based system of stratification and inequality. A view of stratification based on money and consumption is compatible with support for the Labour Party, support for statements of a 'Left' nature about social inequalities and divisions, and self-identification as a member of the working class. This model of social structure is held, in other words, by those who display certain beliefs and behaviour which have been labelled the constituent elements of proletarian traditionalism. It may be the case that a money model conceals the more basic processes of structured inequality based on social power, and that these merely manifest themselves in income and consumption. If this is indeed the perception that lies behind the money model, then a money view would obviously be quite compatible with the definition of traditionalism, with the consequence that both dock workers *and* affluent engineering workers should be labelled traditional proletarians. Alternatively, the 'Left' ideology statements, which are thought to represent a class-conscious and oppositional view of society, may refer merely to a perception of inequality which is not extrapolated into a proletarian consciousness. Such a perception is compatible with the money model because this assumes an unequal distribution of earnings and consumption. Yet a third alternative is that 'Left' ideology and money models may co-exist without there being any necessity that they should reinforce each other in the actor's own world view. Whichever explanation is correct, it is clear that the social imagery of dock workers is similar to that of other working-class groups.

In the second place, the money model in its pure form accounts for just less than half of the sample. Approximately a quarter and one-fifth, respectively, hold models which incorporate power or prestige elements. This indicates the *range* of different images which people within one group can embrace. There may be a central tendency towards one model, but the group as a whole did not display the unanimity of perceptions which 'image' theorists would suppose, given their interest in tracing the ideological concomitants of structural positions.

In the third place, foremen differ from the men in ways which are now predictable. They are more likely to possess models with prestige elements in them and less likely to put forward power elements. In this way, foremen as a group are more likely to manifest character-istics described as middle class than are dock workers. However, foremen display a considerable variety of social images, just as do dock workers.

Lockwood has argued that ideology and imagery vary with the

structural setting, with the result that different types of worker with different types of consciousness are found in different social milieux.[31] One important structural setting is the community in which a person lives, and the main structural component here is the pattern of social relationships. Social interaction is held to have a critical influence on perspectives. Given that foremen and dock workers differed in the extent of their white-collar affiliations, particularly among friends and brothers-in-law, and that the class position of close contacts is thought to have an extremely powerful influence on perspectives, this structural difference may well have accounted for different attitudes. It even appeared possible that the foremen might be so divided by the various degrees of middle-class affiliation within their ranks that those without white-collar contacts would be little different from the men. The structural position of one group of foremen might have hidden the similarity of position and corresponding similarity of perspective between the rest of the foremen and the men.

In order to assess the impact of different types of affiliation and community on social perspectives, I conducted a series of tabulations on the data which tested for association between various indicators of perspective, namely ideology, party attachment, class self-assessment, occupational aspiration and social imagery, and the three variables of affiliation, area of residence and distance from the docks. These last two variables were included in case aspects of community other than the nature of social interaction were important. Details of the associations can be found in Appendix C, where they are placed in order to avoid burdening the text with a complex presentation. They show that different categories of contact are to some extent differently associated with social perspectives. Among the dock worker group, the occupations of brothers were more often related to differences of perspective than those of brothers-in-law or friends. Among foremen, brothers and friends were significantly associated with some indicators of perspective but brothers-in-law were not. The different occupational statuses of friends may be slightly related to some of the perceptual differences between foremen and men.

These associations do provide some support for the argument that perspectives are influenced by social milieux, particularly the character

---

[31] D. Lockwood, 'Some Sources of Variation in Working Class Images of Society', *Sociological Review*, 14, 1966, pp. 249–67, and 'In Search of the Traditional Worker', in M. Bulmer (ed.), op. cit., pp. 444–59. In the second paper, Lockwood distinguishes between ideology and imagery, arguing that they are separate elements of people's cognitive interpretations of society, with the result that imagery may tell us nothing about ideology. The separation of imagery and ideology comes as a surprise after Lockwood's considerable earlier emphasis on the coherence of culture and world views, but such a separation would certainly describe the apparent inconsistencies found in these dock data, though this of course reduces the explanatory value of imagery.

of social relationships. But the extent of this influence was not particularly great, because only a few of the indices were significantly associated, while the associations themselves were mainly slight. The other aspects of community, area and distance, were scarcely related to perspectives at all. In other words, different relational characteristics were sometimes slightly associated with different social perspectives, but there was no evidence of any sharp or consistent variations according to these or other structural differences. The obvious conclusion is that different milieux were not solely or even mainly responsible for different perspectives within or between the two groups.

The preceding chapter demonstrated that occupational membership had some implications for dock workers' lives outside work. The occupation had a significant influence on two aspects of private life, which were the presence of weak forms of occupational community outside work and the kin-based recruitment system which ensured that relatives were often occupational members as well. This contrasts strongly with printing, which has a similarly well-developed work culture but which scarcely touches the lives of occupational members outside work.[32]

This chapter, however, indicates that being a dock worker or foreman is less important in other areas of life outside work. Ideology, imagery and aspirations show that dock workers are little different from other workers and that they often differ among themselves. Where they are more united and extreme than other working-class groups, as in the extent of their support for Labour and some of the ideological statements, then it may be possible to hypothesize that these differences are explained by occupational factors.

The existing attempts to create this linkage, using concepts like those of 'traditional worker' or 'isolated mass', are not very useful for this purpose, however. Neither is sufficiently precise in specifying the evidence required or the concepts involved. Thus the criteria for distinguishing between traditional and other workers, or the bench-marks on some continuum from traditional to modern, are vague. Similarly, the defining characteristics of traditionalism are complex and the ideal type rests on a conflation of numerous traits, with the result that there is ambiguity about which characteristics are the more important for locating groups. In the pure type of traditionalism all the relevant characteristics point the same way and reinforce each other, with the result that there is little need to state which of them are more significant than others, but this situation rarely occurs in practice.

The imprecision makes it difficult to analyse the dock data so as to assess the extent of dock workers' traditionalism. It was found to be unclear whether the occupational communities outside work noted in

[32] I. C. Cannon, 'Ideology and Occupational Community: A Study of Compositors', *Sociology*, 1, 1967, pp. 165–87.

the previous chapter were the sort which traditional occupations are supposed to generate. This was essentially a problem of measurement. There was also a conceptual problem: how traditional is an occupation whose members have a money model of society and privatized patterns of family life together with great commitment to Labour and support for 'Left' political ideology statements? In the absence of any weighting between the various aspects of traditionalism, the place of dock workers is somewhat ambiguous. However, if the proletarian image of society is the single most important element, then there is little prima facie evidence of traditionalism here.

What is clear is that foremen have less solidly working-class patterns of aspiration and perspective than the men, just as their friendships and neighbourhoods were seen to differ earlier. Foremen, indeed, sometimes displayed opinions which had strongly middle-class overtones. Foremen's lives outside work often appeared to differ from the men's and sometimes even from the working class as a whole.

CHAPTER 11

Conclusions

The docks have displayed certain elements characteristic of *gemeinschaft* societies throughout their history. Primordial ties of kin, personal bonds between friends and a sense of moral obligation in industrial relationships have dominated the industrial culture and organization. The docks do not differ totally from other industries nor do they reflect completely outmoded forms of organization, because *gemeinschaft* elements can be found everywhere; but in the docks they are certainly more extreme. The presence of these elements has made possible an effective system of administration which relies little on conventional bureaucratic or formal principles of organization, or on the regulative force of a set of organizational goals and the associated value system. This situation has allowed lower-level employees more real control over their working lives than is common in almost any other setting, except perhaps in the printing industry.

One key element in the social system of the docks has been the culture shared by dock workers, foremen and managers alike. The culture was based firmly in the structural conditions of the casual system of employment. In the first place, many of the specific elements of the culture were directly concerned to regulate relationships within the casual system, notably those between dock workers themselves and between dock workers and foremen. Secondly, casual employment ensured that power lay in the hands of the owners and their agents, with the result that the various customary practices sanctioned by dock culture rarely encroached on the interests of capital at that time. The term 'occupational culture' has been used to describe the shared norms and values found in the industry, but in fact their influence has extended far beyond the men and foremen who make up the occupation.

The culture and typical forms of social regulation had tangible consequences in the primitive organization of the industry, because simple structures existed to administer quite complex tasks. Companies made little attempt to define roles or to ensure the co-ordination of tasks, in the private sector at least, but withdrew from most activities now regarded as the duties of management. Highly personal ties between members of the workforce and foremen and the moral pressures of the social community formed one principle of organization. The coercive potential of the employment relationship was a second, while pride in workmanship, the inheritance of traditional skills from kin and the occupational control of standards was a third. The net result was a private sector organized according to craft principles of administration, which relied heavily on the technical and managerial expertise of the foremen and men, and on their willingness to exercise these abilities with very little managerial intervention.

Structural changes in the industry over the years immediately preceding my investigation had already modified the system in its classic form as just described. Full employment during the sixties, decasualization in 1967 and the retention of the Scheme from the casual era, combined to give the men considerably more power than previously. Many traditional features of the social organization survived these structural changes, at least in attenuated forms: for instance, bonds of kinship, friendship and religion were still important principles of social organization, though they had little affective significance. Some aspects of the occupational culture were modified in the new situation, particularly the shared understandings concerning the authority and role of foremen. Foremen, who had been the central figures in the organization of traditional dock work, moved somewhat to the sidelines during the closing years of the sixties. Ironically, they had sufficient freedom and discretion to redefine their roles, precisely because they had once been so important and managers were accustomed to allowing them to act as they saw fit. Other culturally sanctioned practices were readily given up about this time: the rules concerning work-sharing and flexibility, and the gang system, both of which had played vital roles in the past, were happily renounced for the Phase 2 package deal. Cultural change could also be observed in the men's attempts unilaterally to redefine traditional 'custom and practice' norms of behaviour. The foremen and managers sometimes tried to resist processes of cultural change, but they were not powerful enough to resist for long.

In the long run, a series of further changes imposed on the industry as the result of conditions which are partly outside the control of those working within it, may destroy much of its traditional character. Alterations in the old distribution of power have already led to mutations of the old institutions and customary practices; but wider changes threaten more drastic modifications while, at the same time, they may restore some of management's lost control. These changes threaten the old system of administration, undermine some of the foundations of the men's present strength, and increase pressures for greater formalization and bureaucratization.

Over the last half-century, most notably in the last two decades, industrial work has been subjected to a continuing process of rationalization which has affected the docks relatively less than other industries. The nature of the work people do and the conditions of employment under which they do it have been subjected to a double-pronged attack, which has led to the historically unprecedented extension of managerial authority into the details of production. This managerial initiative has been most noticeable in the more skilled occupations. The consequence has been to reduce the skill requirements of work and the control workers traditionally exercised over their immediate work environment, and to promote the managerial take-over of the planning and monitoring functions previously exercised by shop-floor personnel. The process ultimately deprives manual jobs of most of their remaining intellectual elements, and leaves managers to determine what will be the precise content of tasks and their relationship to each other in the production system. Workers increasingly execute decisions taken elsewhere. The sorts of jobs characteristic of large parts of British industry in the early and middle phases of industrialization, when many workers still performed 'whole' tasks, controlled their own work processes in an autonomous manner and used their brains as well as their hands, are found less and less today except in enclaves like the docks or printing (where many work tasks are more skilled than in the docks). Though most non-manual work in industry has not yet been rationalized in the same way.

But even in the docks the process has begun. As in other industries, one facet of rationalization in the docks has been technological change which 'de-skills' existing work. Technological 'de-skilling' works in two ways: by simplifying work tasks and by making managers responsible for the organization of work processes. Simplification of tasks reduces management's dependence on people with scarce skills and fixed expectations regarding work tasks and control (the result of occupational socialization), which gives managers more freedom to extend their control over production. Conventional work has been simplified over the last twenty-five years, with the spread of palletization and other new methods of packaging cargo, and with the new designs of ships. But the major 'de-skilling' has resulted from the introduction of the new handling techniques and reorganized work processes following unitization: these have destroyed the relevance of traditional occupational skills. Managers have begun to intervene more and have assumed responsibility for the organization of production now that their employees can no longer do this themselves—though there is no likelihood of the work being thrown open to unskilled outsiders in the ports covered by the Scheme. The full implications of technological change will take time to be realized, of course, because conventional work will have a place for some years and most men will continue to use their traditional expertise. There is also the possibility that on-the-job experience may become more important in the new operations, though the prospects of this are not great given the inherent simplicity of the work.

The second facet of the rationalization experienced by other industries has been the development of managerial control systems which impinge more directly on work processes and workers. The control previously exercised by workers and foremen has increasingly been replaced by that of managers, which can be seen in the destruction of the traditional multi-functional supervisory role and the great reduction in the discretion allowed the shopfloor, the growth of functional specialists within management, and the expansion of the numbers of managerial and other supervisory staff in British industry since the war. The visible trend towards more formalized administration is part of the same process of extending managerial control, at the cost of the old, informal administrative patterns which gave foremen and workers great influence. At the same time, the application of a rigid division of labour on the shopfloor by splitting each job into a series of specialized sub-tasks performed by different people, one of the elementary principles of scientific management, means that workers have such fragmented jobs that they are no longer capable of co-ordinating or controlling production. These functions have now to be performed by managers or their agents.

Dock workers have not yet experienced this second development. But pressure from management is likely to increase over the years for two reasons. The mergers of the last two years have led to larger firms operating in London, and it is a commonplace of organizational analysis that increased size leads to increased pressure for more bureaucratic procedures, which may lead dock managers to press more forcefully for more formalized administration. At the same time, dock management may become less insular and in-bred, realizing that other industries have found new ways of doing things and that there is now available a body of knowledge about managerial techniques. The P.L.A. has already shown its awareness of the situation by appointing some senior managers who are not steeped in dock culture and attempting to put into effect various principles of modern management.

The response of the men to the rationalization process is not entirely clear. On the one hand, the insecurity which threatens the occupation as the result of changing cargo transit practices, legal decisions regarding dock work and the financial difficulties of many firms, may weaken the men's resolve to exploit their obvious power. Should the men weaken in this way, then any attempts to introduce a new formalism would be made easier. On the other, while the Scheme continues in its present form dock workers will retain considerable control as long as there are still docks left to employ them. If a sympathetic government should extend the Scheme to all ports or redefine dock work to include the container work now performed in the vicinity of the docks, then the men's power will actually increase. Even without this development, however, dock workers should be able to maintain traditional and non-bureaucratic phenomena such as recruitment on the basis of kinship and friendship, worker control of the shopfloor and joint control of the industry itself for some time to come.

Dock workers enjoy work which is less coercive and gives them more real power than is the case with most working-class occupations. This aspect of their work sets them apart from others and shows them to be privileged by the standards of what is normal in the working class. But dock workers whom I interviewed did *not* differ greatly from other manual workers in their evaluations of the work they had to perform. They all reacted favourably to the environment in which they did their jobs, the freedom and variety which the docks allowed, but they did not necessarily regard the work itself as interesting or creative, though there were differences by age here. Work was not a central life interest: the men saw the work as being less unpleasant than any other manual job open to them and as making few demands for a trade-off between job satisfaction and the satisfaction of their strong instrumental needs, but as little more.

Dock workers differed from the foremen in this respect, because the latter group rated the content of their work higher, though even here work was not a central life interest. Foremen had more responsibility and more interest in their jobs and they saw their work as being skilled and demanding. This supports evidence from other studies that jobs become more satisfying as one moves up the occupational hierarchy, because the division of labour in most industrialized societies is such that lower status work is less interesting and creative than higher. Age cut across the differences between foremen and men but they did not disappear.

Because of the difference between manual and non-manual work, there was a basic difference between the jobs of foremen and dock workers, though the two groups sometimes shared fairly similar feelings about work. In fact, some of the differences were being eroded by the changes occurring in the industry and in some respects foremen were only nominally in a more advantageous position. This can be seen in the analysis of authority at work, when the assumptions that sharp discontinuities occur between manual workers and those who are supposed to control them and that these discontinuities mark a fundamental line of class cleavage were not found to be entirely appropriate in the docks. Foremen obviously had a greater *formal* share in the power structure of their firms, which marked them off from the men, but in reality the difference was less than it might have seemed.

Foremen had lost their power to control the labour force, a fact which on its own did not reflect any change in their relative standing in their firms, because there was a loss of power all the way through the hierarchy. But the increasingly marginal position of foremen as they withdrew from areas of potential conflict suggested that their position was changing. Foremen certainly did not form part of management in any meaningful sense, because interaction with managers was low, promotion opportunities were remote and foremen identified with other foremen, while the men increasingly bypassed their supervisors and dealt directly with managers.

It is scarcely surprising that in the late 1960s and early 1970s workplace relations should have been so harmonious, or rather that the men should have thought them harmonious. Overtly authoritarian and exploitative relationships had not survived decasualization while conflicts arising from the normal disparity of power in industry were fairly infrequent. Here again, dock workers found themselves in a privileged position which minimized the impact of class relations at the workplace: the unusually even distribution of power between the men and the lower echelons of management protected the men from the kinds of social relations of production found in many other industries, though workers were still aware of the obvious conflicts of interest between the parties at the workplace.

The structural settings *other* than work in which class is manifest, for example the family and community, show that dock workers differ very little from other manual workers but that their differences from foremen are more extensive. The accounts of family and community showed how little working-class 'traditionalism' could be found among the men. Home-centred and privatized family life was the norm, and there was little gregariousness within the extended family or the local community. There was some sort of occupational community outside work, but this was incorporated into the privatized style of life and bore little resemblance to old-fashioned, working-class occupational communities. In comparison, foremen were even more remote from traditional patterns and acted in ways similar to those of middle-class groups. They were home-centred and privatized but made little contact with the occupation outside work and had more white-collar friends than the men. They tended to be home-owners and to live in areas with fair numbers of non-manual neighbours. There was no evidence that they formed the élite of a dock-based, proletarian community; though the efforts they made to separate themselves from the men may have resulted from their own feelings of superior status.

What emerged was a picture of dock workers who were solidly working class but were not 'traditional' proletarians and foremen who were less homogeneous as a group and who displayed characteristics typical of both working and middle classes. The attitudes of men and foremen strengthened this image. Dock workers had a strong occupational solidarity which cut across different firms and different docks, but they had overcome the sectionalism implicit in occupational solidarity to feel a wider and more universal sense of solidarity with workers in other industries. They believed in the necessity of collective action and the industrial aims of the union movement, but they rejected the idea of a united industrial and political labour movement. They had no particularly coherent and radical form of consciousness, but put forward scattered, often unrelated and sometimes inconsistent elements of an ideology in an ad hoc manner. As a group, dock workers were to the 'Left' in their replies to statements about inequalities, but these views were unrelated to their views about industry, an area in which more radical views had been anticipated on the basis of popular stereotypes; while individuals obviously did not have any systematic account of the world which linked together the various different spheres of their experience. Or rather, it should be said that their actual experience of industrial relations was more harmonistic than their experience of social inequality outside work, and that this work experience was reflected in their replies to the statements. Social imagery was middle-of-the-road, because very few people supported the radical extreme of a power dichotomy and most preferred some variation of the money image.

Dock workers shared the typically inchoate social consciousness of the British working class, based on a mixture of personal experience, some exposure to radical ideologies, and the conditioning effects of the dominant culture. They were radical to different degrees in different contexts. Those ideological elements which can be traced suggest an oppositional awareness, or so the latent opposition in employment and the recognition of social power and inequality would suggest. There was some evidence that dock workers had a sense of identity with other members of the working class. But this universalism was essentially a trade unionist view, because it laid emphasis on the need for collective solidarity in the industrial sphere alone. It was also an 'economistic' ideology, because it was confined to the protection of material conditions rather than being concerned with, say, the nature of power and control in industry, despite the considerable power dock workers themselves had in their own industry. Unlike some other studies of manual workers, in my research I found little variation by age or locality: people did not become less radical with advancing years, nor were certain communities more proletarian than others. Collective awareness and solidarity of the sort encountered in the docks could, of course, form part of a more all-embracing, oppositional class-consciousness, but this particular ideological development had not occurred at the beginning of the nineteen-seventies.

Foremen shared a collectivist orientation in many cases. But even when age and political affiliation were controlled for, there were fewer foremen with a collective or oppositional view than among the men. They emphasized status images of society more often than the men, condemned the union–political alliance and any extension of industrial solidarity beyond the occupation itself, and had socially more ambitious aspirations. In these ways they marked themselves off from the men and showed some similarity with what we assume to be middle- rather than working-class traits.

Thus dock workers can be placed firmly in the mainstream of the contemporary British working class. Certain aspects of their work are unusual, though their power at the workplace is recent and we cannot tell how long it will continue in the future, but their work tasks and their appraisals of work are recognizably similar to other workers'. They share a distinct occupational culture at the workplace which occasionally spills over into life outside work, but this does not isolate them from the rest of their class nor does it consign them to that particular sub-section (if it exists) which has been labelled 'traditional'. The evidence of dock workers strongly suggests that the working class is more homogeneous than has been allowed for: those who wish to divide it into old and new greatly exaggerate the divisions which actually occur within the ranks of semi-skilled and skilled workers, though there may still be some sectional differences between a few craftsmen, the true heirs of the old 'aristocracy of labour', and the rest of the working class.

Foremen are more ambiguous. Their position is marginal both in their firms and in their occupation, their work situation appears to differ from those of the men and the managers, and they view themselves as a group separate from others. Outside work, they display a mixture of characteristics which belong to both working- and middle-class life styles. They clearly differ from dock workers, yet do not unambiguously belong to the middle class. Indeed, foremen illustrate the problems which analysts face when trying to cope with many groups which are intermediate between the two major classes as historically defined. Yet these occupational groups are now growing in size and importance. The changing manpower requirements of new technologies and the attempted extensions of managerial control into the minutiae of production mean that modern industry employs an ever-increasing proportion of intermediate staff who are neither workers nor managers. As the British occupational structure changes, the class position and social identity of intermediate groups becomes an issue of increasing significance.

Tables

The statistical techniques used throughout this book are from R. J. Senter, *The Analysis of Data* (Glenview, Illinois, 1969). They include the Chi-square statistic, the difference between proportions using z scores, a multiple range test for the analysis of variance, and the Phi contingency coefficient (because the maximum value of Φ is often less than 1, all Φ coefficients are corrected by $\dfrac{\Phi}{\Phi\max.}$ and the resulting statistic interpreted in the same way as a correlation coefficient).

All percentages are rounded off to the nearest whole number, which means in a few cases that the totals fail to add to 100. The following abbreviations are used: DK = Don't Know; DNA = Does Not Apply; NA = No Answer.

TABLE 1.1

Registered Dock Workers

	1967	1968	1969	1970	1971	1972	1973	1974
National Total	57,505	56,563	52,732	46,912	45,491	41,247	34,509	34,606
London Docks								
Surrey[1]	3,005	2,702	2,626	1,912	1,079	1,002	617	526
Pool	2,313	2,044	1,707	796	578	441	98	73
Tilbury and N.' Fleet	2,539	2,742	2,951	2,773	3,413	3,095	3,094	3,181
Royal	7,180	6,821	6,616	6,135	6,934	5,690	4,156	4,068
India and Millwall	3,132	3,171	2,796	2,751	3,177	2,667	2,416	2,443
London and St. Kaths.[2]	2,299	1,658	568	400	224	—	—	—
Lighterage	3,287	3,040	2,604	1,903	1,679	1,567	1,244	1,201
London Total	23,755	22,178	19,868	16,670	17,084	14,462	11,625	11,492

Notes:
(1) Closed down 1970–71.
(2) Closed down 1968.
Source: National Dock Labour Board.

TABLE 1.2

U.K. Container and Roll-on Foreign Trade on Selected Routes
(Imports plus Exports)

	Per Cent Penetration[1]			
	1969 %	1971 %	1973 (Estimate)[2] %	P.a. Growth Rates 1980 (Estimate) on 1971 (Potential)
E.E.C.	59	71	—	7·7
Ireland	52	54	—	3·1
Scandinavia	10	20	—	3·1
North America	13	30	—	4·7
Australasia	—	37	—	1·3
Total all routes[3]	17	27	44	3·7

Notes:
(1) Penetration figures are the actual tonnage as a percentage of the potential. The potential market is what could be achieved if no constraints, such as inadequate facilities, existed. Potential tonnage is Total Trade minus unmilled cereals, sugar, animal feedstuffs and basic materials such as ores, crude fertilizers, sand and gravel.
(2) The actual tonnages achieved in this year are known, but the potential tonnages are not available broken down into particular trades. The only available proportion is for the total trade on these selected routes.
(3) All foreign trade, not only the selected routes above.
Source: National Ports Council.

TABLE 1.3
Earnings[1]

Men				Foremen		
£	%	(N=139)		£	%	(N=93)
Below 1600	11	(15)		Below 1600	1	(1)
1600–1700	11	(15)		1600–1800	53	(49)
1700–1800	12	(17)		1800–2000	30	(28)
1800–1900	15	(21)		2000–2200	9	(8)
1900–2000	13	(18)		2200–2400	2	(2)
2000–2100	16	(22)		2400–2600	2	(2)
2100–2300	10	(13)		2600–3000	2	(2)
2300–2500	6	(9)		3000+	1	(1)
2500–3000	0					
3000+	6	(9)				

Note:
(1) Based on previous six months' earnings and extrapolated into annual income.

TABLE 4.1
Perceptions of the Work Situation

	Men %(N=139)		Foremen %(N=93)		Men: Conventional Hand Work %(N=113)		Crane %(N=25)		Unitized %(N=30)	
	Pace of Work									
Too fast	25	(34)	26	(24)	25	(28)	24	(6)	23	(7)
	Freedom: Speed									
Freedom to work at own speed	81	(112)	53	(49)	80	(90)	76	(19)	77	(23)
	Difference is significant at ·01 level; $z=5·04$									
	Fatigue									
Too tiring	28	(39)	38	(35)	31	(35)	16	(4)	13	(4)
					Difference between Conventional and Crane is significant at ·05 level; $z=2·43$ Difference between Conventional and Unitized is significant at ·06 level; $z=2·34$					
	Control: Way Work is Done									
Can decide how work is done	60	(83)	80	(74)	64	(72)	48	(12)	33	(10)
	Difference is significant at ·01 level; $z=3·36$				Difference between Conventional and Crane is significant at ·05 level; $z=2·78$ Difference between Conventional and Unitized is significant at ·01 level; $z=3·13$					

	Men %(N=139)	Foremen %(N=93)	Men: Conventional Hand Work %(N=113)	Crane %(N=25)	Unitized %(N=30)
Planning					
Well-planned work	22 (31)	54 (50)	18 (20)	12 (3)	67 (20)
	Difference is significant at ·01 level; z=5·04		Difference between Conventional and Unitized is significant at ·01 level; z=5·25		
Monotony					
Work is monotonous	15 (21)	12 (11)	11 (12)	36 (9)	33 (10)
			Difference between Conventional and Crane is significant at ·05 level; z=2·50 Difference between Conventional and Unitized is significant at ·05 level; z=2·52		
Variety					
Sufficient variety	87 (121)	88 (82)	94 (106)	40 (10)	73 (22)
			Difference between Conventional and Crane is significant at ·01 level; z=5·27 Difference between Conventional and Unitized is significant at ·06 level; z=2·35 Difference between Crane and Unitized is significant at ·05 level; z=2·62		
Concentration					
Maintained concentration is required	75 (104)	83 (77)	73 (82)	68 (17)	100 (30)
			Difference between Conventional and Crane is significant at ·01 level; z=6·04 Difference between Conventional and Unitized is significant at ·01 level; z=3·37		
Use of Ideas					
Can try out ideas	59 (82)	84 (78)	64 (72)	28 (7)	47 (14)
	Difference is significant at ·01 level; z=4·4		Difference between Conventional and Crane is significant at ·01 level; z=3·55 Difference between Conventional and Unitized is significant at ·05 level; z=2·59		
Simplicity					
Work is too simple for abilities	31 (43)	25 (23)	28 (32)	56 (14)	27 (8)
			Difference between Conventional and Crane is significant at ·05 level; z=2·56 Difference between Conventional and Unitized is significant at ·06 level; z=2·28		
Freedom of Movement					
Free to leave work place for half hour	81 (112)	87 (81)	82 (93)	48 (12)	80 (24)
			Difference between Conventional and Crane is significant at ·01 level; z=3·32 Difference between Unitized and Crane is significant at ·05 level; z=2·54		
Freedom of Interaction					
Free to interact	82 (114)	86 (80)	85 (96)	16 (4)	57 (17)

TABLE 4.2

Perceptions of Skill

	Men %(N=139)		Foremen %(N=93)		Men: Conventional Hand Work %(N=113)		Crane %(N=25)		Unitized %(N=30)	
Perceived Skill Level										
Skilled	63	(87)	81	(75)	62	(70)	72	(18)	57	(17)
Semi-skilled	27	(37)	6	(6)	29	(33)	28	(7)	27	(8)
Unskilled	10	(14)	13	(12)	9	(10)	—		17	(5)
DK	1	(1)								

Difference in Skilled response is significant at ·01; $z=3·09$

Perceived Learning Process To Do Job Well										
Formal training	24	(33)	3	(3)	20	(23)	28	(7)	47	(14)
Long experience	66	(92)	87	(81)	71	(80)	56	(14)	33	(10)
Short period getting to know ropes	6	(8)	4	(4)	5	(6)	4	(1)	7	(2)
Training and experience mixed	4	(6)	5	(5)	4	(4)	12	(3)	13	(4)

Difference between Training responses is significant at ·01 level; $z=5·12$
Difference between Experience responses is significant at ·01 level; $z=3·94$

Difference between Training responses of Conventional and Unitized is significant at ·05 level; $z=2·67$
Differences between Experience responses of Conventional and Unitized and Conventional and Crane are significant at ·01 level; $z=3·80$, and ·05 level; $z=2·54$

Perceived Exclusivity of Work										
Anyone with experience of dock work could do job	60	(84)	22	(20)	66	(74)	36	(9)	50	(15)

Difference is significant at ·01 level; $z=6·5$

Difference between Conventional and Crane is significant at ·05 level; $z=2·78$

TABLE 4.3

Age and Perceptions of Work

	Men		Foremen	
	Ai	*Aii*	*Bi*	*Bii*
	Below 45	*Above 45*	*Below 45*	*Above 45*
	Years of Age	*Years of Age*	*Years of Age*	*Years of Age*
	%(N=79)	%(N=60)	%(N=22)	%(N=71)
Work is too simple for abilities	39 (31)	20 (12)	32 (7)	23 (16)
	Ai — Aii difference is significant at 0·05; $z = 2·49$			
Can try out ideas	53 (42)	67 (40)	82 (18)	85 (60)
	Ai — Bi difference is significant at 0·05; $z = 2·87$			
	Aii — Bii difference is significant at 0·06; $z = 2·31$			
Maintained concentration is required	71 (56)	80 (48)	73 (16)	86 (61)
Freedom to work at own speed	81 (64)	80 (48)	77 (17)	45 (32)
	Aii — Bii difference is significant at 0·01; $z = 4·48$			
Pace of work is too fast	25 (20)	23 (14)	41 (9)	21 (15)

TABLE 4.4
Age and Perceptions of Skill

Men[1]
Age Groups

	25–34[1] %(N=33)		35–44 %(N=46)		45–54 %(N=40)		55 *and over* %(N=20)	
Skilled	39	(13)	65	(30)	73	(29)	75	(15)
Semi-skilled	39	(13)	26	(12)	18	(7)	25	(5)
Unskilled	19	(6)	9	(4)	10	(4)	—	

Difference of Skilled versus Semi- and Unskilled replies between age group 25–34 years and rest of sample is significant at $0·01$: $X^2 = 8·98$ with 1 degree of freedom.

Difference between 25–44 and 45 and over is significant at $0·05$: $X^2 = 4·80$ with 1 degree of freedom.

Note:
(1) One respondent gave a 'don't know' reply.

Foremen
Age Groups

	25–44[1] %(N=22)		45–54 %(N=38)		55 *and over* %(N=33)	
Skilled	68	(15)	87	(33)	82	(27)
Semi-skilled	9	(2)	5	(2)	6	(2)
Unskilled	23	(5)	8	(3)	10	(4)

Difference of Skilled versus Semi- and Unskilled replies between age group 30–44 and 45 and over is not significant at $0·05$: $X^2 = 2·86$ with 1 degree of freedom.

There is no statistically significant difference between Men and Foremen over the age of 45 years.

Note:
(1) Number of foremen in 25–34 range=3, so this group incorporated with next.

TABLE 4.5

Rating of 17 Items in the Ideal Job[1]

	Men %		Foremen %
(1) Security[2]	95	(1) Security	96
(2) Efficient company	95	(2) Accomplishment	94
(3) Accomplishment	93	(3) Efficient company	93
(4) High pay	92	(4) Control	92
(5) Workmates	91	(5) Superiors (good relations)	91
(6) Personal life	90	(6) High pay	90
=(7) Development	89	(7) Workmates	89
=(7) Working conditions	89	=(8) Responsibility	89
(9) Subordinates	86	=(8) Development	89
(10) Superiors (good relations)	85	(10) Personal life	89
(11) Control	83	=(11) Subordinates	86
(12) Responsibility	80	=(11) Working conditions	86
=(13) Nature of work	76	(13) Supervision	80
=(13) Supervision	76	=(14) Promotion prospects	75
(15) Recognition	73	=(14) Recognition	75
(16) Promotion prospects	64	(16) Nature of work	75
(17) Status and prestige	53	(17) Status and prestige	67

Notes:

(1) Figures expressed as percentages of total possible score. Rank order is based on the figures calculated to two decimal places *prior* to the scores being rounded off.

(2) The categories presented in this table are abbreviated in order to simplify presentation; the full categories are contained in the questionnaire (Appendix A, Section D).

TABLE 4.6

Choice of 3 Most Important of 17 Items[1]

	Men %		Foremen %
(1) High pay	57	(1) Security	47
(2) Security	48	(2) High pay	41
(3) Development	30	(3) Promotion	30
(4) Accomplishment	27	(4) Accomplishment	29
(5) Workmates	25	(5) Responsibility	22
(6) Personal life	21	(6) Development	20
(7) Promotion	18	=(7) Workmates	16
(8) Working conditions	14	=(7) Control	16
(9) Control	12	(9) Superiors (good relations)	14
=(10) Recognition	9	(10) Personal life	13
=(10) Efficient company	9	=(11) Recognition	12
(12) Superiors (good relations)	8	=(11) Efficient company	12
(13) Supervision	6	=(13) Subordinates	8
=(14) Responsibility	4	=(13) Supervision	8
=(14) Nature of work	4	=(13) Working conditions	8
=(16) Subordinates	1	(16) Nature of work	5
=(16) Status and prestige	1	(17) Status and prestige	1

Note:

(1) Percentage of sample giving items as one of 3 most important.

TABLE 4.7

Choice of Three Most Important Items by Age

Men

25–34 (N=33)	%	35–44 (N=46)	%	45–54 (N=40)	%	55 and over (N=20)	%
Pay	67	Pay	65	Pay ⎫		Security	75
Security	49	Security	61	Security ⎬ 43		Pay	50
Personal life	30	Development	40	Accomplishment	35	Accomplishment	45

Foremen

30–44 (N=22)	%	45–54 (N=38)	%	55 and over (N=33)	%
Pay	79	Security	47	Security	49
Promotion	47	Pay	37	Accomplishment	42
Security	37	Promotion ⎫		Pay	27
		Accomplishment ⎬ 30			

TABLE 4.8

'Affective' Involvement By Age

	Men %(of Age Group)		Foremen %(of Age group)	
Upset: 25–44 years	21	(17)	27	(6)
45 and over	22	(13)	52	(37)
Not Upset: 25–44 years	79	(62)	73	(16)
45 and over	78	(47)	47	(34)

TABLE 5.1

Perceptions of Role Behaviour
(Allocation of time to various activities)[1]

	Foremen's Estimate (Mean %)	Management Estimate (Mean %)	Actual (Mean %)
Activity: Supervision	(A)	(B)	
Public (i)	13 (*Ai*)	25 (*Bi*)	1
Private (ii)	21 (*Aii*)	28 (*Bii*)	1
Differences not significant at ·05 level: *Bii* and *Bi*			
Activity: Co-ordination	(A)	(B)	*Actual*
Public	19	10	18
Private	27	34	19
Differences not significant at ·05 level: nil			
Activity: Work Direction	(A)	(B)	*Actual*
Public	20	28	17
Private	38	33	40
Differences not significant at ·05 level: *Aii* and *Bii*; *Bii* and *Bi*; *Bi* and *Ai*			
Activity: Interaction (All)	(A)	(B)	*Actual*
Public	58	72	51
Private	57	62	60
Differences not significant at ·05 level: *Ai* and *Aii*; *Ai* and *Bii*; *Aii* and *Bii*			
Activity: Interaction (Men)	(A)	(B)	*Actual*
Public	16	33	11
Private	19	31	22
Differences not significant at ·05 level: *Ai* and *Bi*; *Aii* and *Ai*			
Activity: Interaction (Boss)	(A)	(B)	*Actual*
Public	7	14	5
Private	14	8	13
Differences not significant at ·05 level: *Ai* and *Bii*; *Aii* and *Bi*			

Note:
(1) Significance assessed by the analysis of variance, using Duncan's new multiple range test to compare individual pairs of groups within the analysis of variance design. Differences between pairs are significant unless otherwise stated.

TABLE 5.2

Openness of Communication with T.O.*/Superintendent[1]

	Public %	Private %
How aware is he of your difficulties?	55	20
How sure are you of order of importance he places?	56	19
How much agreement between you on order of importance?	31	20
Do you usually know how satisfied he is?	55	19
How far do you really understand him?	31	17
Does he mean what he says?	44	18
How far do you reveal your plans?	50	9
How direct are you with him?	19	12
Does he say what he means?	46	20
How likely are you to criticize him directly?	15	12
How often do you give him your true opinion?	19	18
How often do you withhold information?	54	10

Note:
(1) Weighted results expressed as a percentage of total possible score: 100 =
Completely Blocked; 0 = Completely Open.
* T.O. = P.L.A. Traffic Officer.

TABLE 5.3

Role Ambiguity

Degree of Clarity	%	(N = 93)
Always clear	24	(22)
Clear on most things	34	(32)
Fairly clear	30	(28)
Not too clear	12	(11)
Not at all clear	0	

Types of Ambiguity		
Lack of information on technical aspects	42	(39)
Lack of information on authority/responsibility	14	(13)
Inability to predict men's reactions	2	(2)
Conflicting orders from superiors	5	(5)
Other	1	(1)
DNA/DK	36	(33)

Sources of Ambiguity in Lack of Technical
Information Category

	%	(N = 39)
Other port agencies/division of labour	90	(35)
Own management	10	(4)

TABLE 5.4
Role Conflict of Foremen

Nature of Conflicts	%	(N=93)
Inter-Sender:		
Own boss vs. client	36	(33)
Generalized conflict between different parties	8	(7)
	44	(40)
Intra-Sender:		
Focal person vs. own boss/client	20	(19)
Focal person vs. non-client outsiders	3	(3)
Focal person vs. own subordinates	9	(8)
	32	(30)
Other and unclassifiable	5	(5)
DNA	19	(18)
Parties Involved in Conflicts[1]		
Own superiors	50	(46)
Other superiors	6	(6)
Subordinates (own line)	9	(8)
Outsiders (including 'other superiors')	48	(45)
Not specified	8	(7)
DNA	19	(18)
Content of Conflicts		
Technical functions (planning and execution)	74	(69)
Personnel function	2	(2)
Other	4	(4)
DNA	19	(18)

Note:
(1) Total=more than 100 as some replies included in more than one category.

TABLE 6.1

Days Lost per 1,000 Workers in the Docks, as Multiples
of National Average

Period[1]	Multiple	
	All Docks	London Docks
1959–61	8·0	13·1
1960–62	9·2	14·0
1961–63	5·2	9·8
1962–64	5·5	5·7
1963–65	7·0	6·4
1964–66	8·5	8·8
1965–67	17·9	11·8
1966–68	14·7	29·7
1967–69	14·1	21·7
1968–70	11·2	16·9
1969–71	8·6	12·3
1970–72	10·7	16·3
1971–73	6·0	12·7

Note:

(1) Data based on three-year moving averages in order to minimize short-run fluctuations.

Sources: M. Silver, op. cit., *Department of Employment Gazette*, 1974, and National Dock Labour Board.

TABLE 6.2

Evaluation of Company Men

Company No.:	1		2		3		4		6		Total	
	%(N=23)		%(N=16)		%(N=40)		%(N=21)		%(N=39)		%(N=139)	
Favourable Evaluation (Company is 'good')	96	(22)	50	(8)	75	(30)	76	(16)	90	(35)	80	(111)
Reasons:[1]												
Management is fair and reasonable	87	(20)	31	(5)	25	(10)	19	(4)	33	(13)	45	(62)
Company same as others—no particular advantage	0		0		23	(9)	33	(7)	26	(10)	19	(26)
Good pay	13	(3)	25	(4)	20	(8)	33	(7)	21	(8)	22	(32)
Fair work shares	9	(2)	6	(1)	5	(2)	5	(1)	5	(2)	6	(8)
Variety of work	4	(1)	0		3	(1)	0		15	(6)	6	(8)
Other	13	(3)	0		5	(2)	10	(2)	5	(2)	7	(10)
Less Favourable Evaluation[2]	4	(1)	50	(8)	48	(19)	57	(12)	36	(14)	37	(54)

Foremen

Company No.:	1		2		3		4		5		6		7		Total	
	%(N=6)		%(N=6)		%(N=18)		%(N=12)		%(N=24)		%(N=15)		%(N=12)		%(N=93)	
Favourable Evaluation	100		100		94	(17)	75	(9)	83	(20)	80	(12)	100		88	(82)
Reasons:[1]																
Management is fair and reasonable	67	(4)	33	(2)	56	(10)	58	(7)	54	(13)	27	(4)	8	(1)	44	(41)
Company same as others—no advantage	0		17	(1)	6	(1)	8	(1)	17	(4)	40	(6)	0		14	(13)
Pay and security	17	(1)	0		22	(4)	0		4	(1)	7	(1)	42	(5)	13	(12)
Other	17	(1)	50	(3)	11	(2)	8	(1)	8	(2)	7	(1)	50	(6)	17	(16)

Note:

(1) As respondents gave more than one reply, percentages = more than 100.

(2) This combines the company is 'bad' replies with the 'same as others—no particular advantage' replies, to indicate the lack of positive commitment. Thus the latter replies are counted *twice*.

TABLE 6.3

Consideration given to Leaving

Men

Company No.:	1 %(N=23)		2 %(N=16)		3 %(N=40)		4 %(N=21)		6 %(N=39)		Total %(N=139)	
Have considered leaving	9	(2)	63	(10)	50	(20)	29	(6)	39	(15)	38	(53)

Foremen

Company No.:	1 %(N=6)		2 %(N=6)		3 %(N=18)		4 %(N=12)		5 %(N=24)		6 %(N=15)		7 %(N=12)		Total %(N=93)	
Have considered leaving	0		0		6	(1)	17	(2)	4	(1)	7	(1)	8	(1)	6	(6)

TABLE 6.4

Reasons for Staying with Company

Men

Company No.:	1 %(N=23)		2 %(N=16)		3 %(N=40)		4 %(N=21)		6 %(N=39)		Total %(N=139)	
Sum of 'negative' reasons[1]	17	(4)	38	(6)	54	(21)	44	(10)	64	(25)	48	(66)
Sum of 'moral involvement' reasons[2]	44	(10)	6	(1)	8	(3)	14	(3)	13	(5)	16	(22)
Company of workmates	4	(1)	38	(6)	10	(4)	0		0		8	(11)
Intrinsic work interest	13	(3)	0		13	(5)	0		10	(4)	9	(12)
Instrumental (pay/security)	17	(4)	0		10	(4)	29	(6)	10	(4)	13	(18)
Other	4	(1)	19	(3)	8	(3)	14	(3)	0		7	(10)

Foremen

Company No.:	1 %(N=6)		2 %(N=6)		3 %(N=18)		4 %(N=12)		5 %(N=24)		6 %(N=15)		7 %(N=12)		Total %(N=93)	
Sum of 'negative' reasons[1]	17	(1)	0		22	(4)	42	(5)	50	(12)	27	(4)	50	(6)	35	(32)
Sum of 'moral involvement' reasons[2]	33	(2)	33	(2)	39	(7)	33	(4)	29	(7)	40	(6)	8	(1)	31	(29)
Company of workmates	17	(1)	17	(1)	6	(1)	0		0		0		0		3	(3)
Intrinsic work interest	33	(2)	17	(1)	11	(2)	25	(3)	17	(4)	27	(4)	8	(1)	18	(17)
Instrumental (pay/security)	0		17	(1)	17	(3)	0		0		7	(1)	33	(4)	10	(9)
Other	0		17	(1)	6	(1)	0		4	(1)	0		0		3	(3)

Notes:

(1) These include age, inertia, impossibility of changing and the fact that other companies are no better.

(2) These include the quality of human relations and feelings of loyalty, satisfaction and identification.

TABLE 6.5

Images of Employment Relationship

Descriptive	Men %(N=139)		Foremen %(N=93)	
Harmony	56	(78)	33	(31)
Antagonism	41	(57)	66	(61)
DK/Neither	3	(4)	1	(1)
Normative				
Harmony	32	(45)	63	(59)
Antagonism	9	(13)	3	(3)
DK/Neither	2	(3)	0	
DNA	56	(78)	33	(31)

TABLE 7.1

Unions and Respect and Leadership of Members

	Men				Foremen			
	T.G.W.U. %(N=116)		N.A.S.D. %(N=23)		T.G.W.U. %(N=69)		N.A.S.D. %(N=24)	
Yes	23	(27)	56	(13)	33	(23)	62	(15)
No	72	(84)	43	(10)	62	(43)	37	(9)
DK	4	(5)	0		4	(3)	0	

	All			
	T.G.W.U %(N=185)		N.A.S.D. %(N=47)	
Yes	27	(50)	60	(28)
No	69	(127)	40	(19)
DK	4	(8)	0	

TABLE 7.2
Nature of Changes

	Men					
	T.G.W.U. %(N=116)		N.A.S.D. %(N=23)		All %(N=139)	
Regular election of officers (local)	20	(23)	0		17	(23)
New officers (local)	21	(24)	0		17	(24)
Greater union contact with members	24	(28)	0		20	(28)
Union to favour men, not management	9	(10)	0		7	(10)
Election/accountability of *all* officers	2	(2)	0		1	(2)
Consolidated criticism of local officers only	41	(47)	0		34	(47)
Consolidated criticism of general failure of union to represent members' views (including criticisms of local officers)	75	(87)	0		63	(87)
Union to be more progressive	3	(4)	22	(5)	7	(9)
One port union	5	(6)	17	(4)	7	(10)
Stronger line taken with members	2	(3)	0		2	(3)
Other	1	(1)	13	(3)	3	(4)
DK/DNA	13	(15)	48	(11)	19	(26)

	Foremen					
	T.G.W.U. %(N=69)		N.A.S.D. %(N=24)		All %(N=93)	
Regular election of officers (local)	3	(2)	0		2	(2)
New officers (local)	9	(6)	0		6	(6)
Greater union contact with members	33	(23)	8	(2)	27	(25)
Union to favour members, not management	3	(2)	0		2	(2)
Election/accountability of *all* officers	1	(1)	0		1	(1)
Consolidated criticism of local officers only	12	(8)	0		9	(8)
Consolidated criticism of general failure of union to represent members' views	49	(34)	8	(2)	39	(36)
Union to be more progressive	3	(2)	4	(1)	3	(3)
One port union	1	(1)	50	(12)	14	(13)
Stronger line taken with members	15	(10)	17	(4)	15	(14)
Other	10	(7)	13	(3)	11	(10)
DK/DNA	22	(15)	8	(2)	18	(17)

TABLE 7.3

Reasons for Separate Foremen's Section

	T.G.W.U. %(N=69)		Foremen N.A.S.D. %(N=24)		All %(N=93)	
Foremen's interests differ from other groups	57	(39)	29	(7)	49	(46)
Same as above, plus statement that men are hostile to foremen and do not protect interests at branch	16	(11)	50	(12)	25	(23)
Total of separate interest arguments	73	(50)	79	(19)	74	(69)
Men can use branch to discipline foremen	7	(5)	4	(1)	6	(6)
Other	1	(1)	0		1	(1)
DNA	19	(13)	17	(4)	18	(17)

TABLE 7.4

Perceptions of Trade Unions

Men								
	All %(N=139)		By Party Allegiance:	Lab. Constants %(N=95)		Cons. Constants %(N=5)		Changers %(N=19)
Trades unions ought to get members a say in management								
Agree	81	(112)		81	(77)	60	(3)	84	(16)
Neither	5	(7)		5	(5)	0		0	
Disagree	14	(20)		13	(12)	40	(2)	16	(3)
Trades unions have too much power in this country								
Agree	40	(56)		38	(36)	40	(2)	42	(8)
Neither	11	(15)		8	(8)	20	(1)	5	(1)
Disagree	49	(68)		54	(51)	40	(2)	53	(10)
Trades unions ought not to support Labour party								
Agree	61	(85)		57	(54)	60	(3)	58	(11)
Neither	7	(9)		6	(6)	0		0	
Disagree	32	(45)		37	(35)	40	(2)	42	(8)
Trades unions are no longer so necessary as they used to be								
Agree	16	(22)		16	(15)	0		16	(3)
Neither	2	(3)		2	(2)	0		0	
Disagree	82	(114)		82	(78)	100	(5)	84	(16)

Foremen

	All %(N=93)	By Party Allegiance:	Lab. Constants %(N=45)	Cons. Constants %(N=29)	Changers %(N=11)
Trades unions ought to get members a say in management					
Agree	79 (73)		85 (38)	76 (22)	82 (9)
Neither	2 (2)		2 (1)	3 (1)	0
Disagree	19 (18)		13 (6)	21 (6)	18 (2)
Trades unions have too much power in this country					
Agree	67 (62)		55 (25)	79 (23)	73 (8)
Neither	7 (7)		7 (3)	7 (2)	9 (1)
Disagree	26 (24)		38 (17)	14 (4)	18 (2)
Trades unions ought not to support Labour party					
Agree	75 (70)		60 (27)	93 (27)	82 (9)
Neither	8 (7)		7 (3)	3 (1)	18 (2)
Disagree	17 (16)		33 (15)	3 (1)	0
Trades unions are no longer so necessary as they used to be					
Agree	36 (33)		22 (10)	45 (13)	55 (7)
Neither	2 (2)		0	3 (1)	9 (1)
Disagree	62 (58)		78 (35)	52 (15)	36 (4)

TABLE 8.1

Assessment of Most Important Quality of Good Foreman

Men

	%(N=139)	
Knows his own job	42	(58)
Way he treats men—'consideration'	19	(27)
—leaves men alone	10	(14)
Personal qualities not related to men (e.g. decisiveness, honesty, responsibility)	14	(19)
Knows own job + way treats men equally	14	(19)
Other	1	(1)
DK	1	(1)

Foremen

	%(N=93)	
Knows own job	54	(50)
Way he treats men	1	(1)
Personal qualities	27	(25)
Knows own job + personal qualities equally	18	(17)

TABLE 8.2
Dock Workers: Preference for One or Rotation of Foremen

	Total	
	%(N = 139)	
Prefer One Foreman		
Reasons:		
Teamwork (better money; safety)	30	(42)
Better relations with foreman	3	(4)
Teamwork and relations jointly	4	(5)
Other	2	(3)
	39	(54)
Prefer Rotation of Foremen		
Reasons:		
Foremen cannot expect favours	16	(22)
Change breaks boredom	14	(19)
Other	9	(13)
	39	(54)
Irrelevant which method	18	(25)
DK	4	(6)

TABLE 8.3
*Weighted[1] Scores of Foremen's Perceptions of Being
'In the Middle'*

Company	Score	Sector[2]	Score
1	20·8		
2	33·3	Private	15
3	11·1		
4	29·2	Public	31
5	10·4		
6	6·3		
7	31·3		

Notes:
(1) Figures are expressed in such a way that the nearer the score is to zero the *greater* the frequency of conflict (the more often people said 'nearly all the time'). Higher scores indicate less frequent conflict.
(2) Difference between private and public sectors is not statistically significant.

TABLE 8.4
Foremen: Perception of Position in Company

Company No.:	1 %(N=6)	2 %(N=6)	3 %(N=18)	4 %(N=12)	5 %(N=24)	6 %(N=15)	7 %(N=12)	Total %(N=93)
Staff	67 (4)	67 (4)	94 (17)	92 (11)	88 (21)	87 (13)	100 (12)	88 (82)
Management	33 (2)	33 (2)	6 (1)	8 (1)	12 (3)	13 (2)	0	12 (11)
Labour	0	0	0	0	0	0	0	0

TABLE 8.5
Foremen: Perception of Forming Group in Company

Company No.:	1 %(N=6)	2 %(N=6)	3 %(N=18)	4 %(N=12)	5 %(N=24)	6 %(N=15)	7 %(N=12)	Total %(N=93)
Stick together as a group	67 (4)	67 (4)	72 (13)	83 (10)	79 (19)	80 (12)	100	80 (79)

TABLE 9.1
Origins of Dock Friendships

	Men		Foremen			
	Proportion of dock worker friends %(N=142)[1]		Proportion of dock worker friends %(N=25)[2]		Proportion of foremen friends %(N=17)	
Dock-Based						
Via work	23	(33)	8	(2)	47	(8)
Via docks	11	(16)	8	(2)	53	(9)
	34	(49)	16	(4)	100	
Based Outside						
Via pub/club	23	(33)	28	(7)		
Via school	16	(22)	16	(4)		
Via kin	13	(19)	24	(6)		
As neighbours	12	(17)	12	(3)		
Other	1	(2)	4	(1)		
	65	(93)	84	(21)		

Notes:
  (1) Excludes 2 tally clerks and 1 foreman.
  (2) Excludes 2 tally clerks.

TABLE 9.2

Dock Friends as Proportion of All Friends, by Area of Respondent's Residence

		Men (Absolute Nos.)	%		Foremen (Absolute Nos.)	%
Thurrock	(N=150)	74 ⎤		(N=79)	18 ⎤	
Gravesend	(N=11)	6 ⎬	59	(N=12)	3 ⎬	27
East End	(N=63)	33 ⎦		(N=42)	15 ⎦	
Other	(N=119)	32	26	(N=68)	8	12

TABLE 9.3

1961 and 1966 Census Data

1961 Census	Proportion of Dock Workers %
Barking	3·0
Bermondsey	11·7
Bethnal Green	2·1
Camberwell	1·0
Deptford	3·9
East Ham	2·8
Greenwich	1·9
Hackney	0·6
Lewisham	1·4
Poplar	7·3
Shoreditch	0·9
Stepney	7·4
West Ham	4·4
Thurrock	5·4

1966 Census	Proportion of Dock Workers %	Proportion of Non-Manual Workers %
Barking	1·7	24·7
Greenwich	0·9	36·4
Hackney	0·3	24·7
Lambeth	0·1	35·6
Lewisham	1·0	36·2
Newham	2·4	23·5
Redbridge	0·3	50·7
Southwark	1·6	26·4
Tower Hamlets	3·0	18·9
Thurrock	3·0	27·1

TABLE 9.4

Proximity to Dock

	Men			Foremen		
	West India %(N=37)	Tilbury %(N=102)	All %(N=139)	West India %(N=18)	Tilbury %(N=51)	All %(N=93)
−1 mile	19	17	17	11	22	17
1–2 miles	24	11	14	11	18	17
2–4 miles	16	34	30	17	33	25
Over 4	41	38	39	61	27	41

TABLE 9.5

Occupations of Close Friends

	Men %(N=343)		Foremen %(N=194)	
Employers, managers and professionals	6	(20)	18	(34)
Intermediate and junior non-manual	9	(29)	26	(51)
Skilled manual and foremen	20	(69)	26	(51)
Semi-skilled and unskilled manual	63	(217)	29	(56)
Personal service	2	(7)	1	(1)
DK	0[1]	(1)	1	(1)

Note:
(1) Less than 1 per cent.

TABLE 9.6

Origin of Friendships

	Men				Foremen			
	Manual[1] %(N=286)		Non-Manual %(N=49)		Manual[1] %(N=107)		Non-Manual %(N=85)	
Work	17	(49)	8	(4)	6	(6)	2	(2)
Non-Work								
Pub/Club	30	(87)	16	(8)	30	(32)	12	(10)
School	16	(46)	14	(7)	22	(23)	12	(10)
Kin	15	(43)	10	(5)	18	(19)	25	(21)
Neighbours	10	(28)	35	(17)	12	(13)	34	(29)
Other	9	(25)	10	(5)	10	(11)	8	(7)
No Information	3	(8)	6	(3)	3	(3)	7	(6)

Note:
(1) Figures exclude Personal Service and Don't Know categories in previous table.

TABLE 9.7

Proportion of People in Each Area with Manual Affiliations Only

Men

	Thurrock %(N=63)		East End %(N=29)		Other %(N=44)	
Manual worker friends only	86	(54)	69	(20)	55	(24)
Manual worker brothers only	56	(35)	52	(15)	52	(23)
Manual worker brothers-in-law only	71	(45)	48	(14)	64	(28)

Foremen

	%(N=35)		%(N=20)		%(N=33)	
Manual worker friends only	34	(12)	40	(8)	21	(7)
Manual worker brothers only	46	(16)	65	(13)	46	(15)
Manual worker brothers-in-law only	26	(9)	65	(13)	46	(15)

TABLE 9.8

Proportion of People in Each Area who are Home Owners

	Men		%	Foremen		%	Total	%
Thurrock	(N=63)	22	(14)	(N=35)	57	(20)	36	(34)
East End	(N=29)	18	(5)	(N=20)	40	(8)	27	(13)
Other	(N=44)	61	(27)	(N=33)	82	(27)	70	(54)
Gravesend	(N=3)	67	(2)	(N=5)	80	(4)	75	(6)

TABLE 9.9

Desired Friends

	Men %(N=139)		Foremen %(N=93)	
People with good education	19	(27)	36	(33)
People with 'bit of class'	1	(1)	1	(1)
People with similar background	53	(74)	34	(32)
People who are good company (even if common at times)	14	(20)	4	(4)
People with interesting/responsible jobs	12	(17)	25	(23)

TABLE 9.10
Leisure Activities and Husband–Wife Segregation

Men
Type of Activity

Frequency	Visit Pub %	Stay Home %	Outside Entertainment %	Visit Relatives %	Relatives Visiting %	Visit Friends %
0	30	0	70	54	39	71
1	22	5	23	32	37	21
2	24	7	5	9	14	7
3	14	17	1	3	6	1
4	6	22	0	1	3	0
5	1	23	0	0	0	0
6	1	17	0	0	0	0
7	0	9	0	0	0	0
NA	1	1	1	1	1	1
Proportion of Occasions when Wife was Present	41	89	89	63	99	66

Foremen
Type of Activity

Frequency	Visit Pub %	Stay Home %	Outside Entertainment %	Visit Relatives %	Relatives Visiting %	Visit Friends %
0	52	3	61	46	58	61
1	17	3	28	36	28	24
2	13	11	5	13	9	11
3	9	8	2	2	2	1
4	3	26	0	0	0	0
5	0	20	0	0	0	0
6	0	11	0	0	0	0
7	0	15	0	0	0	0
NA	3	3	3	3	3	3
Proportion of Occasions when Wife was Present	47	95	98	97	100	91

TABLE 9.11

Aggregation of Occupational Categories of Close Relatives[1]

| | Men | | | | Foremen | | | |
| | Fathers | Fathers-in-Law | Brothers | Brothers-in-Law | Fathers | Fathers-in-Law | Brothers | Brothers-in-Law |
	%	%	%	%	%	%	%	%
Non-manual	3	14	13	18	4	17	26	39
Manual	92	82	82	70	96	68	71	50
Dock workers	60	23	41	20	58	26	42	9
Dock foremen	7	1	3	1	18[2]	3	8	0
Tally clerks	1	1	1	1	2	1	0	0

Notes:
(1) Figures exclude Personal Service, Don't Know and No Reply.
(2) Equals 21 per cent of private sector foremen.

TABLE 10.1

Rating of Promotion Prospects in Perfect Job

	Men %(N=139)		Foremen %(N=93)	
1. Not at all important	12	(16)	9	(8)
2. Not very important	24	(34)	8	(7)
3. Of some importance	22	(30)	18	(17)
4. Definitely important	17	(24)	25	(23)
5. Extremely important	25	(35)	41	(38)

TABLE 10.2

Extent to Which Promotion Prospects Satisfy or Dissatisfy in Present Job

	Men %(N=139)		Foremen %(N=93)	
Dissatisfy	30	(41)	33	(31)
Satisfy	23	(33)	44	(41)
Irrelevant	47	(65)	23	(21)

TABLE 10.3

Occupational Aspirations for Own Child (where applicable)

	Men %(N=79)		Foremen %(N=35)	
Employers, managers and professionals	15	(12)	63	(22)
Intermediate and junior non-manual	29	(23)	20	(7)
Skilled manual and foremen	17	(13)	11	(4)
Semi- and unskilled manual	6	(5)	0	
Personal service	3	(2)	0	
No preference	30	(24)	6	(2)
Dock worker	6	(5)	0	

Occupational Aspirations for Hypothetical Son

	Men %(N=139)		Foremen %(N=93)	
Employers, managers and professionals	37	(52)	73	(66)
Intermediate and junior non-manual	29	(40)	12	(11)
Skilled manual and foremen	11	(15)	6	(6)
Semi- and unskilled manual	4	(6)	0	
Personal service	1	(1)	0	
No preference	18	(25)	9	(8)
NA	0		2	(2)
Dock worker	2	(3)	0	

TABLE 10.4

Occupations of Children in Work[1]

	Men %(N=100)		Foremen %(N=107)	
Employers, managers and professionals	15	(15)	14	(15)
Intermediate and junior non-manual	31	(31)	39	(42)
Skilled manual and foremen	7	(7)	18	(19)
Semi- and unskilled manual	17	(17)	15	(16)
Personal service	2	(2)	2	(2)
DK[2]	28	(28)	12	(13)
Dock worker	6	(6)	7	(8)
Dock foreman	0		0	
Tally Clerk	1	(1)	2	(2)

Notes:
(1) Including occupations of married daughters' husbands.
(2) Mainly sons-in-law whose job is unknown to respondent.

TABLE 10.5

Desired Improvements in Way of Life

	Men %(N=139)[1]		Foremen %(N=93)[1]	
Better standard of living	50	(69)	25	(23)
More leisure	44	(61)	40	(37)
Better pension	6	(8)	23	(21)
Better working conditions	5	(7)	2	(2)
More security	7	(10)	1	(1)
Other	3	(4)	6	(6)
None	10	(14)	14	(13)

Note:
(1) Percentages equal more than 100, because respondents could give more than one reply.

TABLE 10.6

Occupational Choice If Had Time Again

	Men %(N=139)		Foremen %(N=93)	
Same job	50	(69)	45	(42)
Management in docks	23	(32)	29	(27)
Non-manual outside	25	(35)	26	(24)
Manual outside	2	(3)	0	

TABLE 10.7

Voting Patterns
(Proportions of those eligible to vote)

| | *Men* | | | | | | | |
	1959 %(N=120)		1964 %(N=129)		1966 %(N=134)		Tomorrow %(N=139)	
Lab.	83	(100)	86	(111)	81	(108)	73	(102)
Cons.	8	(9)	5	(6)	6	(8)	10	(14)
Lib.	3	(4)	2	(3)	4	(5)	4	(6)
Com.	—		—		1	(1)	1	(2)
Abstain	4	(5)	5	(7)	6	(10)	9	(12)
NA	2	(2)	2	(2)	2	(2)	1	(2)
DK	—		—		—		1	(1)

| | *Foremen* | | | | | | | |
	1959 %(N=91)		1964 %(N=93)		1966 %(N=93)		Tomorrow %(N=93)	
Lab.	56	(51)	55	(51)	59	(55)	51	(47)
Cons.	37	(34)	36	(33)	32	(30)	41	(38)
Lib.	1	(1)	2	(2)	2	(2)	1	(1)
Com.	—		—		—		—	
Abstain	4	(4)	5	(5)	4	(4)	4	(4)
NA	1	(1)	2	(2)	2	(2)	1	(1)
DK	—		—		—		2	(2)

Nature of Party Attachment

	Men %(N=139)		Foremen %(N=93)	
Lab.[1]	68	(95)	48	(45)
Cons.[1]	4	(5)	31	(29)
Lib.[1]	1	(2)	1	(1)
Change[2]	14	(19)	12	(11)
None[3]	12	(16)	5	(5)
Abstain	—		—	
NA	1	(2)	2	(2)

Notes:
(1) Includes one abstention.
(2) One change between parties.
(3) More than one change.

TABLE 10.8
Reasons for Attachment to Labour Party

	Men %(N=95)		Foremen %(N=45)	
General identification with Labour as working class party	47	(45)	40	(18)
Favours social policies	3	(3)	7	(3)
Family tradition	23	(22)	11	(5)
Better off personally	3	(3)	0	
Labour more efficient	11	(10)	9	(4)
Labour rule in interests of all	6	(6)	18	(8)
Other	6	(6)	15	(7)

TABLE 10.9
Socio-Political Attitudes

		Men				Foremen			
		All %(N=139)		Labour %(N=45)		Cons. %(N=29)		All %(N=93)	
One law	Agree	82	(114)	73	(33)	45	(13)	70	(65)
for rich	Disagree	14	(19)	22	(10)	55	(16)	26	(24)
	Neutral	4	(6)	4	(2)	0		4	(4)
Big business	Agree	81	(113)	67	(30)	35	(10)	56	(52)
power	Disagree	16	(22)	29	(13)	55	(16)	39	(36)
	Neutral	3	(4)	4	(2)	10	(3)	5	(5)
Fair	Agree	73	(101)	58	(26)	31	(9)	45	(42)
shares	Disagree	22	(30)	33	(15)	66	(19)	48	(45)
	Neutral	6	(8)	9	(4)	3	(1)	7	(6)
No social	Agree	19	(27)	33	(15)	48	(14)	40	(37)
classes	Disagree	78	(108)	62	(28)	45	(13)	55	(51)
	Neutral	3	(4)	4	(2)	7	(2)	5	(5)

TABLE 10.10

Correlation Matrix Of Various Ideology Statements

Statements:

		1	2	3	4	5	6	7	8
One law for rich	1								
Big business power excessive	2	·40[1]							
Upper classes prevent fair shares	3	·45[1]	·58[1]						
No social classes	4	*	− ·26[1]	− ·41[1]					
TUs: have too much power	5	*	·23[3]	·26[1]	*				
TUs: should not support Labour	6	*	·28[1]	*	*	·40[1]			
TUs: should get say in management	7	*	*	·29[2]	*	− ·50[3]	*		
TUs: are no longer as necessary	8	*	*	·25[2]	·27[1]	·49[1]	*	− ·22[3]	
Statements:		1	2	3	4	5	6	7	8

Notes:
  (1) Significant at 0·001 level.
  (2) Significant at 0·01 level.
  (3) Significant at 0·05 level.
  (*) Less than ·20 or non-significant.

The statistic used to measure association is the Phi coefficient (Φ). (The replies to the statements are dichotomized by dropping the neutral response from the analysis.)

TABLE 10.11

Nature and Distribution of 'Images' of Structure

	Men %(N=139)		Foremen %(N=93)	
Power	14	(20)	10	(9)
Power-money combined	10	(14)	11	(10)
Money	47	(65)	18	(17)
Money-prestige combined	17	(24)	25	(23)
Prestige	4	(5)	20	(19)
Other	4	(6)	5	(5)
No clear image	4	(5)	11	(10)

APPENDIX A

SECTION A

(1) No. of years in the docks
(2) No. of years as foreman (where applicable)
(3) Job history
(4) Type of work
(5) Age

SECTION B I would like to ask you some questions about the work you do.

(1) Please answer the following questions about work, using these categories

Yes to a great extent	Yes to some extent	Neither Yes or No	No not particularly	No not at all

a. Do you find the pace of the work too fast most of the time
b. Do you find your work monotonous
c. Is the work sufficiently varied
d. Do you usually find the work too tiring
e. Is the work too simple to bring out the best of your abilities
f. Does the work give you a chance to try out your own ideas
g. Does the work require maintained concentration
h. Are accident risks too high in your present work
i. Are there good opportunities for overtime
j. Is the work well planned for practical purposes
k. Can you decide how the work is to be done
l. Is there freedom to work at your own speed

(2) If No to last question, Why can't you work at your own speed

(3) Do you like the work very much; to some extent; neither like nor dislike it; dislike it to some extent; dislike it very much.

(4) a. Would you describe your work as skilled
    b. If yes, What sorts of skills are required

(5) To do your job well, does it require: Formal training; Long experience on the job; A short period getting to know the ropes.

(6) Could anyone with experience of dockwork walk in and do your job

(7) What would you say are the main obstacles to doing your job properly (please list 3)

(8) Is there any other work, either inside or outside your company which you would like better than the work you are doing now

(9) What would you say are the advantages of dockwork compared with work in other industries

FOREMEN ONLY

(10) Do you find that you are always as clear as you would like to be about what you have to do on this job

(11) Which best represents how clear you are: I am always clear; I am clear on most things; I am fairly clear; I am not too clear; I am not clear at all.

(12) Would you give me details of particular things or occasions when you are unclear about what you have to do

(13) Are there times in your job when one person wants you to do one thing and someone else wants you to do something else

(14) Can you give me some details of these occasions

(15) Some people complain that their job puts them in the middle between two sets of people who want different things. For instance, between the men and management or between the customers and the company. How often do you feel in the middle between:
    a. the men and management
    b. the customers and the company:
       Nearly all the time; Quite often; Sometimes; Rarely; Never.
    c. Can you give me some details of these occasions and of what you did

(16) Do you feel that your job imposes stresses and pressures beyond those which most people have to cope with

(17) How did you learn what to do in your job as a foreman (Probe replies)

235

(18) a. How sure are you of the order of importance your T.O./Superintendent
        places on the various aspects of your job
     b. How much agreement is there between you and your T.O./Superintendent
        on the priority of importance of the various aspects of your job
     c. How aware is your T.O./Superintendent of the aspects of your job
        which give you the most difficulty
     d. To what degree do you listen to your T.O./Superintendent with real
        understanding when he is talking to you
     e. In your dealings with your T.O./Superintendent do you feel he really
        means what he <u>says</u>
     f. When you are upset or displeased with something your T.O./
        Superintendent has done, how likely are you to tell him about it
     g. In general, how direct are you with your T.O./Superintendent
     h. How often do you withhold information from your T.O./Superintendent
     i. In talking to your T.O./Superintendent how much do you tend to
        reveal your true complete plans and intentions
     j. In your dealings with your T.O./Superintendent do you feel he <u>says</u>
        what he <u>means</u>
     k. Do you feel you usually know how satisfied he is with what you do

     (Respondents give a 5-point scale for each question, which 1 = perfectly
     open communication and 5 = blocked.)

SECTION C

In this section I would like you to give me your views on the changes going
on in the docks at the present time, and also your views on more general
issues in dockwork.

(1) <u>If on mechanized or unitized work</u>
     a. What differences do you find between your present job and others
        you had before moving onto mechanized work
     b. Do you find that you now have to plan more moves ahead than before
     c. Has mechanization altered the main obstacles to doing your work
        properly
     d. If yes, in what ways
     e. Do you prefer this job to others you've had
     f. Why

(2) <u>Those not on unitized work</u>
     a. Would you prefer to work on containers or other unitized systems
        to your present job
     b. For what reasons do you prefer this type of work

(3) a. Do you think that the new systems of cargo handling, such as
        containers, package timber, and bulk grain are good things for
        the docker/foreman   b. Why

(4) a. Do you think that these new systems are being brought in
        Too rapidly; At the right speed; Too slowly
     b. Why do you say that

(5) a. Do you think you would find working on these systems different,
        for instance more boring, compared with conventional work
     b. Are you worried that unitization may lead to redundancy
     c. Would you say that those men working on the new systems are looked
        up to by others in the docks

DOCK WORKERS ONLY

(6) a. Are you working on a piece-rate basis or a package deal at the
        moment
     b. Which do you prefer, a piece-rate system or a flat wage
     c. Why do you prefer this
     d. Should there be an incentive based on productivity on top of the
        flat wage
     e. Why

(7) a. Which do you prefer, the old system of casual labour or the permanent
        system since Devlin Phase 1
     b. For what reasons do you prefer this
     c. Is there anything you dislike about permanency

(8) a. Before Phase 1 were you a perm for any company or did you get jobs
        from the pool
     b. Did you work most of the time for one company

(9) a. Did you work regularly with one foreman most of the time
     b. Do you work with the same foreman now

(10) a. Did you work with regularly the same workmates in a gang most of the time
     b. Do you work in a gang with the same people now

(11) a. Which would you prefer: to work regularly with one foreman or to rotate between several
     b. Why do you prefer this

(12) a. Would you rather work with a regular gang or have a different one for each job
     b. Why
     c. Do you work in a regular gang now

(13) How would you feel if you were moved to another job in the docks, more or less like the one you do now but away from all the people you work with now.   Would you be:
     Upset; Fairly upset; Not much bothered; Not at all bothered

(14) Would you say that ship and quay work is more difficult than shed work

(15) In your opinion, should men with more skills than others be paid higher wages

FOREMEN ONLY

(6) a. Are your men working on a piece-rate basis or a package deal at the moment
    b. How long have they been on a package deal
    c. Has it altered the way <u>they</u> behave on the job
    d. In what ways
    e. Has it altered the way <u>you</u> treat them
    f. In what ways

(7) a. Which would you prefer your men to have: the present piece-rate system or a package deal
    b. Why do you prefer this
    c. Would you like your men to have an incentive scheme based on productivity on top of the basic wage

(8) a. Which do you as a foreman prefer: the old system of casual labour or the permanent system since Devlin Phase I
    b. For what reasons do you prefer this
    c. Has it had any effect on your job
    d. <u>If YES</u>, what

(9) a. Before decasualization, did you have some men who worked regularly with you on all jobs
    b. Do the same men work regularly with you now

(10) a. Would you prefer to work regularly with only a few men nowadays
     b. Why do you prefer this

(11) a. Has Phase I made any difference to your feelings about your job
     b. What
     c. Are you less satisfied with the job now

SECTION D

People have different ideas as to what they want from a job.   On this page there are listed a number of factors connected with jobs, and I would like you to rate them in terms of the importance you yourself would attach to them when thinking about a job.   Do not consider the extent to which they are present in your present job, but imagine that you were looking for another job outside the docks.   What would you look for in the perfect job? (These factors explained more fully during interview, using more concrete language).

Not at all important	Not very important	Of some importance	Definitely important	Extremely important
1	2	3	4	5

1) Promotion prospects
2) The working conditions
3) Status and prestige
4) A chance to develop your own skills and potential
5) A chance to feel that you are accomplishing the job to the best of your ability
6) Responsibility for the job
7) The type of supervision from your boss
8) The actual nature of the work involved in the job
9) Job security

10) Recognition for what you do
11) Control over the way the job is done
12) Friendly and co-operative workmates
13) Efficient company policy and administration
14) Friendly and co-operative subordinates
15) Good relationships with your superior
16) The way your job affects your personal life
17) High pay

From this list of factors, please list in order of importance the 3 most
important ones that you would look for, starting with the most important.

SECTION E

Now I would like you to think about your present job in this company.
Compared with what you said you wanted in the ideal job in the last
section, how satisfied are you with your present job, in terms of these
same factors? If any of these factors are not important either way,
please say so.

Extremely Dissatisfied	Dissatisfied	Slightly Dissatisfied	Slightly Satisfied	Satisfied	Extremely Satisfied
1	2	3	4	5	6

 1) Promotion prospects
 2) The working conditions
 3) Status and prestige
 4) A chance to develop your own skills and potential
 5) A chance to feel that you are accomplishing the job to the best of
    your ability
 6) Responsibility for the job
 7) The type of supervision from your boss
 8) The actual nature of the work involved in the job
 9) Job security
10) Recognition for what you do
11) Control over the way the job is done
12) Friendly and co-operative workmates
13) Efficient company policy and administration
14) Friendly and co-operative subordinates
15) Good relationships with your superior
16) The way your job affects your personal life
17) High pay

Thinking about your job overall would you say that you are: Extremely
Satisfied; Quite Satisfied; Indifferent; Quite Dissatisfied; Extemely
Dissatisfied.

SECTION F

Now I would like to ask you about your company, its foremen, and
management.

DOCK WORKERS ONLY

(1) a. Would you say that this is a good company to work for
     b. Why

(2) Do you think that you yourself could earn more money in another company
     a. Inside the docks
     b. Outside, say in a factory

(3) Could your company afford to pay you more without harming itself

(4) a. Have you ever thought of leaving your company
     b. What is it that keeps you here in this company

(5) Do you get on well with most of the foremen

(6) a. Do you think that the foremen you work with are by and large good at
        their jobs
     b. Are they important for the ordinary running of the work

(7) Would they try to stick up for you with management

(8) What would you say is the most important quality a good foreman
     should have

(9) a. Could you do the foreman's job if given the chance
     b. If no, why not

(10) a. Would you accept the job of foreman if it were offered to you
     b. If no, why not

(11) a. Should foremen be promoted from the men or from the staff as in
     the PLA
     b. Why

(12) Do you think that the management of your company is good at its job

(13) What would you like to see altered in your company's policy

(14) How far would you say that there are good relations without conflicts
     between the men and the foremen and management in your company
     To a great extent; To some extent; Not really; Not at all.

FOREMEN ONLY

(1) a. Would you say that this is a good company to work for
    b. Why

(2) Do you think that you yourself could earn more money in another job,
    a. Inside the docks
    b. Outside, say in a factory
    c. Could your company afford to pay you more without harming itself

(3) a. Have you ever thought of leaving your company
    b. What is it that keeps you here in this company

(4) Would your T.O./Superintendent stand up for you with
    a. Senior management
    b. The men

(5) In your view, how good is he at his own job

(6) In general, how good are T.O.s/Superintendents at their own jobs
    in this company

(7) Are they important for the ordinary running of the work

(8) a. Could you do the T.O.s/Superintendent's job if given the chance
    b. If NO or DK, Why do you say that

(9) In your opinion, is your management really aware of the importance
    of your job

(10) Do you regard yourself as a part of management, of the staff, or of
     the labour force

(11) a. If not management, Do you think that foremen should be promoted into
     management
     b. Do you think that you have any chance of promotion

(12) Do you know most of the other foremen in your local company

(13) Do you think that the foremen as a group have distinct interests
     different to other groups (probe replies)

(14) In your opinion do foremen tend to stick together as a group in
     your firm

(15) Outside work do you mix socially with any other dock foremen
     A lot; Sometimes; Rarely; Never.

(16) How would you fell if you were moved to another job in the docks,
     more or less like the one you do now, but away from all the people
     you work with now. Would you be
     Upset; Fairly Upset; Not Much Bothered; Not at all Bothered.
     (Probe answers 1 and 2)

FOREMEN ONLY

SECTION G

Now I would like to ask you some questions about the labour

(1) Do you have enough authority over the men to do your job properly

(2) Should foremen have more authority over the men (Probe)

(3) Do you think that your management tries to uphold
    a. Your authority
    b. Your status

(4) How far would you say that there are good relations without conflicts
    between the men and management in your company
    To a great extent; To some extent; Not really; Not at all.

(5) a. Do you ever find a conflict between your duties as a foreman and
    your feelings towards the men
    b. If yes, Would you say that this affects you personally in any way;
    e.g. worry or stress

(6) a. Do you feel that the men have a right for their views to be taken into account when you take a decision
   b. Would you take their views into account if it meant that the men would co-operate more as the result

(7) How well do you get on with the men at a personal level
   Very well; Quite well; Not too well; Not at all well

(8) Would you say that the prestige and status of the foremen have increased, decreased, or stayed the same since you entered the docks

SECTION H

Now I would like to ask you about your union

(1) To which union do you belong

(2) How frequently do you attend Branch meetings
   Regularly; Occasionally; Rarely; Never
   (If rarely/never, Why do you attend rarely/never)

(3) How often do you vote at Branch elections
   Regularly; Occasionally; Rarely; Never

(4) In your opinion has your union the respect and leadership of its members in the sector in which you are employed

(5) a. Is there anything about your union you would like to see changed
   b. If yes, What

(6) (Foremen only)
   a. Should foremen have a section of the union just for themselves
   b. If yes, Why do you say that

(7) a. Would you say that shop stewards are a good thing for the docks
   b. Why

(8) Do you think it right to take industrial action in support of other dock workers, in London or other ports, when your own dock is not directly involved

(9) The unions say that the present ban on new unitized systems will only be lifted when all dock workers in the industry are offered better pay and conditions. Do you support this viewpoint

(10) Do you think it right for dock workers to help other workers outside the docks who are involved in disputes by, for example, blacking cargo

(11) How far do you agree or disagree with the following statements. Please use the following categories to indicate your opinion

Agree to a great extent	Agree to some extent	Neither agree nor disagree	Disagree to some extent	Disagree to a great extent

   a. The Trades Unions have too much power in this country
   b. The Trades Unions ought not to support the Labour Party, but ought to keep themselves separate
   c. Unions ought to try to get their members a say in management
   d. Trade Union action to improve wages and living standards is no longer as necessary as it used to be, as everyone today can raise their own standard of living by hard work and ability

(12) Here are two opposing descriptions of industry generally and I would like you to tell me which you agree with more:
   a. Some people say that a firm is like a football side - because teamwork means success and is to everyone's advantage
   b. Others say that teamwork is impossible in industry - because employers and men are on opposite sides

(13) Do you think that there is a reasonable hope of this changing in the foreseeable future

SECTION I

Now I would like to ask you some slightly more personal questions, in order to get an overall picture of the environmental and social background of people employed within the port transport industry

(1) Would you say that you see much of other dockworkers socially, outside work

(2) a. If YES, Would you say that by and large they are close friends of yours or only acquaintances

b. Are they people you normally work with during the day
c. Where do you normally meet them outside work

(3) a. Please give me the Christian names of the 3 closest people to you who
are not relatives;   that is , your 3 best friends
b. What do they do
c. Are they just your friends, or are they family friends of you and
your wife together

(4) a. Taking your leisure time in detail, what did you do in the last 7
evenings.   Did you at any time
i Go to a pub or club;
ii Stay home for the evening;
iii Go to a cinema or other place of entertainment;
iv Go round to a friend's home;
v Go round to a relative's home.
b. How often did you do i ii iii iv v
c. On which occasions was your wife with you
d. Were these last few days fairly typical or not
e. If not, in what ways were they non-typical

(5) On average, how often a month do you and your wife have friends round
to your home for an evening

(6) a. After work do you talk much to other people about your work or about
the dock industry generally, or do you leave all that behind you at
the dock gates
b. Would you talk about it much if you were with others from the port
industry (Probe affirmative replies)

(7) a. What job does your father have, or did he have if now retired or
dead
b. And your wife's father

(8) a. Do you live near your parents - say 5 minutes away by car
(Please say if both parents are no longer alive)
b. Do you live near your parents-in-law

(9) a. How often do you see your parents: Several times a week; Once
a week; 2 or 3 times a month; Less often
b. And your parents-in-law

(10) a. What jobs do your brothers do
b. What do your sisters' husbands do

(11) a. How many children do you have (specify boys and girls)
b. If at school what sort of school do they go to
c. If in work what jobs do they do

(12) If any child not in work, ask of eldest not in work: What sort of
job would you like him/her to have when he/she starts working

(13) a. Suppose that you had a fairly bright son, aged about 15 years.
What advice would you give him about his future? Would you advise
him to
i Leave school and get a job; ii Leave school and become an
apprentice; iii Stay on at school if he can.
b. If ii or iii why do you say that
c. If ii or iii what sort of job would you like to see him in
eventually

(14) a. Do you own your house or flat
b. Do you have a car
c. Do you have a telephone

(15) a. Where do you live - area
b. How long does it take you to get to work
c. Do many dock workers live in your neighbourhood

(16) Looking ahead, what improvements in your way of life would you most
hope for in the next ten years

(17) How much would you say that your standard of living has risen over
the last ten years?   Would you say that it had risen a great deal;
quite a lot; not very much; not at all.

(18) (Dockworkers only)
Are you better or worse off financially as the result of decasualization

(19) If you had your time again, would you
Go into the docks and do your present job; Go into the docks at a
higher level; Do another job altogether - what job.

(20) a. How did you vote at the last general election (1966)
     b. The one before that (1964)
     c. The one before that (1959)

(21) If there were a general election tomorrow, how would you vote

(22) I would like you to tell me how far you agree or disagree with the
     following statements, using the categories at the bottom
     a. There's one law for the rich and another for the poor
     b. The men who own the big businesses have too much power in this
        country
     c. The upper classes in Britain have always tried to keep the working
        man from getting his fair share
     d. There are no social classes today as everyone is more or less equal
     e. The coloured immigrants threaten our jobs and ought to be sent home

Agree to a great extent	Agree to some extent	Neither agree nor disagree	Disagree to some extent	Disagree to a great extent

(23) a. Do you think it would make any difference which party won the
        next election
     b. If no, why not

SECTION J

A series of semi-structured and unstructured discussions of social imagery,
based on The Affluent Worker questionnaire reproduced in Vol.3 (1969).

The Sample

I interviewed men and foremen in three private firms, as well as some foremen from the P.L.A. at Tilbury. Companies coded as 1 and 2 in the survey results were the Tilbury and West India/Millwall branches of one firm. Numbers 3, 4 and 5 were the Tilbury, West India/Millwall and Royal Group branches of another firm. Number 6 was a firm based solely at Tilbury. Number 7 was the P.L.A. The samples were taken from less than the total populations of the firms, because 'light duty' men and specialist quay foremen were excluded on the grounds that they obviously differed from the others ('light duty' men were unable to work on normal jobs and were allocated cleaning or clerical duties, and accounted for between 8 and 15 per cent of the workforce in the different companies; while specialist quay foremen were found in only one company, where they performed only a part of the normal ship-worker's job). Half the foremen and 1 in 14 of the men were interviewed. The details are as follows:

Company	1		2		3		4		5		6		7	
	SN	TN	SN	TN	SN	TN	SN	TN	SN	TN	SN	TN	SN	TN
Foremen	6	12	6	12	18	36	12	24	24	48	15	30	12	23
Men	23	320	16	220	40	560	21	295	—	—	39	550	—	—

Note: SN = Sample number; TN = Total Number in the relevant branch

The unitized berths operating at Tilbury were so labour-saving that only about 160 men were ever needed in 1970. Only half that number was employed most of the time. I took an additional sample of private sector men at Tilbury, in order to increase the number of people who were working on these berths, and asked them selected questions. Their replies were treated separately in the analysis. They were all people working on packaged timber/paper pulp berths, because the P.L.A. controlled the two container berths.

Tabulations of Perspectives Against Other Variables

What extent of manual or non-manual affiliation would prove significant could not be predicted, so calculations were done in three ways: (i) a simple majority of manual or non-manual in each category of affiliation, (ii) manual only versus manual and non-manual mixed, and (iii) manual only versus non-manual only. This last category was the most extreme case, but the one with the fewest numbers in each cell. Whichever category gives the most significant results in any case is used in the presentation.

The indicators of perspective are the statements about political ideology, political party attachment, self-assessed class position, occupational aspirations ('time again' question) and imagery. (Rather than repeat the ideology statements, these are numbered and the figure in parentheses after each coefficient refers to the number of the statement concerned. 1 = One Law for Rich; 2 = Big Business Power; 3 = Fair Shares; 4 = Social Classes.)

Brothers' Occupations Dock workers showed significant associations of 0·17 and 0·29 at the 0·05 level between occupation and 2 of the 4 ideology statements (4 and 1), and a non-significant association of 0·34 with a third (2), using the manual only versus manual/non-manual mixed classification. Occupation was significantly associated with the combined 'money-prestige' and 'prestige' model: 0·23 at the 0·05 level. Apart from these, there were neither statistically nor substantively significant associations between occupation and the other indicators. Foremen had a significant association of 0·29 at the 0·05 level with 1 of the 4 ideology statements (2), using the manual only versus manual/ non-manual mixed classification. There was a significant association of 0·34 at the 0·05 level between occupation and 'money-prestige' and 'prestige' models combined. There was a significant and large association of 0·57 at the 0·05 level between occupation and party attachment. There was also a large but not statistically significant difference on class assessment (manual only giving 'working class' reply = 55 per cent and manual/non-manual mixed = 36 per cent). Apart from these, there were no other statistically or substantively significant associations.

Holding brothers' occupations constant, the differences between men and foremen remain.

Brothers'-in-Law Occupations Dock workers had slight but non-significant differences on 2 of the 'Left' ideology responses (using manual versus manual/non-manual mixed = 89 vs 69 per cent and 85 vs 66 per cent on statements 1 and 2). There were no other statistically or substantively significant differences. Foremen had large but non-significant differences on party attachment and class assessment (using manual only 'Labour' versus non-manual only 'Labour' = 69 versus 35 per cent; using manual only 'working class' versus non-manual only 'working class' = 64 versus 38 per cent). There were no other statistically or substantively significant differences. Holding brothers'-in-law occupations constant, the differences between foremen and men remain.

Friends' Occupations The occupations of friends produced no differences at all among dock workers. Among foremen, friends' occupations were associated with party attachment: 0·51 at the 0·05 level, using manual and manual/non-manual mixed. There was a slight, non-significant difference on class assessment (using majority manual giving 'working class' versus majority non-manual giving 'working class' = 52 versus 40 per cent). Ideology statement No. 3 produced a significant and reasonable association of 0·47 at the 0·05 level, using manual and manual/non-manual mixed categories. There was an association of 0·31 at the 0·05 level between occupation and the combined 'money-prestige' and 'prestige' models, using manual and manual/non-manual mixed categories. Holding friends' occupations constant, the gap between manual only men and foremen who were attached to Labour closed from the overall figure of 68 versus 48 per cent to 78 versus 72 per cent. The gap on 2 of the ideology statements closes, from 73 versus 45 per cent to 74 versus 69 per cent (2) and from 81 versus 56 to 80 versus 70 per cent (3), holding manual only friends constant. (These changes are substantively rather than statistically significant.) Therefore friends' occupations *do* have some influence on these differences between men and foremen.

Area and Distance There were slight differences in the proportions of Labour supporters by area and distance among both men and foremen. (Area and distance are related.) Among the dock workers, 73, 71 and 59 per cent respectively of those in Thurrock, the East End and the Other areas voted Labour. Below $4\frac{1}{2}$ miles from the docks, 74 per cent voted Labour consistently against 60 per cent over $4\frac{1}{2}$ miles. Among foremen, 46, 55 and 42 per cent respectively of those in the three areas were solidly attached to Labour. Below $4\frac{1}{2}$ miles, 51 per cent were Labour against 41 per cent over this distance. There were no differences on other indicators.

Index